This monograph is particularly timely in the current environment in which the concept of citizenship is the subject of increasing political and ideological conflict and contention. Its well-written essays provide valuable insights about the common and diverse interpretations of social justice expressed by various cultures and faiths. They also make important contributions to our understanding of the implications of social justice for policy and practice by demonstrating how the concept could be applied to such varied fields as education, sports, and children and family services.

– Michael Reisch, *Daniel Thursz Distinguished Professor of Social Justice, University of Maryland*

Everyday Social Justice and Citizenship

Social justice is a concept which is widely touted and lauded as desirable, yet its meaning differs depending on whether its focus is on the underlying values of social justice, the more specific objectives these entail or the actual practices or policies which aim to achieve social justice. In the current global political context, we need to re-examine what we mean by social justice, and demonstrate that 'making a difference' and contributing to human flourishing is more achievable than this context would suggest. The book aims to increase our sense of being able to enact social justice, by showcasing different ways of contributing to social justice and 'making a difference' in different settings and different ways.

Part I introduces a fluid and contextual approach to social justice. Part II examines social justice and faith perspectives, such as Christianity, Judaism, Islam and community organisations. Part III illustrates perspectives on children, the family, sport and local government. Part IV provides perspectives of social justice in education.

Considering concepts of citizenship and social justice from a variety of contemporary perspectives, *Everyday Social Justice and Citizenship* should be considered essential reading for academics and students from a range of social scientific disciplines with an interest in social justice, as well as those working in education, community work, youth work and chaplaincy.

Ann Marie Mealey is a senior lecturer in ethics and moral theology at Leeds Trinity University, where she is currently Academic Group Leader for theology and religious studies, history and politics. She is the author of 'The Identity of Christian Morality' and other scholarly articles that relate to moral conscience, ecofeminism and bioethics. Ann Marie is a member of the leadership team of Leeds Citizens, the Justice and Peace Commission in the Diocese of Leeds and the CAFOD (Catholic Agency for Overseas Development) Theological Reference Group in the United Kingdom.

Pam Jarvis is a chartered psychologist and a historian. Her key research focus is the well-being of children, young people and their families, and the development of social policy to support this. She has numerous publications and is currently Reader in childhood, youth and education at Leeds Trinity University. She is an active campaigner for 'developmentally informed' policy and practice, frequently blogging in *The Huffington Post* on this topic.

Jan Fook is currently Professor of Higher Education Pedagogy at Leeds Trinity University. She has worked in Australia, Canada and the UK and has held several chairs, including at the University of Southampton and Royal Holloway, University of London. She has published twelve books and over 100 book chapters and articles, mostly in the area of critical social work and critical reflection.

Jonathan Doherty is a lecturer in teacher education, where he teaches professional studies to pre-service teachers. Previously he has worked as an educational adviser, as a consultant and as a senior manager in two HEIs. His research is in the areas of educational disadvantage, inclusion and school improvement and he has published extensively in these areas.

Routledge Advances in Social Work

www.routledge.com/Routledge-Advances-in-Social-Work/book-series/RASW

Domestic Violence Perpetrators
Evidence-Informed Responses
John Devaney and Anne Lazenbatt

Transnational Social Work and Social Welfare
Challenges for the Social Work Profession
Edited by Beatrix Schwarzer, Ursula Kämmerer-Rütten, Alexandra Schleyer-Lindemann and Yafang Wang

The Ecosocial Transition of Societies
The Contribution of Social Work and Social Policy
Edited by Aila-Leena Matthies and Kati Närhi

Homelessness and Social Work
An Intersectional Approach
Carole Zufferey

Responsibilization at the Margins of Welfare Services
Edited by Kirsi Juhila, Suvi Raitakari and Christopher Hall

Everyday Social Justice and Citizenship
Perspectives for the 21st Century
Edited by Ann Marie Mealey, Pam Jarvis, Jan Fook and Jonathan Doherty

Forthcoming

Social Work and Research in Advanced Welfare States
Edited by Kjeld Høgsbro and Ian Shaw

Vulnerability and Marginality in Human Services
Mark Henrickson and Christa Fouché

Critical Realism for Welfare Professions
Edited by Monica Kjørstad and May-Britt Solem

Critical Ethics of Care in Social Work
Transforming the Politics and Practices of Caring
Edited by Bob Pease, Anthea Vreugdenhil and Sonya Stanford

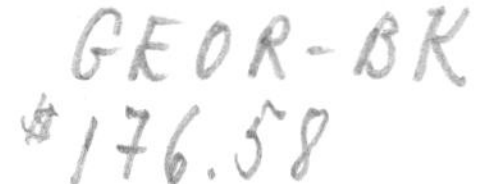

Everyday Social Justice and Citizenship

Perspectives for the 21st Century

Edited by Ann Marie Mealey, Pam Jarvis, Jan Fook and Jonathan Doherty

LONDON AND NEW YORK

First published 2018
by Routledge
2 Park Square, Milton Park, Abingdon, Oxon OX14 4RN

and by Routledge
711 Third Avenue, New York, NY 10017

Routledge is an imprint of the Taylor & Francis Group, an informa business

British Library Cataloguing in Publication Data
A catalogue record for this book is available from the British Library

Library of Congress Cataloging in Publication Data
Names: Mealey, Ann Marie, editor.
Title: Everyday social justice and citizenship : perspectives for the 21st century / edited by Ann Marie Mealey, [and three others].
Description: Abingdon, Oxon ; New York, NY : Routledge, 2018. | Series: Routledge advances in social work | Includes bibliographical references and index.
Identifiers: LCCN 2017026359| ISBN 9781138652804 (hardback) | ISBN 9781315623986 (ebook)
Subjects: LCSH: Social justice. | Citizenship. | Social service.
Classification: LCC HM671 .E94 2018 | DDC 303.3/72–dc23
LC record available at https://lccn.loc.gov/2017026359

ISBN: 978-1-138-65280-4 (hbk)
ISBN: 978-1-315-62398-6 (ebk)

Typeset in Times New Roman
by Wearset Ltd, Boldon, Tyne and Wear

Contents

Contributors

Qari Asim MBE is a senior imam at Leeds's Makkah mosque, and a senior lawyer at DLA Piper. He is an executive member of the British Muslim Forum, the Christian Muslim Forum and the JIF's Imams and Rabbis Council. He is an independent member of the British government's anti-Muslim hatred working group.

Stefano Ba' is a lecturer at Leeds Trinity University, who has a dual national academic background (a taught doctorate from the University of Perugia, Italy, and a PhD from the University of Manchester, United Kingdom) and researches family life, children and job insecurity. He is a sociologist who has grounding in critical theory and recently published in *Capital & Class*. He also contributed to the following peer-reviewed journals: *Sociological Research Online*, *Community Work & Family* and *Quaderni di Teoria Sociale* (*Social Theory Notebooks*).

John Battle was educated at Upholland College and Leeds University. He was the first director of national charity Church Action on Poverty. He served as a local councillor in Leeds 1980–87 and was a Member of Parliament for Leeds West from 1987 to 2010. Now retired, John is active in anti-poverty campaigns and co-chair of Leeds Citizens.

Jonathan Doherty is a lecturer in teacher education, where he teaches professional studies to pre-service teachers. Previously he has worked as an educational adviser, as a consultant and as a senior manager in two HEIs. His research is in the areas of educational disadvantage, inclusion and school improvement and he has published extensively in these areas.

Sue Elmer is Programme Co-ordinator for the MA Family Support programme at Leeds Trinity University, Institute of Childhood and Education, where she is also Head of Programmes for work-based learning programmes. She is an experienced social worker, registered by the Health Care Professions Council, and a Relate-trained and experienced couples counsellor. She is a play therapist and research lead and full member of the British Association of Play Therapists. She is a mixed methods researcher and research supervisor for psychology PhD studies concerning domestic abuse and prosocial identity in girls and young women. She is an external examiner for the University of South Wales (MSc programmes). Her research interests include social work education, integrated practice and innovative approaches to developing HE pedagogy, including sand tray work for problem-solving in entrepreneurial development.

Jan Fook is currently Professor of Higher Education Pedagogy at Leeds Trinity University. She has worked in Australia, Canada and the UK and has held several chairs, including at the University of Southampton and Royal Holloway, University of London. She has published twelve books and over 100 book chapters and articles, mostly in the area of critical social work and critical reflection.

Jonathan Glazzard is currently Head of Academic Development at Leeds Trinity University. He has worked as a teacher in schools and a teacher educator in higher education and he currently leads the academic qualification for teachers in higher education. Jonathan has implemented several initiatives to support academic staff development and to improve the quality of the student experience.

Susan Goodwin is Associate Professor of Policy Studies at the University of Sydney. Her research focuses on social policy, community capacity building and social justice. Recent publications include *Poststructural Policy Analysis: A Guide to Practice* (2016), *Markets, Rights and Power in Australian Social Policy* (2015), *Schools, Communities and Social Inclusion* (2011) and *Social Policy for Social Change* (2010).

Helen Hanna is a lecturer in education studies. Her research and teaching interests are interdisciplinary and international in scope and lie in the area of educational inclusion, particularly of migrant and ethnic minority learners and those with special educational needs. She is fascinated by learners' identities and how these can be explored, supported and celebrated in education.

Ann Marie Hayes is a registered social worker with a wealth of experience in social work within children and families social care, in residential care, youth offending, looked after children, child protection, children in need and family support settings. She qualified as a systemic psychotherapist with families and couples to complement her growing use of and interest in practice that pays attention to the interrelationships between the various contexts of service users and practitioners. She is currently in the second year of her PhD at Leeds Trinity University. She is researching critical reflection and whether it should be considered a contemporary (social work) virtue. She hopes to discover whether and how critical reflection is understood and used by a range of social work practitioners, and what difference it makes for service users, practitioners and organisations. Ann Marie is a graduate teaching assistant and most recently taught a module on ethics and social justice using critical reflection and critical thinking to stimulate learning.

Pam Jarvis is a chartered psychologist and a historian. Her key research focus is the well-being of children, young people and their families, and the development of social policy to support this. She has numerous publications and is currently Reader in childhood, youth and education at Leeds Trinity University. She is an active campaigner for 'developmentally informed' policy and practice, frequently blogging in *The Huffington Post* on this topic.

Patricia Kelly is a senior lecturer at Leeds Trinity University. Her research focuses on ressourcement theology, Joseph Cardijn and the development of Catholic ecclesiology from the nineteenth century.

Ann Marie Mealey is a senior lecturer in ethics and moral theology at Leeds Trinity University, where she is currently Academic Group Leader for theology and religious studies, history and politics. She is the author of 'The Identity of Christian Morality' and other scholarly articles that relate to moral conscience, ecofeminism and bioethics. Ann Marie is a member of the leadership team of Leeds Citizens, the Justice and Peace Commission in the Diocese of Leeds and the CAFOD (Catholic Agency for Overseas Development) Theological Reference Group in the United Kingdom.

Chris Rowley has an academic background in sport psychology, having previously completed a PhD in applied sport psychology. Chris's current research interests include reflective practice, ethnographic methods of inquiry, and the recognition of contextual factors which can affect practice within the applied setting. In addition to this, Chris's prior research has led him to consider the role of student-led enquiry and staff–student collaboration within teaching and learning in higher education.

Graham Turner began his career as a Physical Education Teacher and Physical Preparation Coach (Wolverhampton Wanderers). His experience in the UK includes research and design of National Strategy for Talent Development in Schools (Physical Education and Sport Strategy for Young People); design, delivery and evaluation of Coach Education at Leeds Beckett University (UK Centre for Coaching Excellence in Sport); Founder Member and Director on the Inaugural Board of the UK Strength and Conditioning Association; Technical Consultant for the Start to Move Primary Schools National Programme; and Coach and Athlete Development Consultant at the Northern Territory (AU) Institute of Sport. Graham is currently National Elite Coaching Manager for Gymnastics Australia.

Alana Vincent is Senior Lecturer in Jewish studies at the University of Chester. She is the co-editor of *Jewish Thought, Utopia, and Revolution* (Rodopi, 2014) and author of *Making Memory: Jewish and Christian Explorations in Monument, Narrative, and Liturgy* (Pickwick, 2013) as well as a number of articles and book chapters on modern Judaism, Hannah Arendt and collective memory.

Part I

Introducing social justice

1 Introducing social justice

Jan Fook and Susan Goodwin

Social justice is a concept which is widely touted and lauded as desirable in differing contexts, disciplines and traditions (Reisch 2014). Yet it also has widely differing meanings, even in similar contexts. It is a contested idea and differs depending on whether the focus is on the underlying values of social justice, the more specific objectives these entail or the actual practices or policies which aim to achieve social justice (Fook 2014). Indeed, in the current global political context, it might be argued that we need to re-examine what we mean by social justice, since recent developments such as the British exit from the European Union and the election of Donald Trump in the USA seem to herald a new era of populism which appears to backtrack on many of the social justice gains which we might have taken for granted. For instance, the rise of hate crimes indicates a return to an era of more publicly expressed racism. Trump's attempted undoing of Obamacare, which embodies more equitable access to health care for many Americans, if successful would turn the clock back several generations. Perhaps we are just witnessing an example of the inequitable effects of globalisation which were predicted some time back (Mendoza 2015). For these reasons, we felt it was timely to revisit our multidisciplinary and indeed multiple understandings of social justice, both in theory and in practice. In such a climate, it can also seem that 'making a difference' to social justice, and indeed contributing to human flourishing, is much less achievable than in more optimistic times. The book aims to increase our sense of being able to enact social justice, by showcasing different ways of contributing to social justice and 'making a difference' in different settings and different ways.

In this chapter, we aim to introduce an approach to understanding social justice which might be seen as a more fluid and contextual approach, which recognises the historical development of the concept in relation to different social and cultural contexts. In addition, it also recognises how the enactment of social justice itself might vary, and indeed appear divergent from, the more intellectually espoused version of itself. We deliberately introduce a reflexive approach, one which tries to understand how social justice actions and approaches develop from the experience of social justice exponents themselves. In this sense, this book makes a contribution to our appreciation of how social justice emerges from our own experiences and practices.

The chapter begins with a section which outlines and discusses the development of the concept of social justice, in different historical, social and cultural contexts. The next section outlines a reflexive framework in approaching an understanding of social justice. Lastly, the chapter ends with an overview of the different chapters and how they address the main themes of the book.

The development of the concept of social justice

As the chapters in this book attest, the concept of social justice can be linked to a wide range of traditions, ideals and visions for society and has come to absorb all sorts of meanings, hopes and demands. Writing in the context of social justice advocacy in the United States, Reisch (2002: 343) observed that 'proponents of diametrically opposed visions of society, secular and religious, march under the banner of social justice'. Social justice advocates and researchers themselves often find it hard to specify exactly what they mean by the term, yet they find it a useful way of articulating a wide set of concerns relating to human rights, inequality, citizenship and global justice, among other things (Gil 2004; Goodwin and Robinson 2017). References to social justice are often 'interlaced with the concepts of diversity, equal rights, individual liberty, social responsibility and resource allocation' (Olson *et al.* 2013: 24) and – as can be seen in this book – the 'language of social justice' (Hawkins *et al.* 2001) includes words such as empowerment, advocacy and rights, and dignity. While social justice certainly has multiple meanings, it works as a concept in different registers, across disciplines and across different social and cultural contexts. For this reason, it is useful to examine the emergence of social justice *as a concept*, and to consider how it has been made and remade over time and across space.

Contemporary ideas of social justice are linked in important ways to antecedents in Western political theory and practices, and particularly to the emergence of industrial capitalism, liberal democracy and the development of welfare states. While ideas and discourses about 'justice' can be traced back to Aristotle and Thomas Aquinas, 'social justice' as a term only emerged in the nineteenth century (Jackson 2005). Quite specific political, economic and social arrangements were required in order for the term 'social justice' to make sense, including ideas of 'the social' as well as notions that 'states' or some other authority could and should take responsibility for 'the social'. Originally, social justice had a strong 'distributive meaning', in that it was concerned with addressing the unequal distribution of wealth and resources, and was associated with the development of welfare states. However, with the rise of new social movements in the second half of the twentieth century its meaning has expanded beyond questions of distribution and material equality. In what follows, we discuss these developments in order to capture how and why 'social justice' is linked to notions of redistribution and citizenship. We then discuss more recent constructions of social justice that have emerged with the politicisation of differences *within* societies and *between* societies. In the late twentieth century, social movements actively championed the needs and rights of a range of different identity groups, pluralising the meaning of social justice as a way to argue for *recognition* as well as redistribution. In addition, new pressures for the enactment of global justice and reconstructions of non-Western theories of justice (for example, theories of justice in Islam, in Confucianism and so forth) mean that the term social justice is in greater global use, flourishing outside the boundaries of Western liberal democracies. These developments make sense of the flexibility of the concept and how it manages to signify such a raft of aspirations and ideals. We also briefly discuss contemporary critiques of the politics of social justice, specifically the recurring question about the fit between the politics of social justice and neo-liberal rationalities.

Social justice, industrial capitalism and distributive justice

Brodie (2007) links the emergence of the term 'social justice' to the discovery of the 'social' in industrialising Europe. Through social histories, we know that 'our contemporary understanding of the social, as being synonymous with society and the collective, was shaped during the multiple transformations associated with the emergence of industrial capitalism' (Brodie 2007: 95). It was at this time that progressive social philosophers and political economists turned their attention to what was branded 'the social problem': the poverty and inequality that constituted the 'human costs' of early industrial capitalism. Schwartz (1997) associates the emergence of the concept of social justice with ideas about what it meant to be modern as social reform to alleviate poverty was understood as the mark of a modern, civilised society. Brodie (2007: 97) explains that, with these developments, 'the social way of thinking, representing, and intervening was embedded as a "distinctive idiom" in western politics'. Thus we see the coming together of a number of new ways of thinking, organising and acting: the first formulations that poverty was a problem that was not wholly located in the individual; the rise of the social sciences and intellectual disciplines that privileged ideas of 'progress' and supported beliefs that it might be technically and politically possible to eradicate poverty; and the emergence of social reform movements concerned with devising strategies to deal with 'the social problem' of poverty.

At this time, social justice had had a strong 'distributive meaning' in that it was concerned with resource allocation. Jackson (2005: 358) argues that social justice was 'explicitly aim[ed] to redistribute resources to those disadvantaged by market distribution'. What distinguished social justice from other concepts of justice was that it referred to a social rather than individual obligation; involved meeting people's needs as a matter of justice rather than charity; and placed responsibility on a central authority, presumably government, to redistribute resources and alleviate poverty, address material needs and reduce economic inequality. This was a new way of thinking in Western countries – that the allocation of resources across society is a matter of justice, and that justice involves a distribution of resources that meets everyone's basic needs. The arrival of the term thus both reflected and justified claims that the role of the modern state was to intervene in order to ameliorate economic inequality.

Social justice, social citizenship and the welfare state

The concept social justice entered into mainstream politics and public discourse in the twentieth century, 'when advanced liberal democracies, variously informed by social liberalism and social democratic politics, embraced some form of the welfare state' (Brodie 2007: 95). Across Europe, social democratic parties had gained political force through the progressive extension of civil and democratic rights to the working class, and calls for social justice were attached to the liberal promise of citizen equality. Social justice was to be enacted through the state, and the notion of *social* citizenship provided 'the ideological basis of the modern welfare state' (Pojman 2006: 138). In this conceptualisation, the ideal of citizen equality was expanded to include social citizenship on the basis that the distribution of a whole range of social goods, such as education and health care, should not be left to the market because it was incapable of ensuring fair distribution. Instead, the state, rather than the market or families or charitable organisations, 'had the responsibility for shaping and enforcing the chosen distribution of social resources' (Fleischacker 2004: 7). Various principles were invoked to justify social citizenship: for example, the assertion of the collective over the individual; demands for compensation for structural changes as well as, of course, the injustice of social need; and the fulfilment of rights based on citizenship (Jackson 2005; Pojman 2006).

Fleischacker (2004) argues that social justice became a defining political ideal first in political practice and then later in the debates of political philosophers. Here we see an interesting observation about the relationship between social action and theories of social justice. For example, Fleischacker argues that the well-known theory of justice developed by John Rawls (1971) was in fact an expression of ideas that had already been widely canvassed and enacted by social movements and political actors. Rawlsian ideas of justice, he argues, were an attempt to come to terms 'philosophically' with the dissemination of strong ethical claims about social justice over the course of the twentieth century. In Rawls's theory, social justice is also concerned with the fair or just distribution of social goods in society that can be institutionalised through the application of three principles. First, the equal liberty or freedom principle entitles each person in society to equal rights to basic liberty. Second, the difference principle posits that social and economic inequalities are unjustified unless they are arranged to the greatest benefits of the least disadvantaged. Third, the equal opportunity principle requires that the differences and inequalities in society should be 'attached to offices and positions open to all under conditions of fair equality of opportunity' (Rawls 1971: 302). These kinds of ideas provided philosophical support for many of the institutions and practices of welfare states: the notion of a 'social minimum' (a minimally acceptable level of basic goods and opportunities to which everyone is entitled), a robust social welfare safety net, egalitarian social policies and the principle of non-discrimination in employment. Edgeworth (2012: 31) argues that:

In the Cold War environment in which it appeared, Rawls' approach made a case for social justice that emphasized not merely the importance of both social and liberal justice, but how they need each other's complementary support to thrive in advanced societies.

Social justice, the politics of difference and 'recognition'

In the late twentieth century, social movements actively championed the needs and rights of a range of different identity groups, pluralising the meaning of social justice beyond *the* social problem of class exploitation to include a proliferating field of social problems. This shifted political demands beyond calling on the state to take responsibility for the fair distribution of material goods, or for 'distributive justice', by highlighting other forms of injustice. In addition to pluralising social justice, many social movements were concerned with making ethical claims as oppressed groups, rather than as 'citizens'. For example, social movements argued that the failure to recognise and respect social groups such as women and ethnic and cultural minorities was a central dimension of injustice. In political theory, this shift has been operationalised philosophically through notions of social justice as 'recognition'.

The political philosopher Iris Marian Young (1990), for example, interrogated the ways in which existing social institutions, including welfare state apparatus, empower some groups and oppress others, and her work articulated why the goal of recognition needed to be made central to social justice theories. Nancy Fraser (2001: 21) described 'the politics of recognition' in terms of the goal of 'a difference-friendly world' where 'assimilation to majority or dominant cultural norms is no longer the price of respect'. Examples of claims for recognition of the different perspectives of ethnic, 'racial', sexual and religious groups can be found throughout this volume. In political philosophy, a lively debate has emerged around the possibilities of reconciling justice as redistribution and justice as recognition. The redistribution paradigm is held to conceive of injustice as primarily socio-economic and requiring economic interventions. In contrast, the recognition paradigm conceives of social injustice as a matter of devaluation of group status, requiring cultural or symbolic change. As this collection makes clear, most actual social inequalities are two-dimensional and require integrated strategies that can 'encompass, and harmonize, both dimensions of social justice' (Fraser and Honneth 2003: 26).

Global justice and non-Western reconstructions of social justice

In the twenty-first century, globalisation and contemporary populism have heightened awareness of gaps between the rich and the poor both within countries and between countries. These gulfs focus attention on how social justice can be argued for, enacted and achieved in governing practices on local, national and global scales. The politicisation of the problems created by globalisation such as poverty, unfair trade practices, large-scale exploitation of whole populations and human rights and environmental abuses demand conceptualisations of social justice that can hold true across international and transnational borders. Miller (2003: 367), for example, suggested three principles that could be deployed to promote global justice: 'the obligation to respect human rights worldwide; the obligation to refrain from exploiting vulnerable communities and individuals; and the obligation to provide political communities with the opportunity to achieve self-determination and social justice'. Just as social justice claims based on 'social rights' required the development of welfare institutions by nation states, it was argued that global social justice required international social and economic institutions that can promote more even global development and safeguard universal rights and freedoms. In this sense, recent global events such as the rise of populism and election of people like Trump in the USA, which creates a range of threats to fundamental international cooperation, is of major concern.

However, non-Western reconstructions of social justice have brought to the fore some of the implicit assumptions lodged within such global justice ideals and developments. Amartya Sen (2011), for example, draws on Indian concepts and ethical frameworks to contend that reason, justice and liberty are not uniquely Western ideas that the rest of the world should be invited to adhere to, but instead are part of the common heritage of humanity, albeit expressed through different traditions. In *The Idea of Justice*, Sen (2011) questions the assumption in Western theories of social justice that rules and institutions are essential to its achievement. Sen develops his theory of justice via a Sanskrit concept of *nyaya* – or realised justice – which is linked to 'the world that actually emerges' (2011: 20). In addition, non-Western reconstructions of justice (including, but also beyond Sen) have also been important in shifting focus from the 'management' of the fair distribution of goods and statuses to, for example, enhancing capabilities and opportunities to function (Sen 2011; Piachaud 2008; Kam 2014).

Brodie (2007: 93) claims that 'rallying calls for social justice are growing ever-louder' as the twenty-first century unfolds and it appears that social and political movements calling for social justice are spread across the globe. For example, in January 2011, the activists who occupied Tahrir Square in Egypt called for – among other things – *adala'h ijtima'iya* (a literal translation of 'social justice'), and the large anniversary protests in 2013 were organised partly in response to Morsi's failure to bring about social justice. Robbins and Jamal (2015: 3) state that, rather than calling for 'a specific political system or set of reforms, those on the streets were demanding social justice in its broadest sense – economic justice, political justice and basic human rights for all'. Yet, in Egypt, as elsewhere, the term social justice – even in its 'broadest sense' – is not monolithic and is infused with multiple meanings. In Mittermaier's (2014: 60) analysis of the Egyptian uprising, for example, she argues that 'socialist, communist, liberal, neoliberal and religious trajectories converged in their demand, along with others for which we might not yet have a language'. Thus, regardless of its progeny or the shape of reconstructions, social justice appears to have become a widespread pursuit and accounts of mobilisations across the globe can provide new insights into enactments of social justice.

One key contemporary contention – across contexts – is the relationship between social justice as a concept and neo-liberalism and other oppressive rationalities. For example, commentators have suggested the concept of social justice stands in critical opposition to neo-liberal political rationality, precisely through a focus on 'the social' (Kam 2014; Brodie 2007). On the other hand, concerns have also been raised about the ways in which neo-liberalism can incorporate social justice discourses. For instance, Global South analyses of neo-liberalism have drawn attention to the ways that decolonising social justice aspirations have been compromised through, as Subreenduth (2013) argues, an imperial project of global competition. Taking time to consider these conceptual developments and the theories of social justice that have emerged alongside them provides important background to the accounts of enacting social justice that follow in the book.

A reflexive approach to social justice and an overview of chapters

The concept of reflexivity itself is also contested and is used a wide variety of ways in different disciplines. It is however a very relevant concept in the current social and cultural context, where we are increasingly recognising the difficulties many people have in negotiating their life chances and identities in rapidly changing and fragmented societies. Beck's idea of 'reflexive modernity' (1992) refers to this way of analysing the social worlds in which we now live and, in addition, analysing the ways in which individuals are made in these social contexts. The main features of reflexive modernity include a breakdown of predictable life stages, social rituals and norms because of uncertain social conditions. Additionally, the rise in access to information in many different forms results in shifting social boundaries, categories and borders. These not only give increased opportunities to remake boundaries but also place more emphasis on the importance of individual identity making and life choices. Different social, historical, geographical and cultural contexts become more important and people derive their sense of community from a wide range of different networks. There are different sources of power, which may be less hierarchical and more mixed.

Reflexivity, from this point of view, involves the need to actively keep constructing one's meaning and identity from one's own experiences in different contexts. This of course involves an ability to reflect on personal experiences and actions in order to remake meaning and identity from them. It also means the possibility of interacting with, and creating, different types of power (and indeed different types of social justice and actions to enable it). However, it also involves a more general recognition and valuing of the importance of personal experiences and actions in understanding and defining more abstract or commonly held ideas.

Personal experiences, perspectives and interpretations therefore form an integral part of understanding social justice.

In this book, we take the view that we need to incorporate a reflexive understanding of social justice, and how this is played out in varying settings, historical periods and cultural and ideological contexts. In addition, as we noted earlier in the chapter, we also need to ask how various different interpretations and enactments of social justice have in fact also influenced our understanding of the concept. The first section of this chapter outlined these differing understandings, particularly their development over time. In this section, we will make reference to the broad themes which emerge from the chapters and how they contribute to the aims of the book.

Pam Jarvis's chapter on motherhood provides a stark illustration of how the boundaries and parameters of social justice change. Her analysis of neo-liberal thinking in relation to motherhood, and her exhortation to reuse a feminist analysis remind us how easy it is to lose sight of the theoretical frameworks and principles we might once have assumed were the bulwarks of social justice. In a different way, Sue Elmer's chapter illustrates the practical issues associated with enacting social justice in a local authority setting, when the populations concerned may have limitations in exercising choice.

Although of course we acknowledge different usages in different traditions and settings, there are of course commonalities between the chapters. For instance, there are common ideals associated with social justice in almost all traditions, and these are mentioned in nearly all the chapters. The association of social justice with a value upon human dignity is common. It comes out clearly in Stefano Ba's chapter, where he argues that dignity is fundamental to social justice, especially for families in 'precarious' work situations. This research is especially relevant to social justice as conceived in the present-day UK, where the rhetoric of families who are 'just about managing' has taken hold as a mantra for the site where the current government needs to extent its social justice efforts.

The concept of dignity is also fundamental to the historical development of the UK Citizens movement, which Patricia Kelly argues in her chapter emerged from the Young Christina Workers movement. Current principles are firmly based on ideals of participation, which are also fundamental to groups such as Leeds Citizens (see John Battle's chapter).

The chapters which address faith-based approaches to social justice also draw out the direct connections between social justice and social welfare, and include a clear moral expectation that these faith affiliations also include a moral imperative to contribute to the welfare of all. In different faith traditions this plays out in different ways, of course. The chapter on social justice in the Islamic tradition (by Qari Asim) includes noting how attending to social justice and welfare is also tied with spirituality. But there are also tensions between different approaches to social justice noted in some faith traditions; for example, Ann Marie Mealey notes the debate about whether the Christian tradition is primarily about evangelising or about working for social justice. John Battle posits a tension between a more passive attitude towards suffering caused by societal ills and a more powerful and active pursuit of social justice goals through active community organising. Within the Jewish tradition (see Alana Vincent's chapter), there are different approaches to social justice, one termed 'justice' and the other a more 'advocacy'-oriented approach, which it is argued have developed differently in relation to their different cultural contexts: the former Victorian England and the latter the American civil rights movement.

The argument for identity construction as an integral aspect of social justice is made clearly in Helen Hanna's chapter, by drawing on research in conflict-affected areas (Israel and Northern Ireland), where ethnic division is a historical feature and therefore where citizenship is also contested. She makes a distinction between having an identity and the freedom to make an identity, and she argues that the latter is particularly important in social justice education.

Jonathan Doherty's chapter, while also focusing on education, reminds us of the manifest inequalities in the UK system and very properly exhorts us to return to a critical edge with social justice, and not to water it down by focusing only on issues of inclusion or recognising diversity.

The chapter on introducing a curriculum around social justice and ethical principles in higher education, illustrates some of the difficulties involved in teaching new students about such issues when in fact the school system from which they have just emerged may well not have instilled such principles. Graham Turner's chapter very nicely illustrates how a young person's experience of inclusion or empowerment in a sporting context can vary greatly dependent on nomenclature and also the nature of their engagement with adults in this context. His conclusion that young people's experiences and perspective need to be taken into account more is an important beginning point for many social justice concerns, which is echoed in Pam Jarvis's chapter on children's rights in UK society considered through the lens of the United Nations Convention on the Rights of the Child.

The common thread that runs through all of these chapters clearly indicates that we need to ensure that, whatever social justice we think we are enacting, the views of those we are trying to ensure social justice for need to be elicited and included.

Conclusion

In this chapter we have traced the development of the concept of 'social justice' since its early inception in the West in the nineteenth century and linked it with an understanding of the 'social'. It is however a broad-ranging concept which encompasses many ideas, many of which precede this era and are intertwined with understandings of the concept of 'justice' itself. In the nineteenth century, however, social justice was linked with the emergence of industrial capitalism, liberal democracy and the development of the welfare state. In this era, the concern with poverty and inequality meant that social justice was associated with notions of distributive justice and often had a more explicit material focus.

Into the second half of the twentieth century, however, there were distinct social movements which expanded the concept to include more overtly political notions of citizenship and the idea of 'recognition'. More recently, in the twenty-first century, global and non-Western notions of social justice and citizenship need to be incorporated, especially since there is increasing global awareness of how social injustices are perpetrated on an international scale. This leads us to re-examine some of the fundamental principles implicit in Western notions of social justice, which are perhaps more common across Western and non-Western ways of thinking. In this way, concepts of social justice need to keep developing in order to be relevant globally, and also in very diverse and changing contexts.

Our introduction of a reflexive framework seeks to support this newer approach to understanding social justice, both through the experiences of exponents of social justice in different contexts, but also through a beginning appreciation of the many diverse and multidisciplinary perspectives on it. Perspectives of course differ both within and between disciplines. Clearly it is not possible to illustrate all the ways in which notions of social justice differ and are indicative of different contexts. However, in this book we hope to be able to give you a flavour of how the concept is fluid and complex and *must* keep evolving if we are to hope to address the issues which the very concept of social justice keeps alive for us: how to ensure the dignity, rights, empowerment and inclusion of citizens but also how to address fundamental material equalities which are being undermined globally at this very moment.

References

Beck, U. (1992). *Risk Society: Towards New Modernity*. London: Sage.

Fook, J. (2014). 'Social justice and critical theory', in M. Reisch (ed.) *The International Handbook of Social Justice*. London and New York, NY: Routledge, pp. 160–72.

Fraser, N. (2001). Recognition without ethics? *Theory, Culture & Society, 18*(2–3): 21–42.

Mendoza, K-A. (2015). *Austerity: The Demolition of the Welfare State and the Rise of the Zombie Economy*. Oxford: New Internationalist.

Reisch, M. (ed.). (2014). *The International Handbook of Social Justice*. London and New York, NY: Routledge.

Brodie, J.M. (2007). Reforming social justice in neoliberal times. *Studies in Social Justice, 1*(2): 93–107.

Edgeworth, B. (2012). From Plato to NATO: Law and social justice in historical context, *UNSWLJ, 35*: 417–48.

Fleischacker, S. (2004). *A Short History of Distributive Justice*. Cambridge: Harvard University Press.

Fraser, N. and Honneth, A. (2003). *Redistribution or Recognition?: A Political-Philosophical Exchange*. London: Verso.

Gil, D. (2004). Perspectives on social justice. *Reflections: Narratives of Professional Helping, 10*(4): 1–9.

Goodwin, S. and Robinson, P. (2017). *Colloborative Social Justice Research: Institutional Constraints and Opportunities*. Sydney Social Justice Research Network Report, University of Sydney.

Hawkins, L., Fook, J. and Ryan, M. (2001). Social workers' use of the language of social justice. *The British Journal of Social Work, 31*: 1–13.

Jackson, B. (2005). The conceptual history of social justice. *Political Studies Review*, 3(3): 356–73.

Kam, P.K. (2014). Back to the 'social' of social work: Reviving the social work profession's contribution to the promotion of social justice. *International Social Work, 57*(6): 723–40.

Miller, D. (2003). 'A Response', in D.A. Bell and A. de-Shalit (eds) *Forms of Justice: Critical Perspectives on David Miller's Political Philosophy*. Lanham, MD: Rowman & Littlefield, pp. 349–72.

Mittermaier, A. (2014). Bread, freedom, social justice: the Egyptian uprising and a Sufi Khidma. *Cultural Anthropology, 29*(1): 54–79.

Olson, C.J., Reid, C., Threadgill-Goldson, N., Riffe, H.A. and Ryan, P.A. (2013). Voices from the field: Social workers define and apply social justice. *Journal of Progressive Human Services, 24*(1): 23–42.

Piachaud, D. (2008). 'Social justice and public policy: a social policy perspective', in G. Craig, T. Burchardt and D. Gordon (eds) *Social Justice and Public Policy*. Bristol: Policy Press, pp. 33–51.

Pojman, L.P. (2006). *Justice: An Anthology*. Upper Saddle River, NJ: Pearson Prentice.

Rawls, J. (1971). *A Theory of Justice*. Cambridge: Harvard University Press.

Reisch, M. (2002). Defining social justice in a socially unjust world. *Families in Society: The Journal of Contemporary Social Services, 83*(4): 343–54.

Robbins, M and Jamal, A (2015). *Social Justice and the Arab Uprisings*, Arab Barometer Working Paper, No. 1.

Schwartz, H. (1997). On the Origin of the Phrase 'Social Problems'. *Social Problems, 44*(2): 276–96.

Sen, A. (2011). *The Idea of Justice*. Cambridge: Harvard University Press.

Subreenduth, S. (2013). Theorizing social justice ambiguities in an era of neoliberalism: The case of postapartheid South Africa. *Educational Theory, 63*(6): 581–600.

Young, I.M. (1990). *Justice and the Politics of Difference*. Princeton, NJ: Princeton University Press.

Part II

Social justice and faith perspectives

2 Social justice perspectives in Christianity

Ann Marie Mealey

Introduction

According to Curtis Paul De Young, '[w]herever you find injustice in the world, there are people of faith working for social justice – and often they are Christians' (De Young 2012: 61). Indeed, not only this: one could also say that many Christian denominations have their own social justice tradition, which helps to provide a theoretical framework from which to assess social justice issues. Perhaps the Catholic tradition, with its stress on individual dignity, the common good, solidarity, subsidiarity and, more recently, ecojustice, is a prime example of a faith tradition grappling with issues of poverty, inequality, environment, working conditions, equal pay, international relations etc. (Verstraeten 2013: 231–9). Although the suggestions made may differ from other, perhaps less theological, social justice theories, we can say with some degree of certainty that there is a social justice tradition running through the heart of Catholicism and Christianity.

This chapter will attempt to trace some of the biblical roots which underpin our understanding of social justice and will also raise a question about whether the faith tradition's focus is primarily to evangelise or whether it is to promote social justice. Or are these two at odds? It will also discuss whether the love command overrides any attempt to be just or to adhere to the requirements of social justice. The chapter will end with some examples of Christian practices that help with the development of a good moral character that is concerned with social justice issues as well as matters of worship.

Sacred scripture

Thematically, we get the sense from the biblical texts, from which a large proportion of Catholic social teachings are derived, that we live in an imperfect world where there is an imbalance of wealth and power. The biblical God is one who sees the injustice of our situation and intervenes to address it, either directly or through others. For instance, the book of Deuteronomy tells us that '[i]f in any of the towns in the land that the Lord your God is giving you there is a fellow-Israelite in need, then do not be selfish and refuse to help him. Instead, be generous and lend him as much as he needs' (Deuteronomy 15:7–8).

In the book of Jeremiah, we see God intervening through a prophet to give a message to his people: 'I, the Lord, command you to do what is just and right. Protect the person who is being cheated from the one who is cheating him. Do not ill-treat or oppress foreigners, orphans, or widows; and do not kill innocent people in this holy place' (Jeremiah 22:3).

In a similar vein, the prophet Micah states: 'No, the Lord has told us what is good. What he requires of us is this: to do what is just, to show constant love, and to live in humble fellowship with our God' (Micah 6:8). John tells us that '[r]ich people who see a brother or sister in need, yet close their hearts against them, cannot claim that they love God' (1 John 3:17). The sentiment proposed here is clear: one cannot be a Christian and turn one's back on those in need. As James puts it, '[s]uppose there are brothers or sisters who need clothes and don't have enough to eat. What good is there in your saying to them, "God bless you! Keep warm and eat well!" – if you don't give them the necessities of life?' (James 2:15–16).

Belief in God requires action in the biblical sense. It is clear from the above that one who acknowledges belief in God is not simply meant to acknowledge the presence of this God in their lives but to live out what this God expects in terms of respect for the poor and the needy, the orphan, the oppressed, the widow, the homeless and the foreigner. Luke's Gospel contains a poignant phrase regarding the action of the spirit of the Lord upon him. He claims that '[t]he Spirit of the Lord is upon me, because he has chosen me to bring good news to the poor. He has sent me to proclaim liberty to the captives and recovery of sight to the blind; to set free the oppressed and announce that the time has come when the Lord will save his people' (Luke 4:18–19).

Of course, '[i]t is not only the biblical texts that inspire Christians towards social justice, it is also the narrative history contained in the Bible that informs contemporary Christians regarding how they should live lives of justice and mercy' (De Young 2012: 63). Central to the story is the exodus event, when God liberated the Hebrew people from oppressive slavery (Exodus 1–5). What we find in Christianity is a people who are expected to behave in certain ways regarding social justice issues because they themselves are part of a story of liberation and redemption from slavery. They have experienced being in a position of inferiority and oppression. They were rooted in a context where there was no hope, where dying instead of rising was the main motif. However, through the intervention of God, and God's loving covenantal union with the people of Israel, their dreams of liberation became a reality and they were freed from slavery. Social justice therefore goes to the heart of what divine revelation is all about.

However, there is a question that arises at this point: because of this story of liberation, is the task of a Christian to (1) work for social justice or (2) to evangelise others into this story of liberation from slavery? Or are these two at odds? Or, to put it differently, was Jesus an evangeliser and primarily a prophet or was he a radical social reformer?

The Jesus quest

To answer this question, it is useful to look at the work of Ben Witherington III (1995), *The Jesus Quest: The Third Search for the Jew of Nazareth.* Witherington's text, though now more than twenty years old, is still useful to the beginner trying to find the answer to questions such as those posed in the above.

From analysing the work of Gerd Theissen, Richard A. Horsely and R. David Kaylor, Witherington maintains that scholars tend to see Jesus as being either an eschatological prophet or a social reformer. However, Witherington himself tends to believe that these two can coexist. For Witherington, '[i]t is worth reminding ourselves that these two categories are not necessarily mutually exclusive. At Qumran we find eschatology and, precisely, because of it, a social programme' (Witherington 1995: 160). If we think of it in very basic terms, where there are people believing in a narrative story and in the hope of a future through a story of the past, it is difficult to believe that this could be devoid of expectations about the way things will be in the future. Perhaps we could agree therefore with Witherington that the question is best answered by saying 'both/and' rather than 'either/or'. Many Christians might ask what the point is of believing if it does not impact on behaviour. Then, of course, there are others who might say that belief is not about action, though it is difficult to conceive of a life of devotion, prayer and perhaps piety without suggesting that this could impact positively on behaviour patterns and the virtue of the person engaged in the latter.

But we need also to ask at this point whether the stress on love inherent in the Christian tradition can also accommodate the justice that is required when assessing social justice issues. This leads us to another debate on whether love and justice go together. It could also be expressed by asking whether love usurps justice when the Christian acts.

Love and justice

According to Dominik Markl, '[t]he maintenance of social justice within a society depends largely on the fairness and strength of its legal system …' (Markl 2011, online). But when we square this up with the Christian love motif, we are left with a central question: does love come first and social justice second in the Christian tradition? Or are these two compatible somehow?

The Torah is clear that unjust laws are no laws at all (Leviticus 19:15), but the teachings of Jesus are also clear that love of neighbour is a central motif that overrides all laws (Mark 12:28–34). Does this then mean that in the face of a question of justice that the Christian should choose 'the loving thing'? Or does it indeed mean that whatever the loving thing might be, it is more important than justice or indeed than social justice? Put differently, does 'love thy neighbour' override the need for justice, for instance, in matters of the law and morality?

Ricoeur on love and justice

The work of Paul Ricoeur is useful here. Ricoeur distinguishes between love and justice quite clearly. Justice, for Ricoeur, is at issue when a court is enlisted to decide between opposing parties regarding the nature of their rights and interest (Ricoeur 1995: 321). How this is carried out depends on a judicial structure that includes laws, courts of justice that pass judgment, and individuals who will make an objective and just assessment of the situation. These structures that Ricoeur lists are charged with passing an objective decision and imposing this by force on a given party (Ricoeur 1995: 321).

In this regard, justice contrasts with how Ricoeur interprets love, as he sees love as not arguing in the way that justice does. Justice argues in the way that it searches for the reasons why someone might or might not take a particular course of action. Justice even has its own logic in the sense that it involves two parties who are at odds and requires us to listen to the other side. This is very important for social justice claims, as listening to the other side of a story can often shed light on what is happening to individuals in particular situations. To render someone his/her due therefore is generally how we conceive of justice – *suum cuique tribuere* (Ricoeur 1995: 322).

But how can this drive towards giving others their due be reconciled with the Christian call to love, forgiveness, discipleship in Christ, love of enemies and love of those who hurt you? Is love simply beyond the call of justice or can love and justice coexist?

Ricoeur compares love and justice to the dialectic between the biblical love commandment (Matthew 22:37) and the golden rule (Matthew 7:12) – the former encouraging us to 'just love' and the latter encouraging us to give in order to be treated equally yourself. If we were to follow the logic of just loving all, some actions that pertain to social justice might be justified as we could say they were the loving thing to do – even in cases where this is clearly not so. However, the logic of justice contained in the golden rule prevents this from degenerating into a purely subjective sense – or logic of superabundance, to use Ricoeur's phrase – of what is right or wrong because it focuses on the logic of equivalence: we do unto others as we would have them do unto us. This prevents love from collapsing into a self-serving and potentially dangerous position where many unethical actions could be justified by simply saying they were the loving thing (Ricoeur 1995: 328).

On the other hand, love can prevent justice from falling into a 'one-size-fits all' perspective and encourages justice to become more personal and consider the actual situation that individuals might be living in, or circumstances that they may have had to contend with (Van Stichel 2014). Love can help to soften the demands of cold justice as love enables justice to move away from the threat of a purely utilitarian (i.e. the greatest happiness for the greatest number) approach to questions of social justice. Love can help justice to become more competent to deal with novel situations, minority groups or underrepresented classes in society, to name but a few examples.

When it comes to deciding whether Christians should favour the love commandment over the call to justice when it comes to matters of social justice or social injustice, therefore, it seems that both love and justice are intertwined. One does not supersede the other but they exist in a positive dialectical relationship which prevents justice from become purely utilitarian in approach and prevents love from become love of everything or anything at all. These two limit and reorient each other so that Christians can claim to be both just – and interested in the demands of social justice as and when they arise – and loving in equal measure (Mealey 2009: 82).

Practices and social justice

Of course, linked with the interplay of love and justice and 'doing the loving and/or just thing' in the Christian sense is also supported by various practices of the Church. For instance, practices help us to develop virtues – such as honesty, humility, benevolence, empathy, fortitude, charity and temperance – which help us often to combat instances of social injustice. Listening to the word of God reminds us of our identity as Christians. Repeating stories of liberation from oppression reminds us to be hopeful and full of fortitude when dealing with oppressive situations.

Often, especially where new issues come to the foreground, it is the virtues (and not necessarily a list of rules and principles) that enable individuals to do the right/just thing. Tuning in to the question 'who am I?' is often much more helpful in terms of development of character and ability to respond to new situations of social injustice than a simple hard and fast rule on a matter. Virtues are more flexible and goal-oriented and they allow for the fact that the individual is on a journey towards the truth or the just outcome, rather than being on a quest for simple obedience to rules and principles (Selling 2016).

But practice is thought to make perfect, and help us to strive for excellence in good living. The philosopher Alasdair MacIntyre asserts that practices have an inherent good that enables people to develop virtues and become better people overall. He claims that:

> [a]ny coherent and complex form of socially established cooperative human activity through which goods internal to that form of activity are realised in the course of trying to achieve those standards of excellence which are appropriate to, and partially definitive of that form of activity, with the result that human powers to achieve excellence, and human conceptions to the ends and goods involved, are systematically extended.
>
> (MacIntyre 1984: 187)

Listening to the liturgy of the word, for instance, is a practice for Christians which can awaken concerns for social justice. The act of remembering or 'saying again' or repeating the story of a people who were in unjustly in bondage can bring this event into the present and enable a 're-entering' or a reshaping of our perspectives in the here and now (Adams 1983). Retelling the story of Christ's life, death and resurrection can help us to remember that Christians are born into the thematic cycle of 'dying and rising'. In relation to social justice issues, it can remind us that often we must die to certain propositions and ways of living and rise to other, more fulfilling and life-giving situations. In addition, the story of Christ's death and resurrection makes Christians a people of hope – a people who have a hopeful engagement with the world and who hope despite whatever social injustice might be going on around them.

But another point can be made here in relation to the practice of worship and social justice. As Adams puts it:

> The relationship between the Church's worship and its calling to acts of justice is rooted in Christ, the Christ whom we have called priest and victim. If one sees a body of Christians who neglect acts of justice as inappropriate in favour of liturgical privatism, we must ask, who is the Christ of the Church's liturgy? And if one were to see a body of Christians who spurned praise and common prayers in favour of a 'good deed', we must ask, who is the Christ of the Church's mission?
>
> (Adams 1983: 14)

In short, this implies that it is Christ who expects us not only to preach and tell his story but also to be concerned about social isolation, injustice of any kind, hunger, poverty, mental health etc. While the act of worship itself may not give us all the answers, it certainly awakens the individual to care for what God cares about and to enter into the story of salvation history in an active rather than passive way. This is linked again to the earlier point about whether Christians are called to simply evangelise or whether they are also called to act where there is social injustice of some kind or another. Christians are called in worship to stand against that which is debilitating or undermining for individuals in some way and not only to pray for the alleviation of suffering and injustice but to act for it too.

Conclusion

The biblical texts indicate that love of God should also give rise to love of neighbour. This neighbour is not necessarily the person who we know but can also be the stranger who is unknown to us. In faith, therefore, we are called to care about social justice issues. We are called to care for the other and their place, situation and context in life. Belief in God is not simply a private affair; as has been indicated above, it requires a sense of action for social justice and an application of the love commandment that is coupled with a sense of justice. For the Christian, love and justice coexist in a mutually enhancing and limiting fashion so that one does not overtake the other and lead to an imbalance between doing the loving thing and doing the just thing. The practices of the Church which take place in acts of worship help to formulate the virtues and to remind us of the injustices of the past in the hope that these will not be re-enacted again. The memory of the Church is crucial in tackling social justice issues as it reminds us time and time again not to reengage in a cycle of injustice, hatred or violence. In a world where individualism is on the rise and subjective tendencies drive much of our political views, it is increasingly important for Churches to articulate their messages of love and justice to the world so that the mistakes and injustices of the past do not become the mistakes and social injustices of today. Of course, this is not to say that Christians do not believe in forgiveness for past wrongdoings but the act of remembering along with various other practices of the Church allows them to 're-enter' the past in the present so it becomes a source of wisdom in addressing today's social justice issues.

Bibliography

Adams, W. (1983). A look at Christian worship. *Touchstone*, *1*(2): 6–15.

De Young, C.P. (2012). 'Christianity: contemporary expressions', in M.D. Palmer and S.M. Burgess (eds) *The Wiley-Blackwell Companion to Religion and Social Justice*. Chichester: Blackwell.

MacIntyre, A. (1984). *After Virtue: A Study in Moral Theory*. London: Duckworth.

Markl, D. (2011). Social justice in the Bible. *Thinking Faith*. Online. Available at www.thinkingfaith.org/articles/20111014_1.htm (accessed 2 February 2017).

Mealey, A.M. (2009). *The Identity of Christian Morality*. Farnham: Ashgate.

Ricoeur, P. (1995). *Figuring the Sacred: Religion, Narrative, and Imagination*. Minneapolis, MN: Fortress.

Selling, J. (2016). *Reframing Catholic Theological Ethics*. Oxford: Oxford University Press.

Van Stichel, E. (2014). Love and justice's dialectical relationship: Ricoeur's contribution on the relationship between care and justice within care ethics. *Medicine, Health Care and Philosophy*, *17*(4): 499–508.

Verstraeten, J. (2013). Catholic social thought and the movements: towards social discernment and a transformative presence in the world. *Journal of Catholic Social Thought*, *10*(2): 231–9.

Witherington, B. (1995). *The Jesus Quest: The Third Search for the Jew of Nazareth*. Downers Grove, IL: Intervarsity.

3 'See, Judge, Act'

The foundation of the Citizens Project?

Patricia Kelly

Introduction

One of the stated objectives of the Citizens UK movement is to 'develop the capacity and skills of the members of socially and economically disadvantaged communities … [that they] are better able to identify and meet their needs and participate more fully in society' ('About Us', www.citizensuk.org). The goal is thus to ensure that key decisions affecting communities are made with the participation of those communities, and not by a governing elite, which may be socially or geographically remote from those whose fates it decides. This chapter argues that this model of community organising has its roots in the small Belgian town of Laeken just over a century ago, and owes much to the thought and practice of the Belgian Cardinal, Joseph Cardijn (1882–1967), founder of the Young Christian Workers (YCW).

Now a global movement with millions of members worldwide, as well as members of affiliated movements such as the Young Christian Students and the Movement of Christian Workers, the YCW developed from Cardijn's pastoral work in Laeken between 1912 and 1925. From a working-class family, Cardijn's distress at the situation of his school friends, now employed in factories, while he was at seminary studying for the priesthood informed his life's work.

> I could write a whole book about my discovery of the problems of the working class, particularly the problems of young people, children as I was [in 1891]. Rather than going to the factory like my young schoolmates, I was able to go to the seminary and become a priest.… During my holidays from the seminary, people were always talking about them, and I saw them pass by the house in groups morning and evening, on the way to work. I travelled the length and breadth of the local industrial regions to find out real-life examples of their abandonment and moral degeneration.
>
> (Cardijn 1963a: 20)

Cardijn remained profoundly affected by the plight of the underprivileged working class all his life, acutely aware of how privileged he himself had been to be given the opportunity to study for the priesthood – and this despite his own working-class, relatively underprivileged family background. Having observed from close quarters how poorly this group were treated, he was 'obsessed' by the possibility of helping the disadvantaged to help themselves overcome the disabilities of their social situation. The transformation of the working-class (or underclass) environment, he insisted, 'can only be effected from the inside, by those who live and work there' (Cardijn 1963b: 48). The methodology he developed, the 'See, Judge, Act', thus has a special relevance for Citizens UK.

Having completed his theological studies and been ordained in 1906, Cardijn spent a year studying Social Sciences under the Belgian sociologist Victor Brants (1856–1917) at Leuven. Brants followed the early French sociologist Frédéric Le Play in his methodology. LePlay, an inspector of mines in north-eastern France, and later the *député* (MP) for the region, had introduced legislation to protect workers, which was informed by the data he had collected as an inspector when he interviewed miners and their families. Following LePlay, Brants impressed upon his students the importance of data from the social group under study extracted from interviews with group members themselves. As Gerard and Wils have noted, '[LePlay's] empirical work had shown how necessary such a study of social reality could be' (1999: 38). Brants continued LePlay's work by introducing students 'to social realities through travels, visits, and personal study' (Rezsöhazy 1958: 154).

For Cardijn, there were three key aspects to the YCW. The first was that it would impress upon young workers, and those around them in the Church and society, their inherent dignity as human beings. Young workers, he would often declare, 'are worth more than all the gold in the world, for they are the children of God'. The second was that any movement should be run 'by, with, and for' young workers. The third was the use of the methodology he developed following the example of Brants and LePlay, which remains central to the movement today: the See, Judge, Act, or 'enquiry'. This methodology, often referred to as the pastoral cycle, continues to be widely used in pastoral and ecclesial settings: it underpins Pope Francis's 2016 Apostolic Exhortation on Love in the Family *Amoris Laetitia*, for instance. Yet it also forms the basis, as this chapter will show, for the model of community organising employed by Citizens UK.

Cardijn's research

Following his Social Science studies, Cardijn was sent to teach in a church school for five years. This post was hugely important for his future. First, he learned to teach and to relate to young people, a gift which undoubtedly made the YCW the huge success it later became. Second, the relatively lengthy vacation periods enabled him to conduct research into working conditions in Belgium, Germany and England. This research was published in a series of articles in the *Revue sociale catholique*. In this research, Cardijn investigated the working lives and living and working conditions of those who were largely un-unionised: textile workers in Belgium and Germany and dockers in England. In the wake of the encyclical letter *Rerum Novarum*, published in 1891 by Pope

Leo XIII, workers' rights were discussed more openly, and may be considered to have improved somewhat. In particular, the Pope had called for a fair wage, decent and safe working conditions, and the right to unionise. (It is important to recall here that the ban on public meetings and associations, introduced in France and Belgium under the Napoleonic legal code in 1801, was only lifted in either country in the 1880s. Such a ban was also in place in the UK.) *Rerum Novarum* made a huge impact, with an editorial in *The Times* ('Dalziel' 1891), and no fewer than eight 'popular' translations in Belgium, of which three were in Flemish and five in French (Gérin 1994: 81). One of these would be the version the nine-year-old Cardijn read aloud to his father in the evenings, encouraging his interest in the importance of decent working conditions and unions.

Cardijn's article on workers' organisations in England (Cardijn 1911a, 1911b) demonstrate his understanding of the English unions at the turn of the twentieth century. He had spent weeks in England visiting London, Birmingham and Manchester, investigating the situation of workers' associations. As a good social scientist, his account offers his observations and accounts of conversations, although he had been careful to consult other documentation as well. Cardijn had sought and gained an interview with Ben Tillett, the famous leader of the 1887 dockers' strike (Cardijn 1911a, 1911b). He reported that at that period dockers had been 'day workers', who queued for work each day (1911a: 385) and that they were thought to be, in Tillett's words, unfit for unions. Cardijn noted that British trades' unions at this time were generally profession-based, in the manner of medieval guilds; there would, therefore, be no place for unskilled workers such as dockers. It was the TUC itself, he reported, which resisted unions for dockers and other unskilled workers (Cardijn 1911b: 22).

A similar, though perhaps more invidious situation, was identifiable in Germany, where Cardijn had earlier investigated the situation of 'pieceworkers' in the Rhineland textile industries. Such workers were to all intents and purposes self-employed. They generally worked at home, usually for a single employer, and were paid 'by the piece', or by the work completed. They were thus extremely vulnerable both to exploitation and to the vagaries of the market. They tended to work in their often crowded and unsanitary living quarters, which were made more unhealthy yet by the damp associated with textile work (1907: 11). Cardin observed sharply that the legislation governing pay, working conditions and the payment of the insurance 'stamp' only covered those working in factories, not those – in otherwise identical employer–employee contracts – who worked at home (1907: 13, 16, 17).

Laeken

The difficulties for workers at the bottom of the heap which Cardijn had observed in Germany and the UK were also rife in the town of Laeken, where he was sent as an assistant priest in 1912. The parish may have included the royal palace, but it was also home to a great number of female textile workers – generally pieceworkers – and to factories employing generally unskilled male labour. Cardijn reacted to these issues in two different ways. First, he went visiting around the parish, as was the custom at the time. Typically, the parish priest would make the rounds of the parish, visiting families and the sick, encouraging people to attend church and seek the sacraments. Cardijn's approach was entirely different. As he observed in a 1962 TV interview, 'I didn't know anyone in Laeken'. As the working day ended, therefore, he would take a walk, moving 'against the flow' of the workers streaming home from the factories. Inevitably, he noted, he would catch someone's eye and say hello, and gradually he became a familiar face as he walked about the town. He got to know workers and their families, asking them questions about work, living conditions, whether the wage was sufficient, what their work was like. But problems, issues, questions, he insisted, could only be dealt with via a visit to the presbytery. There, he and the visiting workers would chew over the problem – bullying and harassment, unsafe working conditions, poor pay – and come to a solution which the workers could implement themselves.

Cardijn operated in a similar way with the young needlewomen of the parish. In nineteenth-century Europe, as industrialisation progressed, bringing vast urban immigration in its wake, Catholics had developed various 'works' to help alleviate poverty and distress. Some offered material aid; others offered the chance for workers to develop as a person, with 'study circles' which sought to educate, improving both literacy and numeracy, and in the Catholic faith. Misner (1999) remains the best account of the attempts of wealthy European Catholics to offer material and spiritual salvation to the industrial workers pouring into their cities during the nineteenth century. The group Cardijn was asked to run in the Laeken parish followed similar principles. It had originally offered a space for young needlewomen to learn about their faith, and perhaps some other skills which would help them to be effective housewives. Cardijn developed this group significantly, calling it the 'Syndicat d'Aiguilles', or Needlewomen's Union, from 1913 onwards. In 1915 it was joined by the 'Syndicat d'Apprentis', or Apprentices' Union (Walckiers 1970: xiii–xv).

In these proto-unions for young workers, both male and female, which Cardijn later described as 'the first YCW groups' (Cardijn 1963a: 21), he guided his little flock in formulating and carrying out the surveys which to this day remain at the heart of the YCW. Walckiers notes that he also 'instructed them in the Church's social teaching including *Rerum Novarum*' (Walckiers 1970: xiv). Already before 1915, the Syndicats had carried out sufficient enquiries to be able to 'make many firm requests of the Labour Inspectors' on behalf of young workers in Laeken (JOC 1930: 27), while in 1922 Cardijn worked with young university students to investigate 'the problems of adolescents in the workplace'. Walckiers points to the attention to even the smallest detail which would enable concrete action to be taken (1970: xxiv). When in 1916 and 1917 Cardijn was imprisoned by the occupying German army for having spoken out publicly against forced labour deportations, he sent 'enquiries' out of prison to the tiny groups, encouraging them to continue their enquiring and surveying of the social reality around them. He also 'spent those months in prison thinking, reflecting, and making notes [about the Syndicats]' (Cardijn 1963a: 19).

Central to the proto-YCW of the period between 1913 and 1925 was the development of the SJA methodology, coupled with Cardijn's insistence that the movement was to be 'by, with, and for' young workers only. Walckiers has documented the battles Cardijn fought with leaders of both unions and the Church to keep his fragile young movements in the hands of the young workers, for whose development they were designed. Attempts in the immediate post-war period to draw the Syndicats more closely into Christian unions were strongly resisted by Cardijn, who pointed out that this would discourage young workers from taking on leadership roles in their own organisation (Walckiers 1970: xviii–xxii). By the early 1920s, Church leaders were likewise trying to persuade Cardijn to join the YCW to national associations of young Catholics. Again, he resisted, this time on the basis that the young workers would naturally cede leadership to the middle classes and students who made up the bulk of members (Walckiers 1970: xxv–xxxv). The JOC, rather, was 'a youth organization which would govern its own affairs … each and everyone … was called upon to do their own share to shape the present and the future of their own organization' (Horn 2008: 13). The insistence that it was young working-class people who should lead their own movement was 'truly revolutionary', notes Horn, adding that it was this responsibility which enabled many to 'overcome their psychological and other barriers which had hitherto kept them mostly silent and subservient', allowing them to develop the confidence, patience, and advocacy skills which the JOC required of them (Horn 2008: 15). The See, Judge, Act, meanwhile, was also entirely innovative (Horn 2008: 13), particularly in its emphasis on the responsibility of the membership to carry out the surveys and enquiries which this methodology gave rise to.

See, Judge, Act

The first section of the 1930 *Manuel de la JOC* (JOC 1930) demonstrates how the SJA methodology is to be used by the YCW to develop or influence policy. First comes the 'See', in which the Young Christian Workers ask a question or react to a difficult reality in their lives or the lives of those around them. In the *Manuel*, the underlying question was about the number of young workers in Belgium and their living and working conditions. Other examples might be harassment in the workplace, or the question of homelessness in the local neighbourhood. In this example, the 'See' thus begins with census data about the numbers of young workers in Belgium, and noting that this data is not subdivided into types of employment and does not include the unemployed (JOC 1930: 7–8). The second part of the 'See' is the result of the enquiries, or surveys, undertaken by the Young Christian Workers themselves among their peers, neighbours, and co-workers. The questions they asked, like Cardijn's on his parish visits, were focused on obtaining information about living and working conditions (JOC 1930: 9–17). The information they obtained pointed to young people who had left school with poor qualifications and no opportunities for furthering their education, who suffered great deprivation through having to live

away from their families, who were vulnerable to exploitation, early
isation and so forth.

The next step in the methodology is the 'Judge'. In the *Manuel*, the data are located within their historical, social, economic and religious co and carefully considered from a range of angles (JOC 1930: 18–20). Within Young Christian Workers, data are generally 'judged' within the context of biblical text, or an extract from Catholic social teaching. For the early Young Christian Workers in Belgium in the 1930s, the papal encyclicals *Rerum Novarum* and *Quadragesimo Anno* would have been particularly important. It goes without saying, of course, that the See, Judge, Act methodology implements the principle of subsidiarity which forms a bedrock of both of these encyclicals, and particularly the latter. Subsidiarity – also incidentally a principle underpinning the European Union – argues that the resolution of problems should, wherever possible, be devolved to the smallest or most basic social unit able to resolve the question – the family, the village, the parish council – on the basis that generally local people know their needs and what is best for them.

This principle helped Cardijn to avoid the paternalism which had dogged so many of the circles formed by Social Catholics in the nineteenth century. In returning the power to make change to the young people of the parish, he was putting subsidiarity into action. But he was also motivated by his faith in the dignity of every human person to improve conditions for Young Christian Workers and through them for all young workers. By drawing on 'a working class elite from the working-class masses … the yeast in the dough' (Cardijn 1963b: 50; see, too, JOC 1935: 75–6), who would be capable of leading and advocating for their peers, he was preparing to form them. They knew best what their peers needed. They were best placed to survey their peers, to ask what was good, bad and ugly about their working lives and living conditions (See) and to interpret the data (Judge).

The final stage of Cardijn's revolutionary methodology is the 'Act' – the proposing and implementing of a solution or solutions to the problems which have been identified and analysed. In the *Manuel*, of course, it is rooted in Catholic social teaching and framed in religious language (JOC 1930: 21–3). Its initial focus reminds young workers of their eternal souls and the 'overarching aim' of their lives, which in Catholic theology is 'the glorious life of heaven and eternal happiness'. Yet it also observes that this should be balanced by improving their lot on this Earth, first and foremost by using education to remind them of their rights and responsibilities. By developing their understanding and improving their professional education and training, young workers would be able to improve society around them.

As his predecessors in the Social Catholic movement had done during the nineteenth century, Cardijn called for improved education in Christian faith. It is important, indeed vital, to remember that, for Cardijn, education in the Christian faith was not a matter of proselytism. Rather, because of his emphasis on the creation of each and every human person in the divine image, this was a crucial first step in emphasising the essential human dignity of each young worker,

..ne value of every human life on earth' (Cardijn 1963a: 25). Again and ..ne insisted that 'workers are not machines, not beasts of burden, not ..s: they are the children, co-workers, and heirs of God' (Cardijn 1963b: –7; see too his introductory address in JOC 1935: 63). While framing the ..ssential dignity inherent to every human person in distinctively Christian language may seem odd to contemporary ears, we should expect nothing less from Cardijn, who, after all, was first and foremost a Catholic priest, and indeed from the movement, which was founded under the aegis of the Church. But it was attentiveness to Christian doctrine, and in particular to the Judaeo-Christian emphasis on the human person as created in the divine image, that lay at the heart of Cardijn's theology, and this key doctrine spilled over abundantly into the Young Christian Workers, infusing the movement and its members with a powerful sense of their innate human dignity.

The example of the See, Judge, Act from 1930 thus proceeds as follows. Using census data and data collected from surveys by YCW members of their peers, the Belgian YCW presented a snapshot of the conditions for working-class youth in 1930. They reflected on this data, questioning what it indicated for the future and what potential problems it raised, before proposing action: a new focus on education, both religious and professional. The religious education was key, as it reminded young workers of their eternal destiny and of their reflection of the divine image, thus reinforcing their sense of dignity and self-worth. An emphasis on appropriate education and training in the workplace, such as the call for apprenticeships, meanwhile, would help them to develop professionally. Finally, by organising themselves into small groups they would be able to represent themselves and their peers in demanding better and more appropriate working and living conditions, conditions which should, after all, be worthy of those who are 'children of God'.

Conclusion

We have seen that the innovative methodology of the Young Christian Workers may permit this movement to be described as a precursor of Citizens UK. The methodology has two sides, each as important as the other. First, the principle of subsidiarity is enshrined in the 'by, with, for' mentality of the movement: the insistence young workers know best what they and their peers require in order to live and work in conditions which are worthy of their inherent human dignity as persons created in the divine image – as 'children, co-workers, and heirs of God'. That the movement should be run 'by, with, and for' young people leads in turn to an expectation that they will be able to develop their skills as advocates for and representatives of their peers, in order to transform the world around them for the better, or, in other words, 'to identify and meet their needs and participate more fully in society'. The 'pastoral cycle', or 'See, Judge, Act', meanwhile, encourages the collection and use of data which includes personal experience in order to improve living and working conditions in the locality. Like the Young Christian Workers, Citizens UK seeks to support the disadvantaged in society as they develop their skills and abilities in identifying problems, reflecting on these issues in a range of contexts and proposing viable solutions which will make a real difference to the communities in which they are rooted. The influence of a young priest in a small Belgian town before the outbreak of World War I lives on in Citizens UK.

Bibliography

Cardijn, J. (1907). L'industrie à domicile en Allemagne, *Revue social catholique, 11*: 5–26.

Cardijn, J. (1911a). L'organisation ouvrière anglaise I, *Revue social catholique, 15*: 381–90.

Cardijn, J. (1911b). L'organisation ouvrière anglaise II, *Revue social catholique, 16*: 20–30.

Cardijn, J. (1963a). 'Point de départ d'un cheminement', in *Laïcs en Premiers Lignes*. Paris: Éditions universitaires, pp. 19–28.

Cardijn, J. (1963b). 'L'apostolat des laïcs dans une de ses réalisations concrètes: un laïcat ouvrier', in *Laïcs en Premiers Lignes*. Paris: Éditions universitaires, pp. 45–53 (originally published as 'Le laïcat ouvrier' in 1935).

Citizens UK www.citizensuk.org (accessed 29 January 2017).

Gérin, P. (1994). 'Catholicisme social et démocratie chrétienne (1884–1904)', in E. Gerard and P. Wynants (eds) *Histoire du Mouvement Ouvrier Chrétien en Belgique*, KADOC Studies 16. Leuven: Leuven University Press, pp. I.59–112.

Gerard, E. and Wils, K. (1999). 'Catholics and sociology in Leuven from Désiré Mercier to Jacques Leclercq: a process of appropriation', in L. Voyé and J. Billiet (eds) *Sociology and Religions. An Ambiguous Relationship*, KADOC Studies 23. Leuven: Leuven University Press, pp. 38–56.

Horn, G.-R. (2008). *Western European Liberation Theology 1924–1959. The First Wave*. Oxford: Oxford University Press.

Francis. (2016). Apostolic exhortation on love in the family, *Amoris Laetitia*. Vatican City: Libreria Editrice Vaticana.

JOC (1930). *Manuel de la JOC*. Brussels: Éditions Jocistes.

JOC (1935). *Semaine d'Etudes Internationale de la JOC*. Brussels: Éditions Jocistes.

Leo XIII (1891). Encyclical letter on capital and labour, *Rerum Novarum*. Vatican City: Libreria Editrice Vaticana.

Misner, P. (1999). *Social Catholicism in Europe*. London: DLT.

Rezsöhazy, R. (1958). *Origines et Formation du Catholicisme Social en Belgique 1842–1909*. Leuven: Publications universitaires de Louvain.

Walckiers, M.A. (1970). *Sources Inédites Relatives aux Débuts de la J.O.C. 1919–1925*. Leuven: Éditions Nauwelaerts.

4 Powerful agents and suffering servants

The community organising vocation

John Battle

Introduction: a false start

In April 2008, a small group of us in Leeds invited a wide range of organisations and individuals in the city to look at the feasibility of establishing a community organising venture in Leeds. The invitation letter spelt out that

> community organising is about facilitating local communities to campaign around social justice and societal change. We have spoken to many organisations and individuals around the city and there is a clear gap in terms of an organisation to draw together civil society and draw on its strengths to combat the inequalities we see in Leeds. We envisage that initial campaigns will focus on organising low paid workers to gain a living wage in targeted workplaces, support the campaign to get undocumented workers legally recognised, develop a Citizens Charter to address the city's 'wealth gap' and a wide ranging exercise to draw out the views of Leeds Citizens for future campaigns. We envisage the organisations will draw upon the strengths of the city's faith, trade union, migrant and community organisations in developing our own Leeds brand of community organising.
>
> (Battle 2008)

We held this initial meeting deliberately in Leeds Civic Hall, to reclaim the public space, and invited representatives of the Citizens Foundation organisation (based in London) to guide us through their experiences of establishing London Citizens. Though well over 100 turned up, the meeting did not lead on to constructive follow up. Interestingly, committed individuals and single-issue campaigners (drawing from a specific 'activist' segment of the city) dominated the event, rather than representatives of local community organisations in the city. There was out spoken resistance to the representative from London Citizens linking the ethos of community organising explicitly to 'Catholic social teaching'. Despite the presence of both Catholic and other Christians, a religious tone and presence was not warmly welcomed. But the real downfall was that it was a meeting of interested individuals rather than representatives of groups, organisations and institutions, whether voluntary, faith-based or statutory. Furthermore, despite efforts beforehand at widespread consultation, a 'campaign agenda' had prematurely displaced any emphasis on the structured 'craft' of broad-based community organising developed in America and London. Consequently, the campaign themes were not well rooted in the daily experiences of the communities and there was no 'institutional depth'. In practice there was an urge to rush out with the campaign banners but without ensuring there were any marchers.

But the idea did not dissolve. Again, a small persistent and committed team, interestingly including some (and not by design) strongly rooted in faith-based organisations, continued to work to set up a Leeds-wide community organisation and eventually decided to open up formal negotiations to join up to 'Citizens UK' and officially register as Leeds Citizens following their broad-based practices and craft including sending members to full-scale national training. In 2015, Leeds Citizens, having raised the funds to employ a full-time, trained 'Citizen's Organiser', Tom Chigbo, was formally launched at a founding assembly of over 650 wide-ranging group representatives at Elland Road Stadium.

Leeds Citizens

However, understanding how to do community organising in Leeds needs a context. Leeds, though thriving and spot-on national average figures as a whole, is a deeply divided city, spatially, economically, socially and politically; and economic divisions in particular are increasing. Dissected by a river, a railway and a canal running through the city in parallel, Leeds is sliced into north and south. Moreover, the radial road pattern into the centre from the outer ring road like the spokes of a bike wheel further segments the neighbourhoods of the city. Thus Leeds has remained to a large extent a city of nearly a million people split up into a collection of separate 'urban villages', some of which appear self-contained and rarely cross the radial boundaries.

Communities are therefore separated and rarely come together with any sense of a Leeds community.

Leeds Citizens is a serious attempt to break across the boundaries and get communities in different corners to come together in city-wide 'gatherings', linking groups and institutions that in the past had not met or interacted. Leeds Citizens is therefore an independent alliance of dues-paying faith-based, educational and community organisations working together for the common good of Leeds through the practices and craft of 'community organising'. From seven major founding partners in the city, it has built up an organisation already consisting primarily of some thirty-seven committed organisations (referred to in community organising as 'institutions'). These include all major faith-based communities in Leeds: Christian, Muslim and Jewish schools; colleges and universities; and local resident and community groups. Moreover, Leeds Citizens is part of Citizens UK, the national community organising charity, with Citizens groups in London, Cardiff, Birmingham, Milton Keynes, Nottingham and Tyne and Wear. Citizens UK is itself an offshoot from the broad-based community organising movement initiated in Chicago by Saul Alinsky in the 1930s, now known in America as the Industrial Areas Foundation. The basic initiative was to bring people together in communities so that they could effectively mobilise their power for real change in their circumstances in the face of failing trade union power and increasing corrupt politics. At its founding assembly in Leeds in 2015, Leeds Citizens brought together over 650 representatives from right across the city to address their three priorities; poverty, mental health for young and old and local bus transport that had emerged from deep listening campaigns, house meetings and neighbourhood walks, building on the stories and experiences of ordinary people. Those in power responsible for these policy areas were invited, came and were briefly questioned on their commitment to act on these priorities. They were respectfully presented with cases and publicly and politely called to account and to follow up. As the practice of 'community organising' developed, an insistence on groups (referred to as 'institutions') joining the alliance rather than committed and keen individuals developed. Groups mean depth and support. There was to be no reliance on charismatic individuals. A person had to be in a group to come along as a representative and be able to bring others along with them. Institutions became the door key to come in and group turnout the measure of institutional strength. In other words, 'institutions' and 'relational' work are the framework of community organising.

The American Dora Schrantz defined community organising as 'a set of strategic disciplines and practices to build the capacity of people to participate and shape democratic life' (Schrantz 2013, online). David Walls, in his book *Community Organising*, extends this definition to emphasise that 'participants are serious about building powerful organisations based on their interests and values, in which they are accountable to one another for their contribution towards the common good'. Coming together as representatives of a group or institution (and having to report back) builds in that personal accountability to others often neglected in traditional democratic politics. Walls notes: 'community organising is a process that seeks to build powerful, purposeful, coordinated and disciplined activity by groups of people who support and challenge each other to affirm and advance their values' (Walls 2015: 6). Interestingly, member institutions of Leeds Citizens as well as supporting city-wide common campaigns have also directed their strength at the same time to addressing particular local community issues with some real practical successes.

Member institutions are expected to contribute dues to fund a Leeds-wide trained and skilled organiser and cover organisational overheads including regular local training sessions so that Leeds Citizens is not only totally independent of government, council or lottery grants (which usually dry up) but is also building a shared, sustainable, long-term economic base to rely on. Raising dues from poor communities in Leeds is hard but our aim is long-term independence and survival. In the early days, Saul Alinsky identified the skills required from the ideal 'community organiser' as

> curiosity, irreverence, imagination, sense of humour, a blurred vision of a better world (as opposed to a sharp defined ideologically defined vision) an

> organised personality, a strong ego, an open mind with political relativity and the ability to create the new out of the old.
>
> (Walls 2015: 42)

Our Leeds organiser Tom Chigbo has much of the range.

Our regular 'gatherings' led by the leadership group bring representatives together to evaluate progress on development and campaigns, to share experiences and ideas and to make new connections, while developing the capacity to see wider and join with others in challenging national policies, not least those impacting adversely on Leeds Citizens. In the meantime, it was a real highlight in an evaluation session after a gathering in one of the city's largest mosques to hear a Jewish rabbi comment 'I never imagined I would pray in a mosque.'

Just conversations

But bringing group 'institutions' together is only part of the purpose. The aim is not to corral or simply 'round up' big meetings, in press gang fashion, important though a show of turnout with a large public presence of support can be. There is a deeper personal challenge in the 'craft' of organising. People are called together by building on hundreds of personal 'one-to-one', 'face-to-face' conversations. These are also disciplined, structured and purposeful conversations of about twenty minutes, which are not 'chit chat' but a relatively serious attempt to draw out a 'common interest' in order to build up the institutional strength in depth of Leeds Citizens (which includes strengthening the organisations themselves in terms of members and activity). One-to-one conversations are the antidote to the faux-relational activities of social media. Good though digital connections can be in terms of communication, face-to-face personal interaction remains vital. One-to-one conversations therefore build up and strengthen a web of personal relationships, 'reweaving the fabric of civil society' as the Citizens UK banner puts it. It is detailed regular work. Moreover, one-to-one conversations are not just meant to be initial first- and final-time conversation meetings. They need repeating and repeating to deepen ties and understanding. Without regular 'one-to-ones' taking place by all Leeds Citizens among each other and reaching out, the basic 'relational aim' of building a powerful organisation is unsustainable. Just as some people measure their walking steps each day to ensure there is no underestimation of their healthy living effort, perhaps Leeds Citizens need an 'app' to ensure plenty of regular 'one-to-ones' become part of our weekly lives and common practice.

Catholic social teaching and power

But the purpose cannot be to ensnare others to join. Interestingly, Saul Alinsky was in correspondence with the influential French Catholic philosopher Jacques Maritain, whose work insisted from Catholic social teaching that we are all 'persons in community' first and foremost. Maritain spelt out that an 'active human subject' as a 'social being' should participate in creating the world, acting upon it, rather than being shaped by it. In other words, he was interested in the development of dynamic participatory persons. Alinsky's original community organising work got strong support from the Catholic Church in Chicago and elsewhere in America. Notably the Catholic Church has been strong in the development of London Citizens, led by Bishop Victor Guazelli and Catholic laywoman Bernadette Farrell in the 1980s. Key concepts of Catholic social teaching, such as subsidiarity, solidarity and the common good, are regularly referred to as a theoretical underpinning. But it is not a case of Catholics simply being told to become social and community activists. Relational organising and leadership training are central to the structured craft of community organising, which usually focuses on the practice of the one-to-one conversations, of deep listening in communities and relational building, to develop a powerful organisation which is recognised as having power. Training sessions for organisers and the development of new local leadership are the framework of building a Citizens organisation.

In the 1980s I visited the Industrial Areas Foundation in Chicago and attended an action day in Queens, New York. New to community organising, though steeped in local community development, I dipped in and out as an observer and left feeling that the action was somewhat manipulative, ensuring turnout for the public demonstration but without real participant engagement. People should not be used as a means to an end, however just. I became resistant especially to the suggested notion of 'power' despite it being carefully spelt out as simply 'the ability to act effectively in the world'. Years later, through the Citizens UK training, it became clearer that the goal of community organising was not to 'speak truth to power' but rather to gain power through action to bring about change. For some, that commitment to building a 'power organisation' and using power to bring about change introduces an approach to power that at first sight does not sit easily with traditional Christian theological approaches to service, not least in the spirit of the vulnerable suffering servant in solidarity with the least. Kenotic power, imitating the weakness and vulnerability of Christ, became the way to witness to the Gospel rather than working to get power. That 'kenosis theology' was not to be regarded as compatible with institutional power building and power challenging. More generally, power and love are traditionally set at odds and not only in Christian theology.

Yet powerfully kenotic

In her perceptive essay 'The Dialectics of Democracy', the Catholic theologian Anna Rowlands notes that '[k]enotic political theology sits perhaps more easily with the Christian workers movement than it does with Alinsky-style organising' (Rowlands 2013: 351). Yet that kenotic sense of self-sacrifice and service need not be in opposition to building up institutional and collective power. Interestingly, it was Jacques Maritain who in his letter to Saul Alinsky in 1954 suggested that he should meet up with Fr René Voillaume, the founder of a new religious order, 'The Little Brothers and Sisters Of Jesus', following the inspiration of Little Brother Charles De Foucauld who lived the simplest life of prayer and service as a hermit among the Tuareg people in the Algerian desert (Engel 1998). Charles de Foucauld was the apotheosis of the kenotic tradition and a fight between some Tuaregs ended up with his being killed. The writings of René Voillaume, *Brothers of Men* and *Seeds of the Desert* are his letters of encouragement to the members of his new order of brothers and sisters, who live a contemplative life alongside the poor in communities throughout the world. Until recently there was a community of Little Brothers of Jesus in Leeds. René Voillaume's letters encourage the new communities to sustain their lives of prayer and service to the world in which they live, witnessing to 'contemplation in a world of work and action'. But this quiet, kenotic, small community witness is characterised by a deepening sense of personal self-understanding that becomes explicit and a contributor to personal and community building.

One of the tools in the craft box of community organising that is underemphasised is the 'stick man exercise'. Each person in the training session is at some point invited to draw a stick man outline and attach to it a brief profile of their personal relationships, personal history, priorities, commitments and ambitions. Often this is done as a solitary personal exercise to clarify one's own interests (and not shared with others). But it could be done in twos and threes, as René Voillaume recommended for the fraternities, so that each person's own view of themselves is counterchecked and possibly challenged by a colleague. In other words, the stick man exercise could be a real exercise in developing deeper self-awareness. Built into the community organising craft, therefore, is the potential for developing self-awareness and personal transformation, including discovering that I too might be actually part of the problem as well as part of the solution. That stick man exercise could translate into a kenotic exercise of developing personal accountability to others who view us differently from the way we see ourselves and our particular contributions to the whole.

In other words, the 'theology of kenosis', rather than being discarded and those interested being sent off to work on setting up houses of hospitality, could complement a real development of personal accountability to others within the context of community organising. It is precisely that sense of personal accountability that seems sadly lacking in our currently defective democratic politics. Moreover, the stick man exercise could be a helpful antidote to our cultural narcissistic overdrives.

Power built through the strength of combining and supportive institutions, and developed from within member institutions through deep listening sessions and 'gatherings', moves us away from campaigning as individual single-issue initiatives that so often flare up and die to no practical effect. We can begin to regard ourselves as growing members of a community agency.

Assemblies: the new politics

Citizens assemblies of everyone gathered together are the new politics of effective pressure and accountability. Bringing large groups of a wide range of institutions together with clear policy demands based on personal experiential stories and deep listening campaigns can call politicians and power (and money holders) to account in public. Well-organised, disciplined, respectful and courteous and focused on clear brief questioning and answers can put politicians on the spot much better than a rowdy hustings, an imperious journalist or TV *Question Time*. We did exactly that at the local elections assembly in Leeds, held at Trinity Church this year. Since the central purpose is to remain 'people-focused' and to create space for new leadership and at the same time get real commitments from powerful people, it is important to have developed working relations with them to follow through.

In other words, preparation is all and discipline, especially in terms of time and content is crucial. Of course, throughout this process of using power to challenge power there will be, and should be, tensions, occasional conflicts, dramatic symbolic actions to make a point go home. Tensions may need to be generated to demonstrate that Leeds Citizens has some power through institutional depth. But the aim is not that of a negative, confrontational, protest group. The aim is to win policy and practice change. In Leeds, pressure on the major bus company in the city has already led to a working relationship to get into the details of attitudes, fares and routes. The health authorities are at last recognising that mental health for the young and old is a real priority in our communities (though it is not mentioned in local and national elections) and needs supportive practical responses. Campaigns to displace loan sharks with local credit unions and to enlist real 'living wage employers' (including the city council) is well under way in our local communities, with positive support and continued attention to detail. Building power also means developing confidence, with new leaders emerging, stepping forward to speak up, undergoing training and celebrating community and policy successes.

The recent London Citizens mayoral election assembly was a spectacular example of personal stories, but also of song, drama and pageantry, with the 'march of the key workers' seeking affordable homes, all providing a build-up to a brief tough questioning of two key candidates. Attended by over 6,000 Londoners, power and celebration and accountability danced together to effect. Of course, the sheer scale, diversity and power of London overwhelms efforts elsewhere in the country, where many older towns and cities are still struggling with the after-effects of industrial decline and new migration movements. Moreover, many local communities remain entrenched and feel cut off from civic and political life entirely. Political renewal through community organising in our cities may take on newer and more imaginative forms and take longer than current London manifestations.

Community organising: a long-term project

Developing new local leadership together from the base upwards through a strategic rather than a protest movement really is seen to work at building democratic accountable power for all. It can revitalise public life, strengthen institutions, including local communities, and bring about tangible improvements in the conditions of the poor and excluded in our society. Action campaigns developed through institutional listening and rooted in the real daily concerns of people, and organising and generating power in depth and breadth of support, can be channelled into shaping public policy.

Of course, much though local actions can genuinely transform the quality of life of local communities, real economic and political power can remain elsewhere and the need to address national budgets and policies remains. In turn, that makes cooperation between the Citizens organisations that make up Citizens UK an imperative rather than an optional extra. While cities have their own distinctive histories and characteristics, they cannot escape national and international power forces. The initiatives of Citizens UK in response to the international Syrian and European refugee crisis are good examples of the need for effective coordinated national pressure and action. Together Citizens UK can make a real difference.

In Leeds we need to pay more attention to political, economic and social 'power analysis' of the city, which we should work on more regularly in our institutions and together as Leeds Citizens. Neglecting the power analysis concedes the power.

We need a closer analysis of the forces, often hidden, that are making key decisions for the future shape and direction of our city's structure, employment prospects and cultural development. We need to have a clearer vision of social protection and educational opportunities. Analysis of political opportunities should be an element in that power analysis that all institutions making up Leeds Citizens should undertake and share. That power analysis needs to become part of our regular training.

But we need to continually bear in mind that the 'process' of community organising is as important as the campaigning itself. Moreover, it is rather a more personal, reflexive and reiterative process than it first appears. Perhaps community organising needs to place more explicit emphasis on its long-term vision, spell out its values regularly and counterbalance a view of an emphasis on 'short-term interests' and pragmatism with real possibilities of political renewal including training from potential and elected councillors and representatives. Saul Alinsky was critical of action groups that emphasised short-term mobilisation over long-term organisation and that relied on charismatic leadership rather than patiently developing new local leadership. Promoting grass-roots leadership is a central aim of community organising, which is why transmitting the 'craft' through training and actions is vital. Citizens community organising is here for the long haul. It could make the crucial difference in a world of burnt-out politics.

At an anniversary review of the fifty years since Vatican II, held at Leeds Trinity University, a traditional binary view re-emerged. It was claimed that those in the Church involved in organisations such as Justice and Peace Commissions had turned the Church into a version of social action that betrayed the Church's essential commitment to prayer and liturgy. The real Christians were those praying in Church and the activists were selling the Church short. That tension between contemplation and action has been around from the earliest days, not least represented by the Desert Fathers, who moved out of the stressful cities into the hermitages of the deserts. Tensions between monasticism and mission echoed down the centuries, leading to new 'religious orders' and perhaps best captured in the twentieth century in the seminal work of the Trappist monk Thomas Merton entitled *Contemplation in a World of Action*. Prayer and social action should be harnessed together as a manifestation of expressing both love of God and love of neighbour simultaneously.

Of course, there were stronger background agendas, not least fear of engagement and contamination in a world that was taken to be increasingly hostile to the Christian vision. Liberation theologies became a test bed for a newly integrated approach rooted in the poor south of the Church's experience. In the emerging post-industrial north, particularly in the densely populated manufacturing cities, the pressure of working conditions and the cry for social justice and fair political representation became a concern not least for immigrant-dominated local Churches.

This is an attempt to glance over the history of 'broad-based community organising', which was sparked off in Chicago in the 1930s and strongly supported by the Catholic Church in vision and resourcing and adopted more recently in Britain some twenty years ago developed as London Citizens (again strongly supported by the Catholic Church at parish and the highest levels) before spreading to other towns and cities in Britain, including Leeds. Community organising has constantly claimed the support of basic Catholic social teaching as foundational to its vision and values. In Britain, support for citizens organising has developed as a thoroughly ecumenical and indeed 'inter-faith' and wider movement but for Christians engaging with the practices of 'community organising' there has remained a lingering question of the compatibility of working to build up a 'powerful' challenging organisation, pressing for real change, with a Christian dedication to service in the spirit of the vulnerable and suffering servant Jesus Christ. Self-sacrifice, not power building, and the exercise of power relations and negotiations, are generally considered antithetical to Christian witness. Taking the experience of the development of Leeds Citizens in the last few years, and in particular the development of the 'craft' of organising, expressed and learned together through training workshops, this apparent tension between what is classically called the 'kenotic theology' of the 'suffering servant' and a positive 'theology of power' ('For thine is the power, the kingdom and the glory') is not irreconcilable. Rather, it should be integrated and synthesised through engagement and commitment to the community organising model and developing a new rooted, ground-based, properly and personally accountable and democratic politics for real change, not least for the poor in our societies.

Bibliography

Battle, J. (2008). Letter about community organising in Leeds. Unpublished letter, private archive in Leeds.

Engel, L.J. (1998). The influence of Saul Alinsky on the campaign for human development. *Theological Studies*, *59*: 646.

Maritain, J. (1948). *The Person and the Common Good*. London: Geoffrey Bless.

Merton, T. (1998). *Contemplation in a World of Action*. Notre Dame, IN: University of Notre Dame Press.

Rowlands, A. (2013). The dialectics of democracy: broad based community organising, Catholic social teaching and asylum seeking in a UK Context. *Journal of Catholic Thought*, *10*(2): 351.

Schrantz, D. (2013). Community based organising must change: but how? *Rooflines*. Online. Available at www.rooflines.org/2908 (accessed 23 November 2016).

Voillaume, R. (1966). *Brothers of Men: Letters to the Petits Frères*. London: DLT.

Voillaume, R. (1972). *Seeds of the Desert: The Legacy of Charles de Foucauld*. Lincoln: Anthony Clarke.

Walls, D. (2015). *Community Organising*. Cambridge: Polity Press.

5 *Tzedakah*, *Tikkun*

Jewish approaches to social justice

Alana Vincent

Introduction

This chapter will present a historicised phenomenological account of the two dominant forms of social justice within Judaism: *tzedakah* (justice) and *tikkun* (advocacy, or, literally, 'mending'). *Tzedakah* is a core principle of religious Judaism and also has profound resonances within secular Judaism; the history of the Anglo-Jewish community is illustrative of the manner and extent to which *tzedakah* has shaped Jewish identity. The concept of *tikkun* is conceptually more ambiguous, and even now is understood very differently by different Jewish communities. Liberal Jews understand *tikkun* to be both the action of social justice advocacy (of which charitable giving is only a single component) and, simultaneously, a meta-principle which governs the interpretation of *halakah* (Jewish law) even to the point of overriding particular *halakhic* restrictions which may otherwise impede advocacy activity. Ultra-Orthodox Jews are, conversely, likely to view strict adherence to *halakah*, including the practice of *tzedakah*, as the primary means of *tikkun ha-olam* (the mending of creation).

In addition to the key distinction between liberal and Orthodox social justice activity which emerges when *tzedakah* and *tikkun* are considered as modes of action, this chapter will also explore distinctions between ethnic and religious Judaism which emerge when consideration is given to the particular targets of social justice activity: which causes are self-evidently worthy of either charitable or activist intervention? What language is deployed in attempts to promote a cause through appeals to common (Jewish) values? Through a close examination of these issues, the ways in which different traditions of Judaism construct and enact concepts of social justice within both religious and ethnic frameworks will be discursively explored.

Tzedakah

> Tzedakah, tzedakah you shall pursue.
>
> (Deut 16:20)

There is an ambiguity in the translation of Deuteronomy 16:20 which is central to any discussion of Judaism and social justice. The word {justice צדק}, rendered in most translations of that passage as 'justice' (and in other passages as 'righteousness'), appears in the Torah most often referring to legal judgments, although a notion of economic justice is present in Leviticus 19:36 and Deuteronomy 25:15, which command 'a just weight and a just measure' – one is prohibited from cheating those with whom one does business. The prophetic literature expands on this theme, most clearly in Isaiah (e.g. 11:4: 'But with {justice קדצ} he shall judge the poor, and make equal the meek'), and by the time of the redaction of the Mishnah in 220 CE, the word took on a primarily economic connotation. In rabbinic Judaism, *tzedakah* means specifically action to raise the economic status and human dignity of the poor (Marks, Dollahite and Dew 2009: 21). Its linguistic and scriptural genealogy serve as a potent reminder that this action is not optional but a basic religious obligation – in fact, Midrash describes withholding from charitable giving as 'rob[bing] the poor of that which God has granted them' (Numbers Rabbah 5:1).

The recent Institute for Jewish Policy Research report *Charitable Giving among Britain's Jews* found that 77 per cent of respondents – slightly more than one in four Jews surveyed – rated charitable giving as either 'very important' (36 per cent) or 'fairly important' (41 per cent) to their Jewish identity. By this measure, charitable giving outweighs 'supporting Israel' (69 per cent), 'marrying another Jew' (65 per cent) and 'keeping kosher' (50 per cent) (Graham and Boyd, 2016: 8). The study further found that the level of an individual's religious engagement significantly correlates not only to their general attitude towards and practice of charitable giving but also to their choice of which organisations to give to, with Haredi (ultra-Orthodox) Jews being most likely to give solely to Jewish organisations and non-practising Jews being most likely to give solely to non-Jewish organisations – although the vast majority of Jews surveyed gave to a mix of both Jewish and non-Jewish charitable causes.[1] 'Jewish organisations' are not limited to organisations which promote some aspect of religious life; the majority of the 500 organisations listed in the UK Jewish Charity Guide are concerned with a broad range of secular concerns, including medical research, humanitarian aid, arts and culture and social welfare.[2]

While major philanthropy is conducted through the normal system of cheques and bank transfers, the *tzedekah* box, or *pushke*, as it is called in Yiddish, is an iconic symbol of the practice of charitable giving. The practice of keeping a special box to collect coins for charitable distribution originated among the Hasidim of Eastern Europe in the early nineteenth century. The practice of collecting money for particular causes in a box kept in the home spread with emigrants from the Pale of Settlement over the course of the nineteenth and early twentieth centuries, and the box has become an iconic item of Jewish ritual home furnishing.[3] The Jewish Museum New York boasts two examples in its online catalogue, both designed by contemporary artists, although these are admittedly more images of an object familiar to their creators (and with which their creators expected their audience to be also familiar) than functional objects in their own right. The Israel Museum's substantial collection of Judaica contains quite a few examples – not quite as numerous as the spice boxes used in the *havdalah* ritual, which marks the close of the Sabbath, but sufficient that a viewer is not left in doubt about the boxes forming a standard part of a Jewish home's religious furnishing. The boxes in the collection of the Israel Museum are, however, all examples of fine silver craft; similar to those in the New York Jewish Museum, they appear to have been primarily objects of display, rather than of use – although the same might be said of the vast majority of the other sorts of ritual equipment in the museum's collection.

As the terms and interest of the 2016 Institute for Jewish Policy Research report suggest, the patterns of UK Jewish charitable giving are seen by both charitable organisations and the individuals who give to them as significant markers of integration and ethnic identity. Historically, this is unsurprising; in the nineteenth century, many Jewish charitable organisations began as attempts by the relatives affluent members of the established Jewish community to protect their social position by raising the status of the central European Jewish immigrants who arrived steadily throughout the century. Under the 1601 Poor Relief Act, responsibility for social welfare fell to the parish – and the reforms of the 1843 Poor Law Amendment Act did not alter this; impoverished Jews did not have an easy route of access to the support provided by the workhouse system, and recent immigrants were by and large unlikely to have the social capital necessary to participate in established mutual aid organisations or friendly societies.[4] In response to this, a number of organisations emerged which aimed to provide a parallel system of support, demonstrating the capacity of the Jewish community to self-manage without becoming a drain on government resources.[5] Chief among these was the Jewish Board of Guardians, established in 1859. The Board of Guardians and similar organisations followed the standard pattern of Victorian philanthropy, emphasising aid to the 'deserving poor' rather than the more radical concept of economic justice which modern commentators have drawn from *tzedakah*.[6]

In light of this history, it is notable that there is no *pushke* in the collection of the Jewish Museum London. Nor is there a *tzedakah* box. A diligent search through the online catalogue will eventually reveal precisely five objects which might have borne either label:

1 a small cask,[7] with staves and head made from a silver-coloured metal (materials information is not included in the catalogue listing) and hoops accented with gold, branded in gold with a Magen David and the initials JNF; in the place where a bung hole might be, there is a coin slot. Of the five, this is the one which has the most information about both provenance – it was commissioned from a Jewish owned furniture manufacturer[8] in 1924 for a couple living in the suburbs of London – and social context: JNF stands for 'Jewish National Fund' and the box is presented as signifying the increase of Zionist sentiment among British Jews in the wake of the Balfour Declaration.
2 a very plain, straight-sided tankard made of copper,[9] which is described as a collection box from the Great Synagogue in Duke's Place, and dated in the

late seventeenth or early eighteenth century. There is only one photograph of this object, taken from the side, with the lid closed; the viewer must infer the presence of a coin slot.

3 a very similar tankard,[10] with provenance traced to the Hambro Synagogue; this one is photographed with its lid open and the coin slot thus clearly visible. No date is given for its manufacture, but, as the Hambro community split from the Great Synagogue in 1710 and constructed its own building in 1725, a date of the early eighteenth century can be deduced, and the similarity in design accounted for.

4 a barrel-shaped tankard with a scrolled handle and an ornate botanical design chased on its surface, 'said to have been used in a Sarajevo synagogue and … probably made in the Balkans'.[11] Again, the object is photographed only from the side and the presence of a coin slot on the top must be inferred by the viewer. The means by which the tankard might open to be emptied is not evident.

5 a cylindrical tankard[12] with a square handle and several rows of decorative banding, which might look plain next to the Sarajevo tankard but appears almost fussy compared to the Great Synagogue and Hambro Synagogue examples. This item is photographed both closed and open, to demonstrate its unusual double opening mechanism. The door to the lower compartment is inscribed in Hebrew lettering. Although the angle of the photograph prevents the viewer from deciphering the inscription, the catalogue informs us that it bears a date and the name, 'The Brotherhood for Clothing the Poor', which is presumably the charity responsible for its manufacture.

The collection evidences an equal number of deed and tally boxes associated with particular Jewish charities that operated in and around London in the long nineteenth century (the Bread, Meat and Coal Society, the Jews' Temporary Shelter, the Soup Kitchen for the Jewish Poor, and the Jews Deaf & Dumb Home); both of these collections are dwarfed by the museum's holding of snuff boxes. While it is true that the examples in the Jewish Museum New York and the Israel Museum are, for the most part, objects of display rather than of use, their presence in those collections, and absence from the collection of the JML, speaks not only to the museum's focus on public-facing, masculine expressions of Judaism, but also to the distinctive understanding of *tzedakah* within the Anglo-Jewish community: as a social, rather than spiritual, obligation.

It is notable that item 1, the only item in the Jewish Museum London's collection that fits the classic profile of a *pushke* – that is to say, a box intended to hold private charitable collections which accrue over time – is dedicated specifically to the Jewish National Fund.[13] Shaul Stampfer (2010) connects the development of the *pushke* to the early waves of Eastern European *aliyah* (immigration to the land of Israel). He notes that the *pushke* permitted charitable giving to be both equalised, in that wealthy and poor were both enabled to give according to their means without public display, and also regularised, so that the communities of immigrants dependent on the proceeds of *pushke* campaigns could expect to receive a steady level of continuous financial assistance.[14]

The two needs which the *pushke* addressed reflect the Jewish understanding of charity as a basic religious obligation from which no person is exempt. In the words of the Shulchan Aruch 34:2, 'Every person is obligated to give charity according to his capabilities, even a poor man who gets his living from charity.' This principle is materialised in item 5; the purpose of the double opening mechanism is to permit the user to open up a bottom compartment for receiving alms from others, and then to deposit a portion of their income into the upper compartment for distribution among those in even greater need. There are several rationales available for this understanding. In the first instance, there is the theological conviction that all of creation belongs to God and that humans, acting as stewards, are obliged to share whatever passes into their care with others (Ulmer and Ulmer 2014: 46–7). The second rationale is that one who receives charity should not feel themselves diminished thereby, but should be enabled to maintain full participation in the life of the community. In other words, the practice of *tzedakah* is governed, in part, by the same concern which also underlies much modern discourse about *tikkun olam*: human dignity.

Tikkun Olam

> ... every phrase associated with the idea of Tikkun Olam, phrases like—'light unto the nation,' or 'the Jewish mission,' or 'ethical universalism,' all those things became code words for assimilation, reform, and the whole concept of Tikkun Olam became suspect. What a tragedy that is today.
>
> (Sacks 1997)

Tikkun Ha-olam (literally 'repair of the world') plays many roles within the universe of Jewish thought, but perhaps one of its most important functions is to mark out the conceptual divide between the Orthodox and non-Orthodox denominations. The term makes an appearance in a ruling attributed to Gamaliel the Elder (*c.* first century CE) in the Mishnah[15] tractate Gittin 4:2, where a man's ability to cancel or otherwise invalidate a bill of divorce – invalidating any marriage his former wife might have contracted in the meantime – is constrained 'for the sake of the repair of the world'.[16] In a similar way to *tzedakah*, the mishnaic *tikkun* may be understood as ultimately concerned with economic justice; the distinction between them is that the former is redistributive, while the latter is structural, aiming to prevent individuals from being forced into situations which would cause them to require *tzedakah* – if the cancellation of divorces became a common custom, it would seriously constrain women's ability to remarry, putting them at increased risk of poverty. Jacobs (2007) has suggested that the mishnaic *tikkun* is applied 'in response to situations in which a particular legal detail threatens to overturn an entire system'.

The phrase also makes a relatively early appearance in the text of the Alienu, the closing prayer of the daily prayer service,[17] in a request that God 'repair the world, Your holy kingdom'. There is some dispute over the dating of the Aleinu; it is often attributed to Rav (*c.*175–247 CE), and many scholars have taken this attribution as more likely to be accurate than the folk attribution which suggests the prayer was composed by Joshua on the occasion of the fall of Jericho. Jacob Neusner (1966: 164–7), however, has argued that available evidence suggests that Rav was responsible only for some slight emendations to a much older text – though he does not go quite so far as to attribute the original to Joshua. The question of the date is somewhat significant, insofar as a very early date for the Aleinu would cement the suggestion that the Mishnah is drawing on a previously established principle for its rulings, where an attribution to Rav suggests a concept of *tikkun ha-olam* emerging wholesale from the context of the 1st and 2nd centuries. Regardless of the date, however, in the Aleinu *tikkun olam* does a rather different job than in the Mishnah: rather than depending on a court and witnesses to enact laws permitting an individual to maintain their place in society (by e.g. permitting a woman abandoned by her husband to seek another), the Aleinu's *tikkun olam* looks towards a future in which God acts directly to establish divine sovereignty. These divergent understandings of the concept were reconciled in the medieval period: in the twelfth century, Maimonides posited *tikkun olam* as the underlying principle of all *halakah*, clearing the way for the Zohar's mystical reimagination of the concept.[18] The Kabbalistic system positioned *tikkun* as a cosmic action, through which humans became co-creators, assisting with the mending of the created order through the performance of *mitzvot* (commandments).[19] This performance constitutes what Rabbi Jonathan Sacks (2005: 77) has called 'a redemption of small steps', in which each individual act, no matter how small, takes on cosmic significance. Following the messianic disappointment of the Sabbatean movement, however, the concept slid into obscurity and disrepute. It emerged from the former only in the early twentieth century and, arguably, has never emerged from the latter.

The popularisation of *tikkun olam* in modern Jewish discourse can be traced back to the work of Gershom Scholem, the great historian of Jewish mysticism; the use of the phrase to denote political action dates to the interwar period (Cooper 2013). But it was the Reform rabbi Emil Fackenheim who can be credited with reactivating the concept as a lived religious idea.[20] Broadly progressive Judaism[21] embraced *tikkun olam* as a quasi-mystical, meta-*halakhic* principle; rather than a redemption of small steps, in which the framework of *halakah* infuses everyday activities with cosmic significance, contemporary *tikkun* measures the details of *halakah* against an idealised notion of cosmic redemption, most commonly predetermined by the concerns of human dignity and secular social justice discourse. While critics of this new form of *tikkun* rightly point out that it is an accurate reconstruction of neither the mishnaic nor the medieval concepts, the objections thus raised often fail to account for the degree to which *tikkun* has been a historically unstable concept, always slightly vague, always open to interpretation and reinterpretation depending on the particular needs of its promoters, as well as the degree to which the current usage of the term does retain elements of its earlier incarnations. This continuity, as well as the controversies associated with modern *tikkun*, can be illustrated by an examination of the debate on homosexuality in the rabbinate.

Debate on homosexuality

The debate on homosexuality in the rabbinate is of long standing; the Reform movement's Central Conference for American Rabbis (CCAR) published the Resolution on the Rights of Homosexuals in 1977. This resolution frames the issue in straightforward, syllogistic terms:

> WHEREAS, the Central Conference of American Rabbis has consistently supported civil rights and civil liberties for all people, especially for those from whom these rights and liberties have been withheld, and
>
> WHEREAS, homosexuals have in our society long endured discrimination,
>
> BE IT THEREFORE RESOLVED, that we encourage legislation which decriminalizes homosexual acts between consenting adults, and prohibits discrimination against them as persons, and
>
> BE IT FURTHER RESOLVED, that our Reform Jewish religious organizations undertake programs in cooperation with the total Jewish community to implement the above stand.

The rationale of the 1977 resolution is entirely grounded in the language of civil rights, rather than *halakah*: the Reform movement rejects discrimination; homosexuals are discriminated against; therefore the Reform movement rejects discrimination against homosexuals. This rationale carried forward to the 1990 Resolution on Homosexuality and the Rabbinate, which affirmed that any graduate of the Hebrew Union College Jewish Institute of Religion would be automatically admitted to the rabbinate, and that HUC-JIR would not make admissions decisions solely on the basis of sexual orientation (a roundabout way of saying that it cleared the way for the ordination of gay rabbis), and the 2000 resolution that 'the relationship of a Jewish, same gender couple is worthy of affirmation through appropriate Jewish ritual', followed finally by the 2013 resolution which affirmed that the appropriate Jewish ritual should be understood as *kiddushin*, or marriage. The language of the 1990 report, that 'All human beings are created *betselem Elohim*' and that 'their personhood must therefore be accorded full dignity', has become the movement's key theological teaching on sexuality.

In spite of the movement's sizeable membership, in both the US and the UK Reform views are often dismissed from consideration of 'Jewish attitudes', due to the perception of a permissive, 'anything goes' ethos within the movement – a perception not entirely unjustified, given the early history of Reform as a radically assimilationist movement, although such a perception is both out of date and insufficiently attentive to assimilationist tendencies within other branches of Judaism (including, notably, the Anglo-Orthodox community discussed above). For this reason, the *halakah* of the Conservative movement makes a considerably more instructive case study, in spite of its relatively smaller membership. The Conservative movement originated from a schism within the early American Reform movement, and since its inception it has attempted to balance between the Reform theology of continuous revelation and adherence to the more traditional forms of Jewish belief and practice which still retain spiritual and religious significance for the movement's members. Major issues of *halakah* are decided by the Conservative Rabbinical Assembly's Committee on Jewish Law and Standards, which receives queries from congregational rabbis and instructs its members to compose position papers (called *teshuvot*, or responsa); the entire committee votes on each paper, and those which attain the votes of six or more of the twenty-five members of the committee become official positions of the movement. Thus, the concurrence of less than a quarter of the committee is required to render a position official, and when particularly controversial questions are raised the normal procedure is that multiple responsa are presented, and every single one that attains the minimum number of votes becomes *a halakhic* position available to congregational rabbis.

This is what happened in 2006, when the question of the movement's guidance on the inclusion of Jews in same-sex relationships arose. This was not the first time the question had come; there was a substantial discussion in the early 1990s, with a rare consensus statement, barring the blessing of same-sex marriages and the ordination of homosexual rabbis but welcoming gays and lesbians to participation in 'congregations, youth groups, camps, and schools', issued in 1992, and reaffirmed in response to a question about the placement of an openly gay rabbi in 1993. It's important to emphasise that this debate was entirely about recognition within a religious framework; even in 1992, a significant number of the papers submitted to the committee were at pains to emphasise that their view on *halakah* should not be taken as a statement against campaigning for the legitimacy of same-sex relationships in *civil* law, and to explicitly repudiate suggestions that AIDS should be understood as a divine punishment (e.g. Roth 1992: 674). The rationale behind the consensus statement was a combination of perceived clarity in the extant *halakah* on sexuality and a perceived lack of clarity within scientific understandings of how sexuality functions – the argument about the degree of choice involved in sexual orientation was, even then, considered to have potential *halakhic* significance, and a responsum written by Elliot Dorff recommending further study did pass with eight votes in favour, eight opposed, and seven abstentions.

By 2006, an understanding of sexual orientation as innate and mostly unchosen – and of sexual behaviour as therefore the natural expression of that innate orientation – had become far more widely accepted, and of the five papers presented to the Committee on Jewish Law and Standards, three were strongly in favour of finding some way of legitimating same-sex relationships within the social and legal structures of Conservative Judaism. Of these, two were recorded as dissentions, rather than as official positions of the CJLS. One, however, did pass the vote of the committee, with thirteen votes in favour, twelve opposed, and no abstentions; that paper was authored again by Elliot Dorff, in collaboration with Daniel S. Nevins and Avram I. Reisner – Reisner's participation is especially significant, as he voted **against** the Dorff responsum in 1992.

The 2006 paper considers, first, contemporary theories of sexual orientation, then *halakhic* sources regarding homosexual intimacy, and finally engages in an extended discussion on human dignity before arriving at its conclusions, which 'effectively normalize the status of gay and lesbian Jews in the Jewish community'. While a shift in popular understandings of sexual orientation provides the basis for the paper's consideration, the key to its conclusions is the five-page consideration of precisely what sexual acts are forbidden in Torah. Reviewing a range of sources, but relying heavily on Talmud, Maimonides and the Shulhan Aruch – the three major compendia of traditional *halakah* – the paper examines male–male anal intercourse, oral sex, other forms of intimacy covered under the Talmudic category of 'approach', or 'drawing near', and lesbian sex, which Maimonides refers to as 'rubbing'. The paper acknowledges that all of these have been treated as prohibited acts, but notes that only male-on-male anal intercourse is the subject of a prohibition *d'oratia* – as an integral part of the law given in the revelation at Sinai. All other sexual acts are prohibited by rabbinic interpretation – and that prohibition may be subject to interrogation in a way that a prohibition *d'oratia* may not. The paper then turns briefly to consider the feasibility of celibacy, noting that it is *not* a normative or desirable practice within Judaism, and that to expect gay and lesbian Jews who wish to remain observant to become celibate is, in the eyes of the authors, 'not asking for heroism but inviting failure' (Dorff *et al.* 2006: 9) – before dedicating a further five pages to detailing a number of places in the Talmud where commandments that are normally taken quite seriously (mostly pertaining to ritual purity or Sabbath observance) are superseded by concerns for human dignity.

In other words, the authors of the responsum pursue, by a far more exacting path, the same argument that the CCAR embraced in 1990; the emphasis on human dignity is not a peculiarity of Reform theology. Dorff *et al.*, however, have to answer counterclaims introduced in the intervening years, most notably the claim by Rabbi Joel Roth – the author of the 1992 responsum most closely reflected in the consensus statement – that the principle of human dignity may only permit an individual to suspend an ordinary interpretation of *halakah* for the benefit of another person; dignity may not be the cause for an individual to claim exemption for themselves (Roth 2006: 22). This counterclaim is disposed of first by another flurry of citational argument, but, second, and more importantly, by the argument that:

> Dignity is a social phenomenon. In all of [the cases cited], there is interplay between the dignity of the actor and the dignity of his neighbours.... This, of course, is precisely our point. We are concerned for the dignity of gay and lesbian Jews not only because we are sympathetic to their dilemma, but also because their humiliation is our humiliation.... When gay and lesbian Jews are finally welcomed to take their rightful places in our community,

then we will have safeguarded their dignity as individuals, and our dignity as a community.

(Dorff *et al.* 2006: 16)

None of the authors of the response to the CJLS used the language of *tikkun* outright, but the logic underlying the statements is clear and consistent with the 'tikkunista' view critiqued in March (2010):[22] there are larger concerns which can and must overrule even the most entrenched Jewish tradition as well as the details of *halakah*. The important lesson to take from this is that the conclusions drawn by Dorff *et al.*, or indeed in the 1977 CCAR statement, are drawn not *in spite of* the law, but *because* of the law; they emerge naturally from a very detailed process of *halakhic* reasoning – by which we should understand not only reasoning within the framework provided by traditional *halakhic* texts but also reasoning about *halakah* and its role in the community, informed by the broader concerns of human dignity and social justice. At the same time, it is clear that these rulings are outside of the boundaries of normative Orthodox Judaism, and an appeal to a meta-*halakhic* principle which is similarly outside the boundaries of normative Orthodoxy is unlikely to bridge the gap. This is not to say that there are no meta-*halakhic* principles recognised within Orthodoxy; one might argue the principle of *pikuach nefesh* (the preservation of life) effectively functions as such – but a determined opponent might note that the precedence of *pikuach nefesh* over ritual concerns is explicitly enshrined within traditional *halakah*, and the explicit legal function of *tikkun olam* is limited at best.

To conclude, then, the two major frameworks within which Judaism addresses issues of social justice, while not mutually incompatible, have each developed in response to particular social and political pressures on the communities in which they are dominant. Anglo-Orthodoxy retains the *tzedakah* model as developed in response to the project of assimilation in Victorian England, while American progressive Judaism has become characterised by the *tikkun* model, which was shaped by a project of assimilation undertaken largely during the civil rights era. In spite of claims to the contrary, the *tikkun* model is not substantially more assimilationist than the *tzedakah* model, provided that the former is understood within a broader framework of progressive *halakhic* reasoning and the latter understood within a broader framework of ethnic mutual aid projects, although commentators who are predisposed to view progressive Judaism as itself fundamentally assimilationist and anti-*halakhic* are unlikely to agree with this analysis.

Glossary

Aleinu the closing prayer of the daily prayer service

aliyah literally 'ascent'. Jewish immigration to Israel

betselem Elohim 'in the image of God'

d'oratia a portion of *halakah* which can be traced directly to the revelation at Sinai, which is to say directly to the word of God,

	as opposed to *d'rabannan*, which is *halakah* resulting from rabbinic interpretation
halakah	Jewish law
halakhic	legal
kosher (kashrut)	Jewish dietary laws
Haredi	ultra-Orthodox
havdalah	literally 'separation'. The ritual which marks the end of the Sabbath, just after sundown on Saturday evening
Kabbalah	a system of Jewish mysticism which posits that creation is flawed and human agency is required to effect its repair
Magen David	a six-pointed star formed by two equilateral triangles, a long-recognised symbol of Judaism in general, which in the late nineteenth and early twentieth centuries became particularly associated with Zionism, and is now the chief symbol on the Israeli flag
Maimonides	a Jewish philosopher active in twelfth-century Cordoba, known for his attempts to harmonise *halakah* with Aristotelian philosophy
Mishnah	the earliest written compilation of *halakah*, containing more a record of debates between early rabbis than definitive rulings, redacted in 220 CE
Pale of Settlement	the region of Western Imperial Russia where Jewish settlement was permitted, comprising Latvia, Lithuania, Belarus, Ukraine, Moldova and Poland
pikuach nefesh	the preservation of life
pushke	collection box, particularly for charity
Sabbateanism	a movement in the late seventeenth century which embraced Sabbatai Zevi, a rabbi and a teacher of Kabbalah, as the messiah who would complete the redemption of the world. The movement gained great popularity prior to Zevi's conversion to Islam in 1666
Shulchan Aruch	a reference book containing normative rulings on *halakah*, compiled in the late sixteenth century
tzedakah	charity, or economic justice
tikkun olam	the mending of the world, or the redemption of creation
Zionism	a Jewish ethno-nationalist movement which began in the late nineteenth century
Zohar	The foundation text of Kabbalah, first published by Moses de León in thirteenth-century Iberia

Notes

1 The broad denominational correlations in this report are upheld by the study of American Jewish giving patterns discussed in Waxman (2005: 111–12).
2 See www.jewishcharityguide.co.uk (accessed 2 November 2016).

3 For the educational function of the *pushke*, see Blumberg (2005).
4 See Black (1988); Rozin (1999); Englander (1994).
5 Jewish community charity was also influenced in part by the desire to counter stereotypes of Jewish criminality, as described in Tannenbaum (2003).
6 For a discussion of the development of *tzedakah* as a communal practice in the medieval period, see Barzen (2005).
7 Object number 1990.125. Available at www.jewishmuseum.org.uk/jb-Jewish-National-Fund-collecting-box-1924 (accessed 17 October 2016).
8 In fact, it was designed and made in the firm of Salamon Hille, which at that point had not attained the iconic status that it would at mid-century, under the leadership of Salamon's daughter Ray Hille, and the box shows no hint of the functional, modernist aesthetic that Hille would become known for.
9 Catalogue number C 1985.1.1. Available at http://jewishmuseum.org.uk/search-collections?adlibid=6740&offset=36 (accessed 17 October 2016).
10 Catalogue number JM 580. Available at http://jewishmuseum.org.uk/search-collections?adlibid=8578&offset=66 (accessed 17 October 2016).
11 Catalogue number JM 578. Available at http://jewishmuseum.org.uk/search-collections?adlibid=8579&offset=66 (accessed 17 October 2016).
12 Catalogue number JM 579. Available at http://jewishmuseum.org.uk/search-collections?adlibid=8580&offset=66 (accessed 17 October 2016).
13 It is also worth noting that the single example in the Jewish Museum Berlin is a JNF collection box, catalogue number KGM 98/1/0/1–2. Available at http://objekte.jmberlin.de/object/jmb-obj-106101 (accessed 17 October 2016).
14 Stampfer (2010: 112):

> In the passage from the 1829 letter of Perl cited above, he mentioned the requirement that Jews put a coin in the box before each meal and before lighting the Sabbath candles. An additional practice that developed was to make a donation before taking *halah*, the ritual separation of a portion of dough which a Jewish woman was required to do every time she made bread.

15 The Mishnah was redacted *c.* 220 CE, although many of the rulings within it are attributed to rabbis of the first and second centuries. While there is some dispute over the extent to which the Mishnah reflected normative Jewish practice at the time of its redaction, the fact that *tikkun ha-olam* appears as a principle used to justify a course of action, rather than a subject of debate, suggests that it was recognised at least among the Tannaim.

Rosenthal (2005) notes that the verb {standard תקן} appears three times in Ecclesiastes, referring to repair in a general sense, and the phrase as a whole appears 'a handful of times' the Midrash and Tosefta; Jacobs (2007) argues that within Genesis *Rabbah*, it refers very specifically to the repair of imperfections in the physical world.
16 The following verses of Mishnah make a number of other adjustments, aimed at protecting divorced women and captives from economic mistreatment, for the sake of *tikkun ha-olam*. Dorff (2005: 7) suggests that the purpose of *tikkun* in the Mishnah is 'guarding the established order in the physical or social world (with derivatives *t'kinah* meaning "standardization" and *t'kinut* meaning "normalcy, regularity, orderliness, propriety")'.
17 Also significant is the argument of Mitchell First (2011), who contends that 'the original version of Aleinu read {design כתלן עולם} (= to establish the world under God's sovereignty), and not {fix עולם לתקן} (= to perfect/improve the world under God's sovereignty.)'. However, First's view is decidedly a minority position, and appears to be motivated largely by a desire to distance the text from the later meanings which accrued to *tikkun olam*, discussed below.
18 For a much more complete discussion of this development, see Rosenthal (2005). Rosenthal notes that the vast majority of medieval responsa literature does not utilise

the phrase *tikkun olam*, but rather relies on the concept of public good or community cohesion.

19 For a discussion of the relationship between *tikkun olam* and personal salvation, see Scholem (1973: 40–2).

20 The notion of *tikkun* has been particularly influential in post-Holocaust theology, but is by no means restricted to this field. See e.g. Fackenheim (1988); Blumenthal (1993); Raphael (2003). Without being directly connected (although an argument might be made about nostalgia for the 'lost' 'authentic' Judaism of Eastern Europe) to post-Holocaust theology as such, a trend towards neo-Hasidism in fin de siècle theology has also promoted *tikkun*; see e.g. Green (2003); Fishbane (2008).

21 There is a difficulty in language surrounding Jewish denominations: a broad split between Orthodox and non-Orthodox Judaism obscures both the huge variety of positions within the Orthodox world and the more Orthodox-leaning practices active within the Conservative movement; referring to 'conservative' and 'liberal' Judaism is apt to promote confusion between broad outlooks and the particular Liberal and Conservative movements. 'Progressive Judaism' is mainly associated with Reform and related movements. For simplicity, I have chose here to use the term 'broadly progressive' to encompass Reform, Reconstructionist, Renewal, Liberal, and the more liberal side of Conservative Judaism.

22 For similar critiques, see e.g. Kerbel (2010); Plaut (2002); Korff (2013); Sherwin (2009).

Bibliography

www.jewishcharityguide.co.uk (accessed 2 November 2016).

Barzen, R. (2005). 'The Meaning of "Tzedakah" for Jewish Self-Organization within a Non-Jewish Environment', in *Iggud: Selected Essays in Jewish Studies*, Vol 2: History of the Jewish People and Contemporary Jewish Society.

Black, E. (1988). *The Social Politics of Anglo-Jewry, 1880–1920*. Oxford: Blackwell.

Blumberg, S. (2005). 'The place of Mitzvot in children's spiritual lives', in K.M. Just, A. Johnson, S.E. Sasso and E. Roehlkepartain (eds) *Nurturing Child and Adolescent Spirituality: Perspectives from the World's Religious Traditions*. CITY: Rowman & Littlefield.

Blumenthal, D. (1993). *Facing the Abusing God: A Theology of Protest*. Louisville, KY: Westminster John Knox.

Central Conference of American Rabbis (1977). *Rights of Homosexuals: Resolution Adopted by the CCAR at the 88th Annual Convention of the Central Conference of American Rabbis or Subsequent to that Convention in 1977*. Online. Available at http://ccarnet.org/rabbis-speak/resolutions/all/homosexuals-rights-of-1977 (accessed 1 October 2016).

Central Conference of American Rabbis (1990). *Report of the Ad hoc Committee on Homosexuality and the Rabbinate*. Online. Available at http://ccarnet.org/rabbis-speak/resolutions/all/homosexuality-and-the-rabbinate-1990 (accessed 1 October 2016).

Central Conference of American Rabbis (2000). *Resolution on Same Gender Officiation: Resolution adopted at the 111th Convention of the Central Conference of American Rabbis March, 2000*. Online. Available at www.ccarnet.org/rabbis-speak/resolutions/2000/same-gender-officiation (accessed 1 October 2016).

CCAR (2013). *Same Sex Marriage as* Kiddushin. Online. Available at https://ccarnet.org/responsa/same-sex-marriage-kiddushin (accessed 1 October 2016).

Cooper, L. (2013). The Assimilation of *Tikkun Olam*. *Jewish Political Studies Review*, *25*(3/4): 10–42.

Dorff, E. (1992). *Jewish Norms for Sexual Behaviour: A Responsum Embodying a Proposal.* Online. Available at www.rabbinicalassembly.org/sites/default/files/assets/public/halakhah/teshuvot/19912000/dorff_homosexuality.pdf (accessed 1 October 2016).

Dorff, E. (2005). *The Way into Tikkun Olam (Repairing the World).* Woodstock, VT: Jewish Lights.

Dorff, E., Nevins, D. and Reisner, A. (2006). *Homosexuality, Human Dignity and Halakah: A Combined Responsum for the Committee on Jewish Law and Standards.* Online. Available at www.rabbinicalassembly.org/sites/default/files/assets/public/halakhah/teshuvot/20052010/dorff_nevins_reisner_dignity.pdf (accessed 1 October 2016).

Englander, D. (1994). *A Documentary History of Jewish Immigrants in Britain, 1840–1920.* Leicester: Leicester University Press.

Fackenheim, E. (1988). *To Mend the World: Foundations of Post-Holocaust Jewish Thought.* New York, NY: Schocken.

First, M. (2011). Aleinu: obligation to fix the world or the text? *Hakirah, 11*: 187–97.

Fishbane, M. (2008). *Sacred Attunement: A Jewish Theology.* Chicago, IL: University of Chicago Press.

Graham, D. and Boyd, J. (2016). *Charitable Giving among Britain's Jews: Looking to the Future*, Institute for Jewish Policy Research.

Green, A. (2003). *Seek My Face: A Jewish Mystical Theology.* Woodstock, VT: Jewish Lights.

Jacobs, J. (2007). The History of Tikkun Olam. *Zeek.* Online. Available at www.zeek.net/706tohu/index.php?page=1 (accessed 10 October 2016).

Kerbel, P. (2010). The Tikkun Olam Generation. *Conservative Judaism, 61*(3): 88–91.

Korff, Y. (2013). The fallacy, delusion and myth of Tikkun Olam. *Jewish News Service.* Online. Available at www.jns.org/latest-articles/2013/6/3/the-fallacy-delusion-and-myth-of-tikkun-olam#.WDuVyqKLTeQ= (accessed 8 November 2016).

March, C. (2010). Enough with the 'Big Tent'. *Jewish Advocate.* Online. Available at www.thejewishadvocate.com/news/2010-03-12/Charles_Jacobs/Enough_with_the_big_tent.html (accessed 10 October 2016).

Marks, L., Dollahite, D. and Dew, J. (2009). Enhancing cultural competence in financial counseling and planning: why families make religious contributions. *Journal of Financial Counseling and Planning, 20*(2): 14–26.

Neusner, J. (1966). *History of the Jews in Babylonia: The Early Sasanian Period.* Leiden: Brill.

Plaut, S. (2002). The rise of Tikun Olam paganism. *Israel National News.* Online. Available at www.israelnationalnews.com/Articles/Article.aspx/1760 (accessed 8 November 2016).

Rabbinical Assembly Committee on Jewish Law and Standards (1992). *Consensus Statement on Homosexuality.* Online. Available at www.rabbinicalassembly.org/sites/default/files/assets/public/halakhah/teshuvot/19912000/consensus_homosexual.pdf (accessed 1 October 2016).

Raphael, M. (2003). *The Female Face of God in Auschwitz: A Jewish Feminist Theology of the Holocaust.* New York, NY: Routledge.

Rosenthal, G. (2005). *Tikkun ha-Olam:* The Metamorphosis of a Concept. *The Journal of Religion, 85*(2): 214–40.

Roth, J. (1992). *Homosexuality.* Online. Available at www.rabbinicalassembly.org/sites/default/files/assets/public/halakhah/teshuvot/19912000/roth_homosexual.pdf (accessed 1 October 2016).

Roth, J. (2006). *Homosexuality Revisited.* Online. Available at www.rabbinicalassembly.org/sites/default/files/assets/public/halakhah/teshuvot/20052010/roth_revisited.pdf (accessed 1 October 2016).

Rozin, M. (1999). *The Rich and the Poor, Jewish Philanthropy and Social Control in Nineteenth-Century London.* Brighton: Sussex Academic Press.

Sacks, J. (1997). *Tikkun Olam.* Online. Available at http://advocacy.ou.org/tikkun-olam-orthodoxys-responsibility-to-perfect-g-ds-world (accessed 10 October 2016).

Sacks, J. (2005). *To Heal a Fractured World: The Ethics of Responsibility.* London: Continuum, 2005.

Scholem, G. (1973). *Sabbati Sevi: The Mystical Messiah 1626–1676*, trans. R.J.Z. Werblowsky. Princeton, NJ: Princeton University Press.

Sherwin, B. (2009). *Faith Finding Meaning: A Theology of Judaism.* Oxford: Oxford University Press.

Stampfer, S. (2010). *Families, Rabbis and Education: Traditional Jewish Society in Nineteenth-Century Eastern Europe.* London: Littman.

Tananbaum, S. (2003). '"Morally depraved and abnormally criminal": Jews and crime in London and New York, 1880–1940', in S. Tananbaum and S. Bloom (eds) *Forging Modern Jewish Identities: Public Faces and Private Struggles.* London: Valentine Mitchell.

Ulmer, R. and Ulmer, M. (2014). *Righteous Giving to the Poor:* Tzedakah *('Charity') in Classical Rabbinic Judaism.* Piscataway, NJ: Gorgias.

Waxman, C. (2005). 'Patterns of American Jewish religious behaviour', in D.E. Kaplan (ed.) *The Cambridge Companion to American Judaism.* Cambridge: Cambridge University Press.

6 Social justice in Islam

Qari Asim

Introduction

This chapter explores one of Islam's core values: the provision of social justice in society. It first considers the revolutionary approach that Islam has taken to combining secular and spiritual goals to motivate an individual to give and share one's wealth, time and energies for the benefit of others. Second, the chapter presents various tenets that Islam has propagated to procure the provision of social justice in a society. Finally, the chapter highlights some of the attempts being made by British Muslims to implement this core value of Islam through contributing to society

Social justice in Islam

In the modern world, 'social justice' is about ensuring that all communities, regardless of their race, religion, ethnicity or nationality, have equal access to economic opportunities, legal rights and equal protection from and by state agencies. Whereas 'justice' requires the protection of life, liberty, property and freedoms of all people, 'social justice' demands that opportunities are provided for the most vulnerable in society.

In Islam, wealth must serve a useful purpose and should be grown through traffic and trade (Qur'an 4: 29). Islam recognises that human beings are generally motivated by self-interest. This self-interest can lead to an ever-widening gap between the rich and the poor. Islam resolves the potential conflict between self-interest and the collective good by expanding the usually narrow concept of self-interest to include not only the desire to have a luxurious life in this world, but also the desire for a luxurious life in the next world (Chapra 1979: 28).

In Islam, self-interest cannot be served except by fulfilling one's social obligations and by working for social and economic justice in society. Accordingly, a Muslim's desire for the accumulation of wealth will be kept in check by one's greater desire for paradise, resulting in a synthesis of the material and the spiritual. Further, the concept of being held accountable in front of God is a motivation for establishing social justice for the welfare of fellow human beings. This accountability, which does not exist in secular economic systems, motivates a Muslim citizen as well as the governing authorities to be more equitable in how they use the wealth and resources at their disposal.

The Qur'an adopts a revolutionary approach in that it integrates what was traditionally understood as sacred with the secular. In Islam, the traditional acts of devotion as well as one's personal, financial, social and political affairs have all been considered *ibadat* (worship). This integrated approach is provided in the context of social welfare and well-being.

The Qur'an integrates the meaning and purpose of five daily devotional prayers (*salah*) with socially uplifting policies and concern for the welfare of the community. The strategy for ensuring the welfare of all citizens is by harmonising the spiritual and material pursuit of life. The concept of welfare can neither be exclusively worldly nor be purely focused in the hereafter but rather a seamless combination of both to achieve the maximum welfare in this life (material) and the next life (spiritual). This is of course a general indication of what is implied by welfare in Islam.

The critical place that social justice has in the overall message of Islam is evidenced by the fact that in the Farewell Pilgrimage delivered by Prophet Muhammad social justice was distinctly the unmistakable and overarching tenor of the message.[1]

Dimensions of social justice

The Islamic concept of social justice is inherently flexible but there are three dimensions to it which help to achieve its objectives, namely dignity, equality and well-being.

All human beings are created as dignified individuals and the dignity of human life is so important that the Qur'an states: 'and whoever saves one [life], it is as if he had saved mankind entirely …'.[2] The Qur'an does not say that only Muslims or those who have faith in God deserve dignity or rights that are associated with dignity. Rather it refers to the concept in broader terms and declares that no one has a right to deny humans their dignity.[3] Further, it is the moral responsibility of an individual to live a dignified life, catering for his own needs through his own efforts. The emphasis on individual freedom, self-esteem and the value of working hard is to be embedded in a society. To this end, Islam condemns begging and becoming dependent on others, including the state.[4] However, if someone is physically unable to work or cannot find work, then that should not affect their dignity as a human being. A belief in human dignity will lead a citizen to reject all forms of racism, ethnocentrism and hatred towards the 'other', which in turn is likely to lead to giving, sharing and caring for others in society.

With regards to equality, in the sight of God, all human beings are equal, irrespective of their colour, social background or financial status.[5] The Qur'an states: 'He created you (all) from a single person: then created, of like nature, his mate …'.[6] It is imperative in Islam that a state secures aspects of social justice for its citizens equally. Security, freedoms, education and other such facilities must be available to all citizens of a state equally. However, an Islamic state cannot go so far as to advocate absolute equality, for such a notion is clearly at odds with the different capabilities and talents that God has blessed individuals with. Further, absolute equality could only come about at the expense of the individual economic freedom that God has granted us.[7]

Finally, social justice is also about ensuring the well-being of citizens. It is about assisting them to achieve inner peace as well as outward physical well-being. After protecting the well-being of oneself, a citizen is inspired to care for the well-being of the family and wider society. The ultimate goal of social justice is to secure a peaceful society, so that each family can protect the interests of the individuals in it and help towards achieving their true potential. The unity of humanity, the dignity, the justice and the universality of human resources pave the path for peace.[8] There can be no social peace – on either an individual or a collective level – without the firm establishment of social justice (Ramadan 2010, online).

Establishment of social justice in society

Social justice is established through the wealthy members of society contributing towards the welfare of other citizens. This contribution can take the form of the payment of minimum obligatory charity (*zakat*), as well as giving of over and above the minimum level in the forms of compassion and benevolence for others (*sadaqa*), altruism and selflessness (*ithar*).

Zakat

Zakat forms the bedrock of the social welfare state in Islam.[9] The Qur'an commands Muslims to 'establish the prayer, and give *zakat*, and they obey God and His Messenger'.[10] Zakat is payable by those who have an annual income above a prescribed threshold (The Zakat Foundation of America 2007, online).[11] Those who have to give charity share the benefit of their prosperity with those who have fallen short.[12] *Zakat* is therefore seen as the mandatory Islamic contribution to social justice (Mannan 1986).

One of the objectives of the payment of *zakat* is to create a more just and equitable society. It is to help the beneficiaries of *zakat* to be autonomous, and there comes a point when they transition from being recipients of *zakat* to being dispensers of *zakat*. The payment of *zakat* is considered to be a minimum acceptable moral standard for a society. Not only does it enshrine the right of help for the community's vulnerable but, in so doing, it builds a relationship of consideration and appreciation between society's members.

Sadaqah *(charity)*

In addition to payment of the mandatory *zakat* on those with the prescribed means, Islam encourages charity and acts of benevolence.[13] Spending in the way of God is referred to as 'a beautiful [profitable] loan'.[14] The concept of compassion going beyond, and prevailing over, justice is perfectly illustrated in a story from the lifetime of the Prophet Muhammad (peace be upon him). A young orphan came to the Prophet to complain that one of the Prophet's close companions, Abu Lubabah, had taken a palm tree from him that had long belonged to him. The Prophet made some investigations and deemed that the tree did in fact rightly belong to Abu Lubabah; nevertheless, he asked Abu Lubabah to gift the tree to the young orphan. The Prophet sought to establish the principle that in some instances compassion renders it necessary to look beyond one's own legal rights for the sake of the moral or equitable rights of others. Abu Lubabah declined the Prophet's offer to give the asset in question to the orphan. Abu Lubabah's concern for justice at face value meant that, in this instance, he did not reach the superior level of justness of the heart: excellence, generosity, giving. Eventually, another companion, who had observed the whole incident, offered Abu Lubabah an entire orchard in exchange for that single palm tree, which he then gave away to the young orphan.[15] This incident demonstrates that justice is not an end per se. It is a condition and a means to achieving compassionate and caring relationships in society.

In Islam, *Sadaqa* is much more than just giving money in charity; it is also about giving up time and making an effort, reaching out to others, working with others – from all backgrounds, faiths or none – to bring about positive change in society. Islam strongly emphasises the importance of caring for others and refers to those living in surrounding areas as 'neighbours'. A 'neighbour' is not necessarily just a person living next door, but a street is a neighbour to the next street, a district is a neighbour to the next district. This creates a sense of togetherness and shared responsibility in a town or a city. People living in a neighbourhood may be of different backgrounds and/or social and financial statuses but they should be united by procuring social justice in society.

Altruism

Islam recognises a level higher than being charitable – altruism. The Qur'an praises altruistic characteristic of the believers, stating that '[the Believers] prefer the needy to their own selves in spite of the fact that they are themselves in pressing need'.[16] The Prophet Muhammad recalled the significance of the quality of selflessness when he said: 'None of you truly believes until he loves for his brother, what he loves for himself.'[17]

The early Muslims were keen to heed the advice of the Messenger and demonstrate selflessness by placing others above themselves.[18]

Social justice in Muslim countries

The rulers who came after the Prophet practised the same principle of selflessness so that the citizens of the state could be inspired by their example. 'Umar bin Khattab, the second caliph, lived a simple life; he wore worn-out shoes and was usually clad in patched-up garments.[19] While these specific actions of early Muslims were not based on any specific Islamic laws, they were in keeping with the spirit of the Qur'an to establish social justice. Infusing the empire with the ideals of egalitarianism and justice would not have been possible unless government officials set the best of examples. 'Umar recognised the class distinction that have always existed in the world but aspired to erase class distinctions which might inevitably lead to conflict in society.[20]

The majority of Muslim countries have always aspired to implementing the concept of social justice in their states. This desire is said to have been one of the key reasons for the creation of Pakistan, in which principles of Islamic social justice could find free play.[21] However, despite the aspiration, unfortunately many Muslim majority states have not taken the issue of social justice seriously. It is argued that these states have failed in taking an active role in establishing social justice in their societies (Moten 2013, online). Increasingly, there are calls that Muslim countries must establish, or re-establish, social justice (Bandial 2013, online)

Although the states may not have been successful in implementing social justice in societies, a system of endowment, known as *awqaf*, has been popular among Muslims throughout the centuries. *Awqaf* is a form of perpetual charity holding certain property and preserving it for the confined benefit of certain philanthropic purposes. Currently, there are a number of British Muslim institutions that are rendering a wide range of services by providing religious education, community services and maintenance of the mosques through the *awqaf* model, similar to institutions in North America (Hassan 2010, online).

So much emphasis is placed on establishing social justice in Islam that in order to attract Muslims to the territory under their control even the violent cult Daesh (also known as ISIS/ISIL), who claim to have created an 'Islamic State' (although it is widely acknowledged that their actions are contrary to Islamic teachings), claim to have established a welfare state based on the principles of social justice (Revkin 2016, online). This seems to be one of the allures for young people to travel to Daesh-ruled territory (Zelin 2014, online).

British Muslims and social justice

British Muslims have a long history of contributing to social justice; sometimes these initiatives are exclusively Muslim; at other times, different community groups are brought together to work as one in implementing shared values. Through those initiatives, British Muslims have been able to impact on areas of high social need, respond to local priorities, increase volunteering and work in the spirit of localism. One example of responding to local priorities is the involvement of Muslims in the UK's largest civic alliance, Citizens UK (see www.citizensuk.org). Some of these initiatives are long-term while others are short-term.

An ICM poll has shown that British Muslim are more generous than other communities, and many millions are raised and donated each year.[22] Since its inception in 2013 (Iqbal 2013, online), the 'Give A Gift' initiative (see http://giveagift.org.uk) has raised over £70,000 and donated over 1,300 toys for charities in Leeds, including Martin House Children's Hospice and the Children's Heart Surgery Fund in Leeds.

Another key initiative that is championed by Muslims is feeding the homeless. International charities such as PennyAppeal are also involved in a range of social action initiatives in the UK, ranging from providing hot meals to giving out Christmas presents in flood-affected areas (Pilling 2015, online). Young Muslim volunteers in Leeds have handed out an estimated 5,000 meals since the initiative started.[23]

These social actions go beyond just feeding the needy in their neighbourhoods. 'Sadaqa Day',[24] a Muslim-led day of social action, encourages people to demonstrate the universal values, as well as the British values, of giving, sharing and caring for others by donating cash, baking cakes, helping others with their shopping, painting a nursery garden, feeding a homeless person or a refugee, cleaning up the streets or sitting by the side of a sick person, and many such other actions. On the 2016 Sadaqa Day, Leeds-based Muslim organisations collected hundreds of food parcels for the poor and vulnerable.[25] Toys and/or money donations were also collected to give to vulnerable children in the care of Child Friendly Leeds (Asim 2016, online).

The establishment of social justice in Islam is an individual and communal responsibility and ultimately the responsibility of the state. In the current political climate, when violence is associated with Islam and Muslims are labelled as terrorists (Asim 2016, online; Jenkins 2016, online), or are considered by some a 'fifth column' (White 2015, online), it may surprise some people that social justice is one of the core values of Islam. Muslims, whether they are living in a Muslim country or otherwise, aim to contribute towards establishing social justice. They aim to create an environment in which all citizens are able to flourish and their needs are met. The community services provided by British Muslims including the operation of mosques, or partnerships formed with civic society, are all done based on the principle that 'the best of the people are those who are most beneficial to others' (Tabrani 1999: No. 5937).

Notes

1 The Farewell Pilgrimage brought together the largest ever gathering of followers during the Prophet's life time. The key tenets of the Farewell Pilgrimage can be listed as follows: (1) freedom to all; (2) sanctity of life, wealth and property; (3) equality of all races; (4) justice before the law and before God; (5) no exploitation or monopoly. The rich are not to be made richer while the poor become poorer; (6) women's rights and obligations; and (7) rights of others are to be preserved and to be delivered (Pirzada, M. 2009:157).

2 Qur'an 5:32.

3 The Qur'an provides: 'We have bestowed dignity on the children of Adam; provided them with transport on land and sea; given them for sustenance things good and pure; and conferred on them special favours, above a great part of our creation.' (Qur'an 17:70).

4 The Prophet said: 'a man has not earned better income than that which is from his own hard work.' (Abu Dawud 2008).
5 This equality in creation in the sight of God is no better demonstrated than during the Hajj pilgrimage, during which every Muslim adheres to the same dress code and stands before God using the same words as his or her fellow pilgrims to invoke God's mercy. The resulting scene is perhaps the most striking physical demonstration of the concept of equality.
6 Qur'an 39:6. Further, the Qur'an states:

> O mankind! Reverence your Guardian-Lord, who created you from a single soul, created, of like nature, the mate, and from them twain scattered [like seeds] countless men and women;– reverence Allah, through whom ye demand your mutual [rights], and [reverence] the wombs [that bore you]: for Allah ever watches over you.
>
> (Qur'an 4:1)

7 The Qur'an acknowledges the inevitable existence of inequality: 'God has bestowed His gifts of sustenance more freely on some of you than on others' (Qur'an 16:71). Therefore, the goal of the Islamic state is not to abolish inequality but rather to minimise its impact as much as possible.
8 The Qur'an says that 'God shows unto all that seek His goodly acceptance the paths leading to peace and, by His grace, brings them out of the depths of darkness into the light and guides them onto a straight way' (Qur'an 5: 16).
9 *Zakat* is obligatory for every adult, mentally stable, free and financially able Muslim, as mentioned in the Qur'an:

> The alms are only for the poor and the needy, and those who collect them, and those whose hearts are to be reconciled, and to free the captives and the debtors, and for the cause of Allah, and [for] the wayfarers; a duty imposed by Allah. Allah is knower, Wise.
>
> (Qur'an 9:60)

10 Qur'an 9:71.
11 Generally 2.5 per cent is payable on annual savings.
12 When Mu'adh was appointed governor of Yemen, he was instructed by the Prophet Muhammad to take *zakat* from the rich and distribute it to the poor (Bukhari 1997: Book 9, Hadith 218).
13 The Prophet is reported to have said:

> Every day the sun rises, charity is due on every joint on a person: administering justice between two people is a charity; assisting a man to mount his beast, or helping him load his luggage on it is a charity; a good word is a charity; every step that you take for prayer is a charity; and removing harmful things from the road is a charity.
>
> (Nawawi, I. 1999: Book 1, Hadith 122)

14 'Who is he that will lend to Allah a goodly loan so that He may multiply it to him many times? And it is Allah that decreases or increases (your provisions), and unto Him you shall return.' (Qur'an 2:245). When this verse was revealed, one of the companions, Abu Ad-Dahdah Al-Ansari, asked, 'O Allah's Messenger! Does Allah ask us for a loan?' The Prophet said, 'Yes, O Abu Ad-Dahdah.' He said: 'Give me your hand, O Allah's Messenger' and the Prophet placed his hand in his hand. Abu Ad-Dahdah said, 'Verily, I have given my garden as a loan to my Lord.' Abu Ad-Dahdah had a garden that contained 600 date trees; his wife and children were living in that garden too. Abu Ad-Dahdah went to his wife and called her: 'Umm Ad-Dahdah!' She said, 'Here I am.' He said: 'Leave the garden, because I have given it as a loan to my Lord, the Exalted and Most Honored.' She said, 'That is a successful trade, O Abu

Ad-Dahdah!' She then transferred her goods and children. The Messenger of Allah said, 'How plentiful are the sweet date clusters that Abu Ad-Dahdah has in Paradise!' In another narration, the Prophet said, 'How many a date tree that has lowered down its clusters, which are full of pearls and gems in Paradise for Abu Ad-Dahdah!' (Qur'an 57:11; Ibn Kathir, I. 2000, online).

15 The Prophet rejoiced at that outcome and did not resent Abu Lubabah's attitude (Ramadan, T. 2007:133).

16 Qur'an 59:9. Further, the Qur'an states: 'And they give food, in spite of their love for it [or for the love of God], to poor, thc orphan, and thc captive, [saying,] "We feed you seeking Allah's Countenance only. We wish for no reward, nor thanks from you"' (Qur'an 76:8–9).

17 Bukhari, M. 2000a: Vol. 1 Book 2, Hadith No. 7. The altruism of the early community can be demonstrated through the example of an incident that took place during the time of the Prophet. A very hungry man came to the Prophet (peace and blessings be upon him) seeking food. The Prophet was the ruler of the Islamic State at that time but he did not amass wealth for himself, although Islam does not forbid capitalism to an extent, therefore he did not have any food in his house. The Prophet made a general request to his companions at the mosque and one of the citizens of Medina volunteered to take the man home, despite the fact that he did not have enough food for his own family. As they sat down for their meal, the host extinguished the light and gave the impression that he and his family were partaking in the meal alongside the guest. But in reality, they did not eat much so that their guest could eat to his fill. The next morning the Prophet informed the host that God was pleased with his family's act of selflessness (Bukhari, M. 2000b: 727–8).

18 One of the best examples of selflessness is reflected by the treatment of Muslims from Medina, known as Ansar (Helpers), of the migrants (Muhajirun) from Mecca. When Muslims fled persecution and violence in Mecca and took sanctuary in Medina, the migrants had no belongings. They had left all of their wealth in Mecca and came to Mecca as refugees. To alleviate the suffering of the migrants, the Prophet (peace and blessings be upon him) paired each migrant with a family in Medina. The bond between the migrants and the Ansar was so tight that, for a time, they were even allowed to inherit from one another. The Ansar demonstrated such altruism towards the migrants that they once went to the Prophet (peace and blessings be upon him) and offered to give the migrants half of their date groves. When the Prophet (peace and blessings be upon him) refused to accept this offer, the Ansar offered a cooperative work agreement that allowed the migrants to work in the date grove and share in the profits (Salahi, A. 1998: 218).

19 In one particularly telling instance, some of 'Umar's companions were waiting outside for him and were curious as to why the caliph was taking so long to come out. They later found out that 'Umar had no clothes to wear. He only had one outfit in his possession, which had been washed (Ya'qub, A. 1352AH: 387).

20 Under 'Umar, strict administrative policies ensured that all forms of charity – such as *zakat*, *'ushr* (tax on agricultural land), *sadaqah* (charity), *jizyah* (tax on non-Muslims for providing their security) and others were collected, gathered and distributed to uphold social justice in society. Every citizen of the state, who had a need and was a dependent, received their fair share from the welfare system. 'Umar's welfare policies provided: aid to the poor and disabled; education to children; benefits for the elderly; investments for the elderly; *shari'ah*-based loans to aid economic growth; debt clearance payments for people under obligation; social insurance to pay blood money for unintentional homicide; allowances to widows, married and unmarried women, young men and immigrants (who were in need); food aid during serious drought or famines; pensions to soldiers of the state; and medical aid (Nomani 2001).

21 The founder of Pakistan, Muhammad Ali Jinnah, is quoted to have said 'We should have a State in which … principles of Islamic social justice could find free play' (Shah 2013, online).

22 (Gledhill 2013, online). JustGiving, an online charity platform, has reported an increase in digital giving by British Muslims, particularly during Ramadan, over the last few years. The charity noted that Muslims also gave large amounts of donations to non-religious charities such as Macmillan, the British Heart Foundation and Cancer Research UK. See *The Huffington Post UK*.
23 *Yorkshire Evening Post* (2015).
24 www.MySadaqDay.org.
25 The food parcels were donated to PAFRAS – Positive Action for Refuges and Asylum Seekers. Available at www.pafras.org.uk.

Bibliography

Abu Dawud, S. (2008). *Sunan Abu Dawud*. Riyadh: Dar-us-Salam Publications, vol. 1, 382.

Asim, Q. (2016). Bringing faiths together in a day of positive action. *Yorkshire Post*, 18 March. Online. Available at www.yorkshirepost.co.uk/news/opinion/qari-asim-bringing-faiths-together-in-a-day-of-positive-action-1-7803767 and www.yorkshireeveningpost.co.uk/your-leeds/giving-back/leeds-day-of-social-action-by-young-muslims-is-a-winner-1-7809733 (accessed 25 March 2016).

Asim, Q. (2016). Suicide bombers are not following a path to paradise. *The Huffington Post UK*. Online. Available at www.huffingtonpost.co.uk/qari-asim-/suicide-bombers-are-notf_b_8593074.html (accessed 25 March 2016).

Bandial, Q-A. (2013). Muslim countries must promote social justice. *The Brunei Times*, November. Online. Available at www.bt.com.bn/news-national/2013/11/01/%E2%80%98muslim-countries-must-promote-social-justice%E2%80%99 (accessed 25 March 2016).

Bukhari, M. (1997). *Sahih al-Bukhari: The Translation of the Meanings of Sahih Al Bukhari Arabic English*, trans. M. Muhsin Khan. Riyadh: Dar-us-Salam, Book 9, Hadith 218.

Bukhari, M. (2000a). *Sahih al-Bukhari*. Cairo: Theasurus Islamicus Foundation, Vol. 1 Book 2, Hadith No. 7.

Bukhari, M. (2000b). *Sahih al-Bukhari*. Cairo: Theasurus Islamicus Foundation. Summarized *Sahih Al-Bukhari*, trans. A. Khan (1994). Riyadh: Maktaba Dar-us-Salam. pp. 727–8.

Chapra, M. (1979). *Umar, The Islamic Welfare State and its Role in the Economy*. Leicester: Islamic Foundation.

Gledhill, R. (2013). Muslims 'are Britain's top charity givers'. *The Times*, 20 July. Online. Available at www.thetimes.co.uk/tto/faith/article3820522.ece (accessed 25 March 2016).

Hassan, M. (2010). *Role of Zakat and Awqaf in Reducing Poverty: A Case for Zakat-Awqaf-Based Institutional Setting of Micro-finance*. Paper read at the Seventh International Conference – The Tawhidi Epistemology: Zakat and Waqf Economy, Bangi, 2010. Online. Available at www.ukm.my/hadhari/wp-content/uploads/2014/09/proceedings-seminar-waqf-tawhidi.pdf#page=266 (accessed 25 March 2016).

Iqbal, A. (2013). Ramadhan gifts given to children in Leeds hospital. *Yorkshire Evening Post*, 10 August. Online. Available at www.yorkshireeveningpost.co.uk/news/yep125/ramadhan-gifts-given-to-children-in-leeds-hospital-1-5940025 (accessed 25 March 2016).

Ibn Kathir, I. (2000). *Tafsir Ibn Kathir*. Riyadh: Dar-us-Salam, vol 9. p. 476. Online. Available at www.qtafsir.com/index.php?option=com_content&task=view&id=1643&Itemid=113 (accessed 25 March 2016).

Jenkins, N. (2015). *Muslims Speak Out Against Terrorist Attacks in Paris*. Time.com. Online. Available at http://time.com/4112830/muslims-paris-terror-attacks-islam-condemn (accessed 25 March 2016).

Mannan, M.A. (1986). *Islamic Economics: Theory and Practice*. London: Hodder and Stoughton.

Moten, A. (2013). Social justice, Islamic State and Muslim countries. *Cultural International Journal of Philosophy of Culture and Axiology*, *10*(1): 7–24.

Nawawi, I. (1999). *Riyad As Salihin: The Gardens of the Righteous*. Riyadh, Dar-us-Salam, Book 1, Hadith 122.

Nomani, S. (2001). *Life of Omar, The Great (Al-Farooq)*. Delhi: Adam.

Pilling, K. (2015). Amir Khan takes time out of his schedule to help flood-affected areas in Carlisle. *Mail Online*, 12 December. Online. Available at www.dailymail.co.uk/sport/boxing/article-3357305/Amir-Khan-takes-time-schedule-help-flood-affected-areasCarlisle.html (accessed 25 March 2016).

Pirzada, M. (2009). *Human Rights in Light of the Qur'an & Sunnah*. Retford: Al-Karam.

Ramadan, T. (December 2010). *Social Justice: An Islamic Perspective*. Online. Available at http://icnacsj.org/wp-content/uploads/2015/02/Social-Justice-Booklet.pdf (accessed 25 March 2016).

Ramadan, T. (2007). *The Messenger: The Meaning of the Life of Muhammad*. Oxford: Penguin and Oxford University Press.

Revkin, M. (2016). ISIS' social contract. *Foreign Affairs*, 10 January. Online. Available at www.foreignaffairs.com/articles/syria/2016-01-10/isis-social-contract (accessed 25 March 2016).

Salahi, A. (1998). *Muhammad: Man and Prophet*. Shaftesbury and Rockport, MA: Element.

Shah, Z. (2013). Social justice for a slave-nation. *Pakistan Today*, 29 October. Online. Available at www.pakistantoday.com.pk/2013/10/29/business/social-justice-for-a-slave-nation-2 (accessed 25 March 2016).

Tabrani, S.A. (1999). *Mu'jam Al-Awsat*. Beirut: DKI, vol. 1, No. 5937.

The Huffington Post (2013). Muslims 'give most to charity', ahead of Christians, Jews and atheists, poll finds. *The Huffington Post UK*, 27 July. Online. Available at www.huffingtonpost.co.uk/2013/07/21/muslims-give-most_n_3630830.html (accessed 25 March 2016).

The Zakat Foundation of America (2007). *Zakat Handbook: A Practical Guide for Muslims in the West*. Online. Available at www.zakat.org/downloads/zakat_book.pdf (accessed 25 March 2006).

White, M. (12 March 2015). Nigel Farage on anti-discrimination laws: a lazy appeal to lazy voters. *Guardian*. Online. Available at www.theguardian.com/politics/blog/2015/mar/12/nigel-farage-anti-discrimination-laws-lazy-ukip (accessed 25 March 2016).

Ya'qub, A. (1352AH). *Kitab al-Kharaj*, 2nd Ed., Cairo: al-Matba'ah al-Salafiyyah.

Yorkshire Evening Post (13 July 2015). Volunteers hand out 5,000 meals to Leeds' neediest. *The Yorkshire Evening Post*. Online. Available at www.yorkshireeveningpost.co.uk/news/volunteers-hand-out-5-000-meals-to-leeds-neediest-1-7355352 (accessed 25 March 2016).

Zelin, A. (2014). The Islamic State of Iraq and Syria has a consumer protection office. *The Atlantic*, 13 June. Online. Available at www.theatlantic.com/international/archive/2014/06/the-isis-guide-to-building-an-islamic-state/372769 (accessed 25 March 2016).

Part III

Perspectives on children, the family and sport

7 Social justice for children and young people in England

Citizens or drones?

Pam Jarvis

Introduction

This chapter will explore the creation of children's rights charters in history and in geography, initially considering the Geneva Declaration of Rights of the Child (UN Documents 1924), the United Nations Declaration on the Rights of the Child (UNICEF 1959) and the United Nations Convention on the Rights of the Child (UNCRC, UNICEF 1989), all of which have defined the child in ways that reflect Western ideals of individual rights. It will also explore the African Charter on the Rights and Welfare of the Child (UNICEF 1999), which constructs the child in a slightly different fashion, as a socially embedded individual with both rights *and* responsibilities. The chapter will consider how social justice is mediated for children in the neo-liberal environment of the contemporary UK, from the 'Every Child Matters' (DFES 2003) perspective, followed by some practical illustrations of policy. It will close with a consideration of mental health issues that have arisen for children and young people in the UK at the dawn of the twenty-first century, finally posing some questions for the reader to contemplate with respect to improving children's access to social justice in England.

What are children's rights?

In order to begin to answer this question, we first have to consider concepts of 'human rights'. The term first arises in history in the 'Cyrus Cylinder' (539 BCE), in which Cyrus the Great of Persia banned slavery and racial/religious intolerance. It can then be followed through the history of Western society in various examples of charters such as the 1215 English Magna Carta, the 1628 English Petition of Right, the 1787 United States Constitution, the 1789 French Declaration of the Rights of Man and of the Citizen and the 1791 United States Bill of Rights (United for Human Rights 2016). All of these charters recognise aspects of citizens' basic rights to equality but construct the human being from the perspective of an adult male. Mary Wollstonecraft produced the treatise *A Vindication of the Rights of Woman* (1792) in order to illustrate the female rights agenda. In this she implicitly raises the concept of the inherent 'difference' of children:

'Men, indeed, appear to me to act in a very unphilosophical manner when they try to secure the good conduct of women by attempting to keep them always *in a state of childhood'* (Wollstonecraft 1792, online). In this, then, we see an awakening to the idea of the child as a being with specific, additional needs that are rooted in developmental difference.

This concept was taken forward into a general Victorian discourse relating to the nature of children and childhood, eventually resulting in a series of Acts of Parliament to prevent children from working in industry, followed by the Education Act of 1870, which made it compulsory (and free) for children aged between five and ten to attend school. The subsequent Children Act of 1889, the first piece of British legislation to impose penalties on adults who mistreated children, demonstrated the arrival of British society at the conscious notion of children as particularly vulnerable human beings who, in terms of social justice, should be provided with care, education and protection under the law (Jarvis 2016a).

In Europe, the twentieth century became a period in which war on an industrial scale was waged not once but twice, with devastating consequences for the continent's children. At the end of World War I in 1918, the victorious allies created a blockade against the losing side, which resulted in famine in Germany and Austria. Enraged by the suffering caused to children by this situation, philanthropist Egalantyne Jebb handed out leaflets in London's Trafalgar Square, which contained pictures of emaciated German and Austrian children. The document's headline read: 'our blockade has caused this – millions of children are starving to death'. Jebb had been raised in a family of Victorian social reformers and may therefore not have been particularly surprised by her subsequent arrest and trial for distributing papers that had not been cleared by the Defence of the Realm Act (Mulley 2009) but she could not have predicted the emergent result: the judge went on to commend her for her social conscience, and reimbursed her from his own pocket for the fine that he was compelled to impose. Jebb, as a lady from a wealthy family, decided to pay her own fine and use the money donated to her by the judge to set up the now world-famous charity Save the Children. In 1924, she wrote a 'Declaration of the Rights of the Child', now known as the *Geneva* Declaration of the Rights of the Child (United Nations Documents 2016, online). It was adopted on 26 September 1924 by the League of Nations, which had been set up in Geneva in 1920 (Save the Children 2016).

Judged by the scale of later documents, the Geneva Declaration of the Rights of the Child (1924) was relatively brief. It proposed that children should 'be given the means requisite for … normal development, both materially and spiritually' to include nursing when sick, education when 'backward', guidance when 'delinquent' and food and shelter when destitute. It also went on to propose that children should be the first to receive aid in times of national and international distress and be protected from exploitation. It also had one section that was not repeated in further European declarations but which was subsequently raised in a slightly different context in the African Charter on the Rights and Welfare of the Child (UNICEF 1999): the idea that children should be raised in the spirit of dedicating their talents to the service of others in society (United Nations Documents 2016, online).

The League of Nations came to an effective end in the international bickering which preceded World War II, and there was subsequently very little recognition of the rights of children in wartime Europe, with huge atrocities committed upon the children of nations occupied by the German Nazi state, including their inclusion in the Jewish genocide. Other notable suffering imposed upon the continent's children included the Dutch Hunger Winter of 1944, which imposed lifelong health problems upon children, including those who had been conceived but not yet born during that year (Stein *et al.* 2009). In 1945, the final year of the war, representatives of fifty nations met in San Francisco to draw up the United Nations (UN) Charter, which was signed on 26 June 1945 (United Nations 2016). The UN's first action was to produce the Universal Declaration of Human Rights in 1948 (United Nations 1948), followed by the Declaration of the Rights of the Child in 1959 (United Nations 1959). This was a more extensive document than the Geneva Declaration, additionally recognising the psychological suffering of children in a 'total war' situation, including the negation of rights to a settled home and family life. The evidence on this aspect was given by England's Dr John Bowlby (1952), who had studied the psychological effects of children's removal from their families in the evacuation process carried out within the United Kingdom during World War II, a European nation which had never been subjugated to Nazi rule. His resulting theory of 'maternal deprivation' (Bowlby 1988) continues to develop and pose further questions in the twenty-first century (Jarvis 2016b).

The United Nations International Children's Emergency Fund (UNICEF) grew out of the International Children's Fund, which was created in 1946 to provide aid for children whose lives had been impaired by World War II. Since its adoption by the United Nations in 1947, UNICEF has managed myriad relief programmes for children and young people in nations at war. It also acts to promote child health in all nations without discriminating on the basis of religion, nationality, status or political belief (United Nations 2016). From this basis, an impetus gradually arose to extend the scope of the Declaration of the Rights of the Child, which finally came to fruition in a more comprehensive rights document for children and young people, the United Nations Convention on the Rights of the Child (UNCRC, UNICEF 1989). The Convention lists fifty-four articles, which outline a comprehensive set of international rights for children. Here are some of the most important points relating to the promotion of social justice for children living in rich, post-industrial nations such as the UK:

Article 3: All organisations concerned with children should work towards what is best for each individual child.

Article 27: Children have a right to a standard of living that is good enough to meet their physical and mental needs. The government should help families who cannot afford to provide this.

Article 29: Education should develop each child's personality and talents to the full.

Article 31: All children have a right to relax and play, and to join in a wide range of activities.

Article 40: Children who are accused of breaking the law have the right to legal help and fair treatment in a justice system that respects their rights. Governments are required to set a minimum age below which children cannot be held criminally responsible (UNICEF 2016, online).

The vast majority of nations in the world have both signed and ratified the UNCRC, including the United Kingdom. However, the United States of America, despite playing a large part in the construction of the UNCRC and signing it in 1995, ultimately failed to finally ratify it (that is, be bound by it within national laws). This is due in large part to ongoing objections to its ratification from Republicans within the US Senate (*The Economist* 2013), which are most likely to stem from the US's difficulties in fulfilling some of the more socially democratic aspects of the UNCRC, Article 27 in particular, under their right wing neo-liberal socio-economic policies.

So, with the exception of the US, the world's view of children's rights and, by implication, the construction of social justice for children is largely framed by the UNCRC. While the vast majority of African nations have both signed and ratified the UNCRC, questions were raised by them with respect to the highly individualistic nature of its narrative. This eventually led to the production of an independent children's rights charter by the Organisation of African Unity: the African Charter on the Rights and Welfare of the Child (UNICEF 1999). The most striking difference between the African CRWC and the UNCRC is the discrete section on the child's *responsibilities* in the African CRWC, in which the following duties are specified:

- To work for the cohesion of the family, to respect parents, superiors and elders at all times and to assist them in case of need;
- To serve the national community by placing their physical and intellectual abilities at its service.

(UNICEF 1999, online)

In this charter, then, we see the continuation of Jebb's concept of children's service to others in society, from a different cultural perspective. This leads to reflection upon why Western social altruism did not move forward into the UNCRC. This issue will be explored below in the context of the construction of childhood within the post-industrial, neo-liberal culture of the contemporary UK.

One of the problems of considering a UK-wide approach to social justice for children is that, since a range of devolved powers for the UK nations was granted by the New Labour government of 1997–2010, education curricula and other services for children, young people and their families may differ between England and the devolved policies of Scotland, Wales and Northern Ireland; in particular, there are some quite marked differences between Scotland and the other three UK nations (Jarvis 2016a). As such, this chapter will focus principally on policy and practice in England, which houses over 80 per cent of the population of the UK.

Education for the economy

Education has long been viewed within British society as a process through which to progress national social justice, and, in the more immediate sense for children and young people, with respect to their developmental needs. For example, in 1923, a year before the Geneva Declaration of Children's Rights was adopted by the League of Nations, early years educator Grace Owen wrote:

> The environment of the nursery is planned for children only ... the small furniture, the choice of pictures and objects of interest, the arrangement of these so that everything is within reach ... give an environment which the little child can master and feel to be his own ... thus the nursery is able to give the children a wider field for the full exercise of their powers than is usually possible at home.
>
> (Owen 1923: 19–20)

This socially democratic, developmentally informed construction of early years' education is still alive in the Nordic nations, for example Brostrom and Hansen (2010) outline the Danish Social Service Act (1998), which requires that early years practitioners provide space and opportunities for young children to play, learn, investigate, engage in physical exercise and socialise with each other. Greve and Solheim (2010: 161) describe the early years education tradition in Norway as 'built on a social pedagogical foundation more than on preparing for school', while Hannikainen (2010) comments that in Finland the early years' education tradition involves intertwining dimensions of care, education and teaching that promotes positive self-image, expressive, interactive skills and development of thinking. Johansson and Emilson (2010) propose that Swedish early years' education is based on a model of the child as a vulnerable individual, who nevertheless has his/her own recognised areas of competence and individual rights as a citizen of the Swedish nation. Children in the Nordic nations do not start school until they are six or seven years old (seven in Finland and Sweden; six in Denmark and Norway) and even then they are given ample time for free play and are not expected to learn within a formal or centralised curriculum.

However, over the past three decades the sociopolitical milieu in England and the US has evolved in a very different direction to that of the socially democratic Nordic nations, becoming increasingly 'neo-liberal', a sociocultural philosophy introduced into the UK by the Conservative government of 1979–97, which subjugates the needs of the nation's human population to the requirements of the national and international economy. In this way, human beings become defined primarily as 'capital', leading to the implicit construction of childhood as a drain on the economy that needs to be 'dealt with'; the goal is to transform children into capital in the most expedient manner. There are only three effective ways in which to do this:

- Marketing products for children to their parents and/or directly to children in order to ignite 'pester power';

- The provision of profit-generating services for children and families;
- A highly market-focused, expedient programme of education to turn children into worker-consumers via the most parsimonious process available.

This last imperative has had a great impact upon state education, which has developed into a process of 'transmit and test' (Rogoff and Toma 1997). The core focus of the currently Conservative Department for Education (DFE) is upon developing processes through which children can be most expediently primed to fill roles in the adult labour force that will amass capital for themselves, their employer and their nation. The New Labour government of 1997–2010 also enthusiastically embraced neo-liberal policies, producing the flagship 'Every Child Matters' policy (DFES 2003), in which children's rights are structured primarily in terms of skills development and academic achievement, leading to the 'economic well-being', it is implied, of the individual, but within the omnipresence of the national and international economy. The central government agency OFSTED was set up in 1992 to evaluate state schools against these overarching targets through the results of 'key stage' statutory testing. Additionally, despite childcare for children from birth to five being largely provided by commercial enterprise (fulfilling the neo-liberal goal of profit generation in services for children), these too were restructured through the 'Every Child Matters' agenda as an integral part of the preparation for work system, and are also inspected by OFSTED, which places an overwhelming focus upon the acceleration of children's intellectual development even at this very early stage, in the pursuit of 'school readiness'. The first year in the school, 'Reception' class, then marks the transition to the next stage in the race from birth to produce worker-consumers for the economy (Jarvis 2015). Indeed, a very similar process within the US education system was named 'The Race to the Top' by the federal government (The White House 2009).

England's stringently curriculumised education and care system is consequently the source of much concern. It begins effectively from birth, with an Early Years Foundation Stage in which seventeen early learning goals are stipulated for children from birth to five, against which a progress report must be made at age two, and a summative assessment must be made at transfer to the National Curriculum at the conclusion of the school year in which the child becomes five. England's average school entry age of four-and-a half is one of the earliest in the world, and because each 'year group' cohort encompasses children born between September and August across two calendar years, children born in July and August, the 'summer birthdays', are admitted to school when they are between 48 and 49 months old.

Statutory testing takes place at regular intervals throughout a child's education. The original system placed these assessments at the end of each 'key stage' in the education years in which the child passed their seventh, eleventh, fourteenth and sixteenth birthdays, the results of which were communicated to the Department for Education and collectively used to evaluate the performance of the relevant school, with adult workers within the system being individually evaluated on the basis of children's statutory test results ('performance managed'). This inevitably led to much 'teaching to test' as schools attempted to 'game' the system (*Guardian* 2015).

In this sense, then, the whole system was constructed to operate in a highly 'top-down' fashion, viewing children as adults under construction via the most parsimonious strategy, and, consequently, much of the developmentally informed practice outlined by Grace Owen at the beginning of this section has been gradually lost from the system. The most recent notion that has emerged from the Department for Education (DFE) at time of writing (May 2017) is a plan to allocate one overall numerical score to each child through a statutory assessment of literacy and numeracy skills undertaken at the beginning of the Reception year to create a 'baseline' against which achievement at the end of primary school would be compared. The school and its teachers would then be evaluated on the resulting statistic, a so-called 'accountability' measure (DFE 2017). However, this practice has no basis in empiricism and has been subject to a range of criticisms from parents, academics and teachers (see https://morethanascore.co.uk).

Education targets have therefore been become framed by a neo-liberal view of 'social justice', in the sense that measured progress within a particular narrow skills frame is every child's right within an (apparently) predictable pathway to 'economic well-being', a concept that has unleashed a wave of criticism on the basis that 'targets presented as rights' is contrary to the social democratic rights to which the UNCRC signatory nations have committed. Ken Spours, writing in *The New Statesman*, comments:

> The abiding metaphor of education is now a race, a global race in which every country and every person has to become ever more competitive. The best nursery, followed by the best school, the best university all to get the highest paying job. Along the way we learn to compete and to be in debt. Our children and their teachers become stressed and anxious in this arms race that can never end.
>
> (Spours 2015, online)

Others have proposed that children's rights are in fact being *crushed* within such an approach, with the focus firmly upon what is best for the national and international economy rather than what is best for the child as a holistic human being. Stephen (2006) proposes that justification of practice from a perspective of future development does not focus upon the individual but is in fact a politically dominated approach, while Campbell-Barr (2012: 424) comments that 'future returns are based on the acquisition of human capital (principally in the form of laying the foundations for later learning) and the contribution that this can make to the knowledge economy'. Alderson (2008: 53) similarly commented that the Every Child Matters Charter 'appears to be more concerned with the national economy than with the welfare and protection of young children'.

England thus currently struggles with notions of social justice within its education system, finding it difficult to effectively frame children's holistic rights within an economy-focused, neo-liberal culture. In particular, we can further reflect upon issues arising with respect to UNCRC Articles 3 (best interests of the child), 29 (development of the child's personality, talents and mental and physical abilities to their fullest potential) and 31 (play, cultural life and the arts) (UNCRC 2016). The manner in which they are addressed or, more accurately, fail to be addressed in the current state education system gives rise to the question of whether we aim to produce independent, self-motivated citizens or human drones programmed to serve in national and international markets under the guise of individual self-advancement.

Rush little baby

The UNCRC focuses squarely upon the core children's right to be recognised *as* children, in that social justice cannot be achieved without the recognition of children's needs within the context of developmental difference. It has already been illustrated above, however, that the English education system seeks to parsimoniously accelerate the child into being an economically productive adult as quickly as possible. This section now turns to the question of how infants – children under three – fit into the neo-liberal discourse, and this begins from the perspective of what such governments expect from their parents.

One of the emergent results of the construction of human beings primarily as human capital for paid labour was a discontinuity with the previous culture of infant parenting, in which the mother was expected to be the principal carer for the pre-school child. In the mid-twentieth century, this practice was underpinned by the maternal deprivation hypothesis of John Bowlby (1952), which warned of the inadvisability of early separation of the infant from the mother, the core feature of the advice that he gave to the United Nations. Later empirical findings indicated that, in fact, infants could thrive in a situation where care was provided by a small circle of adults to whom they had affectionate attachments (Schaffer and Emerson 1964). The fall of the classic maternal deprivation hypothesis was then capitalised upon by the neo-liberal orientation to working mothers: 'more women in the workforce boosts GDP, increases income from taxes, and reduces welfare costs' (UNICEF 2008: 4) (see Chapter 9).

The principal solution for the 'child care gap' that consequently evolved over the latter third of the twentieth century was one of commercial mass day care for the infants of families in which, owing to absence in the workplace, there was no adult available to provide home-based care. However, spending long hours in collective day care has recently been empirically demonstrated to have a negative impact upon infants and, potentially, their lifelong mental health. A range of studies discovered abnormally raised levels of the stress hormone cortisol in infants placed in such mass care facilities (e.g. Dettling *et al.* 1999; Dettling *et al.* 2000; Watamura *et al.* 2003; Vermeer and Van IJzendoorn 2006; Watamura *et al.* 2009), and it is proposed that this reaction is principally triggered by the lack of emotional bonds between infants and the typically transient population of adult practitioners in such settings, the vast majority of whom are employed on very low wages (Nursery World 2015). The pre-eminence of the economy over the needs of the young human being comes into very sharp relief in this policy and practice example, because the need of the infant for consistent, affectionate care from a small, stable circle of 'emotionally bonded' adults is wholly incommensurate with the human capital culture of a neo-liberal economy.

> Logically, the only way in which children can be economically generative is in a situation where their working parents pay another adult a wage to take care of them – but profit can only be realised if the adults providing care do so at a cost below that of the wage of the average adult in the society in question.... It is now past time for Anglo-American governments to concede that the 'childcare gap' that 21st century families face is an emergent factor from neo-liberal policies and practices, narrowly predicated upon human beings as 'capital'.
>
> (Jarvis 2016c: 8)

Neo-liberalism therefore poses a formidable double bind for families, particularly those in which both parents (or one single parent) work long hours for low wages. Crowley (2014: 117) comments that adults, mothers in particular, in such situations experience 'extreme cognitive dissonance ... continually pushed and pulled between their work and home worlds'. When asked what matters most of all to them, the vast majority of parents report that they would like to have the ability to spend sufficient time with their children to create the deeply bonded relationships that provide them with lifelong emotional security (Mumsnet 2016). Towards the end of his life, John Bowlby reflected:

> Man and woman power devoted to the production of material goods counts a plus in all our economic indices. Man and woman power devoted to the production of happy, healthy and self-reliant children in their own homes does not count at all. We have created a topsy-turvy world.
>
> (Bowlby 1988: 2)

This issue, it could be argued, creates a fundamental lack of social justice for both children *and* their families in contemporary English society. It also provides further evidence that neo-liberalism is incompatible with the construction of developmentally informed policies for children, raising a number of issues that impact upon their developmental rights and, consequently, their access to social justice.

An English childhood in the twenty-first century: 'stop behaving like a kid'

We have seen in the previous section that, in modern family lives within Britain and the US, the neo-liberal culture of 'all adults in paid work' requires that many infants are routinely cared for in non-domestic, professional settings. Many children over five are also routinely cared for in similar settings before and after school, which are inspected by OFSTED under a similar agenda to the one that is applied to schools and early years care, narrowly focused upon the development of children's intellectual abilities, narrowly focused on literacy and numeracy.

This is a dramatically different environment to that in which previous generations were raised, in which children of school age typically engaged in free independent socialisation within their local neighbourhoods whenever they were not in school. British researchers Opie and Opie carried out a range of studies of children's free play in streets and playgrounds during the 1950s and 1960s involving approximately 10,000 children across England, Scotland and Wales. In 1969, they reported 'there is no town or city known to us where street games do not flourish' (Opie and Opie 1969: vi). Since then, however, children have moved into professional care settings, out-of-school play spaces have been increasingly encroached upon by motor vehicles, and the advent of an omnipresent online news media has increased parental fear of predatory stranger abduction. All of this has resulted in an 'adult colonisation of children's lives' (Corsaro 1997: 38), greatly reducing children's opportunities for independent, collaborative free play. The drive for 'achievement' in education has also resulted in a decrease in breaktimes (or playtimes) in English schools to give children and teachers more time to engage with the adult-defined, outcome-based learning demands of the decreed National Curriculum (*Guardian* 2015).

Yet again, the rights of children, this time to leisure and peer socialisation, have been trampled by a narrow focus upon the requirements of the economy. Reducing children's time and space for socialisation in turn reduces their opportunities to develop the core human social skills of competition, collaboration and cooperation (Jarvis *et al.* 2014). Even more worryingly, surveys increasingly find that as neighbourhood children have less frequently encountered playing together around local neighbourhoods, adults have become increasingly intolerant towards children's normal 'childish' behaviour. In 2007, the Joseph Rowntree Foundation commissioned a research project which gathered children's perspectives on this topic, which abundantly illustrated such an adult orientation. One of the participants of this study bleakly commented 'if the police catch you they take you back to your house' (Sutton *et al.* 2007: 29). David Bond of Project Wild Thing (see https://vimeo.com/68072823) reports a series of examples illustrating adult intolerance of active play within public areas, proposing that Britain is currently experiencing a 'perfect storm' of factors which 'stop children roaming free' (*Guardian* 2013, online). O'Brien *et al.* (2000: 273) commented: 'letting children play out is becoming a marker of neglectful or irresponsible parenting'.

This leads on to this chapter's final example of England's intolerance of children's developmental difference: the manner in which English society currently manages serious misbehaviour in childhood and adolescence. Prior to 1998, the legal system in England was premised upon the provision of social justice for children under fourteen through the ancient principle of *doli incapax* – the duty of a judge presiding over a case where criminal charges have been brought against a child between ten and fourteen to carefully examine whether the child understood that what s/he had done was in fact criminal and not just 'naughty'. *Doli incapax* was summarily removed in 1998 by the New Labour Crime and Disorder Act (*Guardian* 2007), setting the unitary age of criminal responsibility at ten years.

Here again we see an impatience with children's developmental difference as the impetus for a neo-liberal regime to overrule more developmentally informed considerations, which in this case had been in place for many centuries before being summarily removed by modern legislation. In 2010, problems arising made national headlines when two eleven-year-old boys were placed on the sex offenders register for attempted rape (*Guardian* 2010) as a result of an episode of inappropriate play which occurred when they were ten years old. Such practices do not only flout the more developmentally informed practices of our ancestors, but additionally disregard findings from recent bio-neurological research which indicate that the last areas of the human brain to mature, over the period of mid- to late adolescence, are those that deal with impulse control and complex social understanding (Blakemore 2012).

Although the national spotlight focuses far less frequently upon this area of practice with children and young people than it does upon education, this is perhaps the thinnest end of the developmentally ill-informed wedge that runs beneath contemporary policies for children in the scale of its utter disregard for social justice. The criminalising of children blights young lives with criminal records issued for behaviour that, owing to their stage of maturation, the person in question was unable to fully consider or even comprehend in terms of the offence committed. The clearly erroneous presumption that children have a fully developed understanding of criminal behaviour from the age of ten years is an issue that has been frequently raised with England by the United Nations with respect to its compliance with the UNCRC, and efforts to create a more developmentally informed policy in this area are ongoing (Halsbury's Law Exchange 2015).

Conclusion: working towards developmentally informed practice for social justice

Looking back over the examples outlined by this chapter, we can deduce a contemporary national impetus to construct children and childhood from a highly 'adulterated' perspective. We expect infants to separate from adults to whom they are emotionally bonded at a very early stage, despite a body of bio-psychological research findings that suggests that this is damaging to the developing stress-coping system; by the time children are four years old, we expect them to engage in a 'transmit and test' education system rooted in individual 'performance' and competition rather than collaboration and cooperation, and in later childhood we provide insufficient opportunities for them to freely associate with peers within a society which imposes draconian, developmentally inappropriate punishments for behaviour violations that may in large part stem from immature impulse control and misunderstanding rather than from criminality. This poses a stark picture of how it actually *feels* to be a child in contemporary England, and there is much empirical evidence to suggest that English childhood is currently in a state of crisis.

One in ten children is currently diagnosed with a mental health disorder, with nearly 80,000 children and young people suffering from severe depression, including 8,000 children aged under ten years of age (Young Minds 2016, online); 20 per cent of young people currently living in the UK deliberately harm themselves (*Guardian* 2014) and there has been a huge increase in admissions to hospital for this reason (Young Minds 2011, online). In 2007, a comparison of child well-being in rich Western nations carried out by UNICEF put Britain at the bottom of on a scale of child well-being (UNICEF 2007). A further study carried out by the Children's Society and the University of York estimated that about 'half a million children in the UK in the eight to 15 age range have low well-being at any point in time' (The Children's Society, 2012: 5). In 2013, UNICEF renewed its examination of children's sense of well-being in rich nations, and found the UK in sixteenth place, still well behind the Nordic nations and all the other Northern European nations apart from Austria, which ranked eighteenth (UNICEF 2013). A study carried out by the New Economics Foundation found that British sixteen- to twenty-four-year-olds demonstrated the lowest levels of trust and belonging in Europe (New Economics Foundation 2009). Twenge (2000: 1018) proposed that a steep rise in juvenile mental health problems in the similarly neo-liberal US after 1980 were largely due to 'low social connectedness and high environmental threat', concluding that 'until people feel both safe and connected to others, anxiety is likely to remain high' (Twenge, 2000: 1017).

So how can we enhance our children's feelings of security and social connection? Creating taxation systems that help families to provide care for children under three in small groups of adults within domestic environments, with professional support for families in need to call upon would optimise the healthy emotional development of infants; more time and space for social free play would help children to build 'social hardiness' (Jarvis 2014, p. 209) and less 'high-stakes' testing in school would comprise a good start in terms of better addressing UNCRC Articles 3, 27, 29 and 31. Raising the age of criminal responsibility, alongside the introduction of a comprehensive national guidance service for teenagers whose behaviour is causing concern would also better fulfil the requirements of Article 40. Such an initiative could be further enhanced by the inclusion of the altruistic perspective of service to others. This would more fully recapture the spirit within the world's first formal declaration of children's rights, in the nation of the originator's birth.

To effectively provide social justice for children, we need an overarching culture which authentically embraces childhood on its own terms as an integral life stage, rather than viewing it through a lens which constructs it as an inconvenient journey to a work-consumed adulthood within a wealth-obsessed society. A deep knowledge of the human developmental process will always be an essential component of policy development for children and their families in nations that start with a genuine intention to promote social justice for their child citizens of the present – who, of course, will be their adult citizens of the future.

Reflection points

- Consider Jebb's avocation to develop children's impetus to use their talents to benefit wider society, and why this might have been lost from the current English discourse of childhood.
- Consider how the recognition of the need to create policy from a developmentally informed perspective might positively impact upon such apparently disparate policies as the provision of care of children under three, the education of children aged three to seven and policies relating to youth justice.
- Why might current policy and practice for children and young people in England/the UK have had a negative impact upon their mental health and sense of 'well-being'?
- What is the value of time and space for free play for children and young people? Should this be considered a fundamental childhood right?
- When and how should we test children in state education?
- How do the rights of children and young people intertwine with the rights of their parents and families? Might the rights of individuals within families and within wider societal environments sometimes be difficult to negotiate?

References

Alderson, P. (2008). *Young Children's Rights* (2nd Ed.). London: Jessica Kingsley.

Blakemore, S.J. (2012). The mysterious workings of the adolescent brain. *TED Talks*. Online. Available at www.ted.com/talks/sarah_jayne_blakemore_the_mysterious_workings_of_the_adolescent_brain?language=en.

Bowlby, J. (1952). *Maternal Care and Mental Health*, WHO report. Online. Available at http://apps.who.int/iris/bitstream/10665/40724/1/WHO_MONO_2_%28part1%29.pdf.

Bowlby, J. (1988). *A Secure Base*. London: Routledge.

Brostrom, S. and Hansen, O.H. (2010). Care and education in the Danish creche. *International Journal of Early Childhood*, *42*: 87–100.

Campbell-Barr, V. (2012). Early years education and the value for money folklore. *European Early Childhood Education Research Journal*, *20*(3): 423–37.

Corsaro, W. (1997). *The Sociology of Childhood*. Thousand Oaks, CA: Pine Forge.

Crowley, J.E. (2014). Staying at home or working for pay. *Sociological Spectrum*, *34*(2): 114–35.

Dettling, A.C., Gunnar, M.R. and Donzella, B. (1999). Cortisol levels of young children in full-day childcare centers: Relations with age and temperament. *Psychoneuroendocrinology*, *24*: 519–36.

Dettling, A.C., Parker, S.W., Lane, S., Sebanc, A. and Gunnar, M.R. (2000). Quality of care and temperament determine changes in cortisol concentrations over the day for young children in childcare, *Psychoneuroendocrinology*, *25*: 819–36.

DFE (2017). *Primary Assessment in England: Government Consultation*. Online. Available at https://consult.education.gov.uk/assessment-policy-and-development/primary-assessment/supporting_documents/Primary%20assessment%20in%20England.pdf (accessed 9 May 2017).

DFES (2003). *Every Child Matters*, Green Paper. London: Stationery Office.

Greve, A. and Solheim, M. (2010). Research on children in ECEC under three in Norway: increased volume, yet invisible. *International Journal of Early Childhood, 42*: 155–63.

Guardian (2007). At what age can you be a criminal? *Guardian*. Online. Available at www.theguardian.com/society/2007/sep/04/youthjustice.childrensservices.

Guardian (2010). Supervision order for 11-year-old boys convicted of attempting to rape girl, 8. *Guardian*. Online. Available at www.theguardian.com/uk/2010/aug/18/boys-attempted-rape-girl-eight-supervision-order.

Guardian (2013). No freedom to play or explore outside for children. *Guardian*. Online. Available at www.theguardian.com/lifeandstyle/2013/jul/13/no-freedom-play-outside-children.

Guardian (2014). Shock figures show extent of self harm in English teenagers. *Guardian*. Online. Available at www.theguardian.com/society/2014/may/21/shock-figures-self-harm-england-teenagers.

Guardian (2015). Playtime is crucial for a child's development – cut it at your peril. *Guardian*. Online. Available at www.theguardian.com/teacher-network/2015/sep/17/playtime-child-development-learning-cut-at-peril.

Halsbury's Law Exchange (2015). *It's Time to Raise the Age of Criminal Responsibility*. Online. Available at www.halsburyslawexchange.co.uk/its-time-to-raise-the-minimum-age-of-criminal-responsibility.

Hannikainen, M. (2010). 1 to 3-year-old children in day care centres in Finland: an overview of eight doctoral dissertations. *International Journal of Early Childhood, 42*: 101–15.

Jarvis, P. (2016a). 'The child, the family and the state: international perspectives', in P. Jarvis, J. George, W. Holland and J. Doherty, J (eds) *The Complete Companion for Teaching and Leading Practice in the Early Years*. Abingdon: Routledge.

Jarvis, P. (2016b). Critical maternalism: a window on the 21st century. *Early Years Educator, 18*(2): 38–44. Online. Available at www.magonlinelibrary.com.libezproxy.open.ac.uk/doi/pdf/10.12968/eyed.2016.18.2.38. doi: http://dx.doi.org/10.12968/eyed.2016.18.2.38.

Jarvis, P. (2016c). Doing the fundamental things. *Early Years Educator*, 17(11): 8. Online. Available at www.magonlinelibrary.com/doi/10.12968/eyed.2016.17.11.8. doi: http://dx.doi.org/10.12968/eyed.2016.17.11.8.

Jarvis, P. (2015). It's against human nature to send two year olds to school. *The Conversation*. Online. Available at https://theconversation.com/its-against-human-nature-to-send-two-year-olds-to-school-37180.

Jarvis, P. (2014). 'Building "social hardiness" for life: rough and tumble play in the early years of primary school', in A. Brock, P. Jarvis and Y. Olusoga (eds) *Perspectives on Play: Learning for Life*. Abingdon: Routledge.

Jarvis, P., Newman, S. and Swiniarski, L. (2014). On 'becoming social': the importance of collaborative free play in childhood. *International Journal of Play, 3*(1): 53–68. Online. Available at www.tandfonline.com/doi/pdf/10.1080/21594937.2013.863440. doi:10.1080/21594937.2013.863440.

Johansson, E. and Emilson, A. (2010). Toddlers' life in Swedish preschool. *International Journal of Early Childhood, 42*: 165–79.

Mulley, C. (2009). *The Woman Who Saved the Children*. Oxford: One World.

O'Brien, M., Jones, D., Sloan, D. and Rustin, M. (2000). Children's independent spatial mobility in the urban public realm. *Childhood, 7*(3): 257–77.

Opie, I. and Opie, P. (1969). *Children's Games in Street and Playground.* London: Oxford University Press.

Owen, G. (1923). *Nursery School Education* (2nd Ed.). London: Methuen.

New Economics Foundation (2009). *Backing the Future*. Online. Available at www.new-economics.org/publications/entry/backing-the-future.

Nursery World (2015). *Danger of Childcare Workforce Shortage without Wage Increase*. Online. Available at www.nurseryworld.co.uk/nursery-world/news/1152769/danger-of-childcare-workforce-shortage-without-wage-increase.

Rogoff, B. and Toma, C. (1997). Shared thinking: Community and institutional variations. *Discourse Processes, 23*(3): 471–97.

Save the Children (2016). *Eglantyne Jebb: A True Children's Champion.* Online. Available at www.savethechildren.org/site/c.8rKLIXMGIpI4E/b.9198313/k.B10/Eglantyne_Jebb_A_True_Childrens_Champion.htm.

Schaffer, H.R. and. Emerson. P. (1964). The development of social attachments in infancy. *Monographs of the Society for Research in Child Development, 29*(3): 1–77.

Spours, K. (2015). Forget the global race. Education is about more than that. *The New Statesman.* Online. Available at www.newstatesman.com/politics/2015/03/forget-global-race-education-about-more (accessed 27 May 2015).

Stein, A.D., Pierik, F.H., Verrips, G.H.W., Susser, E.S. and Lumey, L.H. (2009). Maternal exposure to the Dutch Famine before conception and during pregnancy: quality of life and depressive symptoms in adult offspring. *Epidemiology, 20*(6). Online. doi: http://doi.org/10.1097/EDE.0b013e3181b5f227. Available at www.ncbi.nlm.nih.gov/pmc/articles/PMC3850290/pdf/nihms528204.pdf.

Stephen, C. (2006). *Early Years Education: Perspectives from a Review of the International Literature*. Edinburgh: The Scottish Executive. Online. Available at: www.gov.scot/Resource/Doc/92395/0022116.pdf (accessed 27 May 2015).

Sutton, E., Smith, N., Deardon, C. and Middleton, S. (2007). *A Child's Eye View of Social Difference*. Online. Available at https://core.ac.uk/download/files/66/67152.pdf.

The Children's Society (2012). *The Good Childhood Report 2012: A Review of our Chil dren's Well-Being*. Leeds: The Children's Society. Online. Available at www.childrens society.org.uk/sites/default/files/tcs/good_childhood_report_2012_final_0.pdf.

The Economist (2013). Why won't America ratify the UN convention on children's rights? *The Economist*. Online. Available at www.economist.com/blogs/economist-explains/2013/10/economist-explains-2.

The White House (2009). *Fact Sheet: Race to the Top*. Online. Available at www.white house.gov/the-press-office/fact-sheet-race-top.

Twenge, J. (2000). The age of anxiety? Birth cohort change in anxiety and neuroticism, 1952–1993. *Journal of Personality and Social Psychology, 79*(6): 1007–21. doi:10.1037//0022-3514.79.6.1007.

UNCRC (2016). *Facts Sheet: A Summary of Rights under the Convention on the Rights of the Child.* Online. Available at www.unicef.org/crc/files/Rights_overview.pdf.

UN Documents (1924). Geneva Declaration of the Rights of the Child. Online. Available at www.un-documents.net/gdrc1924.htm.

UNICEF (1959). United Nations Declaration on the Rights of the Child. Online. Available at www.unicef.org/malaysia/1959-Declaration-of-the-Rights-of-the-Child.pdf.

UNICEF (1989). United Nations Convention on the Rights of the Child. Online. Available at www.unicef.org.uk/Documents/Publication-pdfs/UNCRC_PRESS200910web.pdf.

UNICEF (1999). African Charter on the Rights and Welfare of the Child (1999). Online. Available at www.unicef.org/esaro/African_Charter_articles_in_full.pdf.

UNICEF (2007). *An Overview of Child Well-Being in Rich Countries*. Florence: UNICEF. Online. Available at www.unicef-icdc.org/presscentre/presskit/reportcard7/rc7_eng.pdf.

UNICEF (2008). *The Child Care Transition: A League Table of Early Childhood Education and Care in Economically Advanced Countries*. Online. Available at www.unicef-irc.org/publications/pdf/rc8_eng.pdf.

UNICEF (2013). *Child Well-Being in Rich Countries: A Comparative Overview*. Florence: UNICEF. Online. Available at www.unicef-irc.org/publications/pdf/rc11_eng.pdf.

United Nations (1948). Declaration of Human Rights. Online. Available at www.ohchr.org/EN/UDHR/Documents/UDHR_Translations/eng.pdf.

United Nations (1959). *Declaration of the Child*. www.unicef.org/lac/spbarbados/Legal/global/General/declaration_child1959.pdf.

United Nations (2016). *History of the United Nations*. Online. Available at www.un.org/en/aboutun/history.

United for Human Rights (2016). *A Brief History of Human Rights*. Online. Available at www.humanrights.com/what-are-human-rights/brief-history/cyrus-cylinder.html.

Vermeer, H. and van IJzendoorn, M. (2006). Children's elevated cortisol levels at daycare: A review and meta-analysis. *Early Childhood Research Quarterly*, *21*: 390–401. Online. Available at www.researchgate.net/profile/Marinus_Van_IJzendoorn/publication/222525572_Children's_elevated_cortisol_levels_at_daycare_A_review_and_meta-analysis/links/0fcfd5112319d8264d000000.pdf/download?version=vtp.

Watamura, S.E., Donzella, B., Alwin, J. and Gunnar, M.R. (2003). Morning-to-afternoon increases in cortisol concentrations for infants and toddlers at child care: Age differences and behavioral correlates. *Child Development*, 74: 1006–20.

Watamura, S.E., Kryzer, E.M. and Robertson, S.S. (2009). Cortisol patterns at home and child care: Afternoon differences and evening recovery in children attending very high quality full-day center-based child care. *Journal of Applied Developmental Psychology*, *30*: 475–85.

Wollstonecraft, M. (1792). *Vindication of the Rights of Woman*. Online. Available at www.bartleby.com/144.

Young Minds. (2011). *100,000 Children and Young People Could Be Hospitalised due to Self-Harm by 2020 Warns Young Minds*. Online. Available at http://news.cision.com/youngminds/r/100-000-children-and-young-people-could-be-hospitalised-due-to-self-harm-by-2020-warns-youngminds,c9194954.

Young Minds (2016). *Mental Health Statistics*. Online. Available at www.youngminds.org.uk/training_services/policy/mental_health_statistics.

8 Families with young children, precarious work and social justice

Stefano Ba'

Introduction

This chapter considers how job insecurity (here also referred to as 'precarity' or 'precarious employment'; see Standing (2011)) affects the life of parents, but also how the social life of families transform and constitute a shared reality. It is important to understand that parents in precarious employment conditions are not simply victims of the economic system and to consider the ways in which their actions constitute fundamental social links. Pivotal to understanding their social life is the concept of social justice. This chapter will make a comparison of literature assessing the social relations of 'precarious parents' (parents in insecure jobs) in different countries (principally Italy, Great Britain and the USA, but also France and Mexico).

In the first section, Adorno's reflection in *Minima Moralia* (2005 [1951]) is used with the intent to show that an unjust economic system is in place now, as it was in the last century, while the review of critical literature around the 'Great Recession' (which occurred between approximately 2009 and 2011) and the role of capitalism provides the context and the justification for this assertion. Here, one central proposition is that the 'commodification of labour' (that is, reducing people's capability to work to a commodity that can be simply sold and bought, like any other commodity) is setting the conditions for the intimate life of families as well as for their 'economic life'.

In the second section, features of life for parents in precarious employment are explored through a critical lens; the main emphasis will be on the theme of mothers struggling through 'precarity'. In this section, the daily lives of mothers are understood as something that is not just about adapting to precarious circumstances. However, it is in the last section that the concept of 'adaptation' is explored: parents do not simply adapt to given situations but struggle through them, attempting to maintain their sense of dignity. Dignity is suggested to be a fundamental concept, substantiating social justice through the social action of the people who are less privileged.

Box 8.1 'Jam'

Just about managing (Jam) families was the term used by officials in Great Britain at the Autumn Statement of 2016 to indicate six million working-age households on low to middle incomes. The Treasury did not have a formal definition of Jams, but from a statement of the prime minister, Theresa May, these Jams were directly linked to job insecurity. Most of the incomes of Jam families come from work, but they are especially vulnerable to weak income growth and rising cost of life, all factors affecting people in insecure jobs.

From BBC news: www.bbc.co.uk/news/uk-politics-38049245, accessed 14 March 2017

Job insecurity, capitalism and 'private life'

At the beginning of his book on social transformation and personal life, the philosopher and sociologist Adorno (2005 [1951]: 14) observed that, at the beginning of the twentieth century, societies failed to develop an economic way of life in the sense of a more just state of affairs. This simple fact had horrific consequences. He referred to how the socialist movement was first derailed by World War I and then suffocated by fascism in continental Europe and by the Great Depression (in the 1930s) in Great Britain and North America. The economic form Adorno was referring to is capitalism, which, now as a hundred years ago, keeps creating endless spirals of contradictions and crises,[1] as well as booms and busts. For him, the fact that society did not evolve towards a more just system affected profoundly the private life of individuals.

The recent Great Recession has been read in a number of ways, but a renewed focus on the internal contradictions of the capitalist system has gained a reputable relevance (Callinicos 2010; Giacché 2012; Foster and Magdoff 2009; Harvey 2011; Radice 2011). For the context of parents in insecure jobs, here it is important to observe that this literature not only points at the crisis for the capability of the system to renew its profit rate (Bellofiore 2012) but individuates workers' spontaneous actions as the key problem for capital; that is, in their daily lives people have priorities (like a family life) that do not match the interests of capital and this is in the long term a cause for crisis for the economic system (Holloway 2010). This section argues that understanding capitalism is fundamental to locating issues of social justice for families in insecure work.

The Great Recession and precarious work

In addressing issues around families and job insecurity, it is important to start with the Great Recession and austerity,[2] because according to a number of studies these political and economic factors made work less secure. On the one hand, the rise of unemployment created pressures on job security as employers had stronger bargaining positions (Clark and Heath: 80–95, 147–62; Fumagalli

2011) and, on the other, austerity made the unions weaker and created the conditions for the increase of casual and temporary jobs in the labour market (O'Hara 2015; Morini 2012; Tyler 2013). Thus, for the less protected part of the population the Great Recession reinforced trends that keep their wages low and their employment positions less secure (Bellofiore 2012; Holloway 2010; Radice 2011). Put simply, the Great Recession made the most vulnerable part of the population more exposed to the fluctuations of the labour markets. In the language of critical theory (Holloway 2010), within capitalism we all (or at least the 99 per cent of us) have to sell our 'labour skills' in order to get the 'means of subsistence' (Bonefeld 2014). We need an employer to hire us, so we can get a wage in return. Failing that, we are in dire straits.

Why is it important to make these observations about precarious work and family life?

Because here the focus is on how the 'private lives' of families have been marked by recent economic changes. There is of course evidence that recession and then austerity produce material misery for people at the bottom of the social stratification (Clark and Heath 2015), but how might this be an issue linked to structural inequalities, rather than a timeless issue about particular individuals in society? That is, how can we link economic facts (like job insecurity) to the everyday life of parents?

The point of view endorsed here is that economic facts (like job insecurity) always represent social relations and that in social life there are no 'economic laws' that affect people in an automatic, direct way (Bonefeld 2014; Holloway 2010). Here, we propose that economic constraints are not something natural but something social and political, something that has to do with people's social relations. Families in precarious employment create their reality out of conditions that are not of their choosing; however, if these conditions are not 'natural' but rooted within their social relations, how is it possible that these social relations can bring forth something not just? Does the above imply that these parents are somehow responsible for the state of social injustice? To explain this part we briefly recur to the concept of 'exchange value' and the commodification of labour.

'Exchange value' and the commodification of labour as features of capitalism

Exchange value is a basic capitalist mechanism that gives value to things: to goods as well as to what people do for living. Human activities are measured through the mechanism of exchange: what we do is measured and then exchanged for money (e.g. wages or prices of goods). But this mechanism has a tendency to overflow the limits of the market. 'Exchange value' as a quantity measuring mechanism tends to spill over into society as the worker who does a job for living doing or producing something which is measured and considered valuable only through market terms; in this way, her or his value becomes measured through the same principle (Benzer 2011; Holloway 2010; Illouz 2008;

Tischler 2008). A society based on the exchange form of social relations easily produces the 'commodification of labour' (Bonefeld 2014; Standing 2011: 26): work and human activities in general are quantified for profit in market capitalism. Through the consideration of the concept of 'exchange value', we reach a point at which we are able to evaluate this other important concept, which is vital to understand the experience of family in precarious labour conditions.

Commodification of labour understands a person's work or activity only in terms of the monetary value that this work assumes in the market. In a society where almost everything is exchangeable, the activities of a person (work or otherwise) must immediately demonstrate their monetary worth.

Commodification of labour is an experience that deeply impacts upon people in precarious work (Cingolani 1986, 2005), causing them to become continuously anxious about their own employability in the market and the possibility of getting a wage for themselves and for their family. It is about being conscious of the possibility of selling their work skills at 'all cost' and therefore about a price tag that may be attached not only to their work skills but also to themselves as persons (Cooper 2014; Murgia 2010; Pugh 2015; Standing 2011). There is nothing essentially 'economic' about this; rather, the point of view expressed here represents the critique of economics and how capitalism distorts human activities into things (Bonefeld 2014).

Precarious labour and job insecurity are the effects of the economic mechanism that commodifies labour. Indeed, after the Great Recession, 'precarity' and job insecurity have become the default mode for (especially young) people operating in the labour market (Cooper 2014; Giannini and Orientale Caputo 2011; Murgia and Armano 2014; Standing 2011).

Box 8.2 Precarious work in Britain

At the end of 2016, the Trades Union Congress (TUC) published a report about the alarming spread of insecure jobs in Britain. The report said that 10 per cent of British workers are now in precarious work. The number of people in insecure jobs has doubled in the last 10 years. According to the TUC report, there are three forms of insecure job that penalise the most workers: zero-hours contracts, self-employment and casual contracts.

From TUC report, available at www.tuc.org.uk/economic-issues/labour-market/32-million-uk-workers-1-10-are-now-precarious-work (accessed 15 March 2017)

The precarious parent is mainly the mother

This perspective on parenting and insecure employment maintains that it is not just about the psychological damage to a person who may be afraid or anxious about her employment perspectives that matters here. The form that this precariousness takes in society means that people in insecure jobs actively promote their transformation into individuals whose main aim is to produce their own price tag. Thus, parents in job insecurity have the triple burden of having to produce the 'price tag', work (when they find it) and raise children. The commodification of labour then sets not only the conditions of existence for the labourer but also the social form of her life. In this chapter, the feminine pronoun is used when discussing the worker because it is clear that women are the main emergent group within the labour force that live and operate in precarious conditions (Standing 2011). Both as labourers in an increasingly insecure, flexible economy and as the operators of domestic and care work inside the private sphere, women are at the centre of social pressure to work in paid jobs and to be good mothers (Pugh 2015; Murgia 2010).

Are then 'precarious parents' victims of an adverse economic system? Or are they able to forge their own lives, even in the face of 'objective' difficulties? In other words, how can we think about parents' agency, that is, their capability to act on their own accord and their capability to decide about their future?

Adaptation or creativity?

The concept of the commodification of labour reveals that the precariousness of family life is rooted within impersonal mechanisms. Parents' social relations are dependent *from* the very possibility of this commodification, in that they need work to get a wage. However, the fact that parents in insecure jobs control their destiny *through* this impersonal mechanism does not make their lives less personal. Indeed, the most advanced studies (Cooper 2014; Giannini and Orientale Caputo 2011; Murgia and Armano 2014; Pugh 2015; Standing 2011) would not see parents in precarious employment simply as victims of an adverse economic system, nor as simply adapting to precarious circumstances. Surely they are not privileged by the current social order, but recent studies stress their power in constructing meaningful daily lives and document their ability in creating resources out of scarcity (e.g. Wilson and Yochim 2015). However, this creativity from 'below', which is largely about being in control of their own lives, usually enters in conflict with constituted interests. Indeed, this creativity has not much to do with 'freedom of choice'. Precarious employment, under the term 'flexibility', is sold by market capitalism as a form of freedom: freedom of fashioning employment relations according to the individual person's needs and freedom of customising employment schedules according to the individual's preferences. This can be quite handy for parents, when they try to combine childcare and work commitments. So is this flexibility a valued part of parents' strategy for taking control over their 'work and life balance'?

The answer to this question is more complicated than may be perceived, if the answer should come from a standpoint of caring for social justice and the emancipation of the less privileged. Indeed, features of 'precarity', chiefly self-employment, are sometimes connected to struggles against subordination (e.g. oppressive managerial structures). These features are also connected to groups of workers in flexible jobs or self-employment who may be determined in achieving or keeping a certain degree of autonomy, even if the trade-off for it is an insecure flow of income (Standing 2011). These features show that parents in insecure jobs are active (and creative) in trying to fashion their own personal work and family schedules.

Interestingly, in Giannini's analysis (2012), adaptation, denial of long-term perspectives, and withdrawal in traditional ways of constructing solidarities are never simply a regression; they may also represent the social construction of bonds, social relations generated outside the commodification of labour discussed here. Hence adaptation in that sense may represent forms of creativity from 'below', or even resistance. For the purposes of this chapter, it is important to conclude that adaptation and social justice are not simply mutually exclusive concepts (Giannini 2012). This is also where this chapter contributes to this edited book: the everyday lives of parents in insecure jobs are informed not just by simple adaptation but by a type of social creativity that later on will be linked to social justice.

Precarious lives of families with young children

Setting up a family, as a communal project, is never an individualised task, either in terms of investment of money or in shared understanding of emotions. It often happens in a context where previous generations pass resources (money, time or mobilisation of networks of solidarity) to the next ones and where forms of welfare state still operate, even in minimal form. A brief look to comparative cases from the British, American and Italian contexts (Cooper 2014; Family and Childcare Trust 2013; Fumagalli 2011; Gallie *et al.* 2017; Giannini 2016; Giannini and Orientale Caputo 2011, Hardgrove *et al.* 2015; Murgia and Armano 2014; Piccone Stella 2007; Pugh 2015; Standing 2011; Toscano 2007) will show that there are elements of diversity. However, commonalities among these different contexts tell clearly how the evolution of the Great Recession, combined with austerity, has made a profound indent in all involved societies.

Starting a family in precarious conditions

Lack of resources and the uncertainties of precarious employment are directly linked to procrastinations about setting up a family for many young people (Clark and Heath 2015; Giannini and Orientale Caputo 2011; Hardgrove *et al.* 2015; Murgia and Armano 2014; Piccone Stella 2007): young women in particular are simply too unsure about incomes and resources available to plan for births and babies. Here, resources mainly mean housing and financial independence: precarious, insecure employment means difficulties in affording a place called home and with it the symbolic space for new life (Giannini and Orientale Caputo 2011). It is exactly when we examine the individual planning involved in giving birth to children that the social context of employment relations is immediately relevant: women in precarious employment are caught between the necessity for planning for setting up a family and the impossibility for planning for the long term, given the precarious conditions of this class (Cooper 2014). If for resources we understand means of subsistence, the story of capitalism then does not appear to have changed, despite all the so-called progress: struggle over means of subsistence is still the objective reality of less privileged classes (Holloway 2010; Bonefeld 2014). Research on family life and the Great Recession (and, with it, the spread of insecure jobs) confirms the difficulty of couples for forming or keeping family life together in the face of economic difficulties (Clark and Heath 2015; Pugh 2015). Qualitative research suggests that economic insecurity may lead couples to delay starting a family or, where they already have children, to separation or divorce (Piccone Stella 2007).

However, the 'weakening of ties' explained above is only one part of the story: research also suggests that (in Italy as in the English-speaking world) families respond to these events by huddling close and strengthening intergenerational dependences as well as stretching them at the same time (Giannini 2012, 2016; Pugh 2015). This ambivalence is important: it is not about not having enough data or the right data to decide which one is 'true'. If the important category here is 'struggle' (in its broadest sense), then it makes sense that people on precarious living conditions may both argue between themselves and get closer to each other; this represents a struggle to form and confirm social ties that are vital for their well-being, if not for their survival. But what do they argue about? Or, why do they need to get closer to each other? What would the reason be?

Families in job insecurity: everyday struggles

Studies on the British case, from Ipsos Mori (2013), suggest a crude answer to the question just above: money. This study isolates a number of key items of fragility of family daily life in precarious employment conditions, which can be connected to the cost of living (Ipsos Mori 2013; Family and Childcare Trust 2013). The perception of the cost of living does not match official statistics about inflation. Quite the contrary: families complained about rising cost of living and their lack of means of subsistence (indeed, a critical analysis of inflation shows that prices are going up faster for the less advantaged: Clark and Heath 2015: xiii). Families interviewed for the Ipsos Mori study (2013: 19) reported having to go without food at times, either after periods of extra expenses (like Christmas) or because children were given priority for getting healthy meals. Getting into debt is then a common strategy for British families living through recession and so-called recovery. Indeed, British people are among the most privately indebted in the world[3] and this is an important difference with other social contexts (for instance, Italy; see Giacché 2012; Family and Childcare Trust 2013). Cars as daily means of transport, facilitating people getting to work, are as much a resource as an expense for families who cannot afford new, reliable cars and do not have easy access to (still expensive) 'public' transport. Moreover, lack of affordable childcare is said to prevent women returning to work (Ipsos Mori 2013: 12), and thus it is important to point at the continuous intergenerational support that allows typically unpaid childcare arrangements to be made within the familial group (usually grandparents), freeing up mothers for paid employment (this is especially the case for Italy; see Piccone Stella 2007).

How are these practical issues affecting the relationships in the families involved? A number of studies from the British, American and Italian contexts report that families are keen on arranging quality time together: precarious employment makes it difficult, in the sense that there may be either unsocial hours and long commutes on the one hand or lack of employment altogether on the other, and with it lack of money and anxiety about the future (Cooper 2014; Giannini 2012; Ipsos Mori 2013; Piccone Stella 2007). The same studies report of accounts from parents in insecure jobs who narrate their strategies to find time together, to look after each other and to take care of their children. These strategies involve securing free time together as a family in periods of occupation and valuing it in periods 'in between jobs' (Piccone Stella 2007), recurring sometimes to the mechanism of the 'switching off' (Ba' forthcoming). This mechanism is used by couple deliberately when trying to arrange 'quality family time'. These accounts from couples can be seen as stemming from naïve representations of ideals of family, but it is worth considering how these accounts may be the reflection of their struggles to create a dignified life. As we have seen in the first section, for these parents adaptation to given conditions is not a passive mode of action and adaptation is not exclusive of ideals of social justice, because, as we will argue later on, these everyday strategies tend to form a private life which is not immediately affected by the economic system, a life which may be the reflection of their personal qualities.

Box 8.3 Money problem

This is an excerpt from a family interviewed for the *Living Precariously* report. A mother talks about being short of money because of their precarious job situation: 'The money side of things makes things difficult. They [the children] want to go out and I can't afford it. It was Haifa's birthday and she's only 4 and she was going on about it.... I do feel bad sometimes ... that's what the arguments are about ... not having enough money.'

From Family and Childcare Trust (2013: 76).

'Bonding capital' and everyday life

The specialised literature, in assessing intergenerational dependencies, can be moralistic about who owes to whom, how and why, especially in terms of financial support (e.g. Ispos Mori 2013). What emerges with accounting pedantry from this literature is the need to interrogate subjects, hold them to credit liability and question their capability to fully repay what is owned. This is the case of the younger generation getting financial support from the older generation: the 'new parents', those in insecure jobs, often get financial help from their parents, whom in many cases enjoyed the benefits of 'jobs for life' (Cooper 2014; Hardgrove *et al.* 2015; Piccone Stella 2007).

However, when we filter the data from this judgemental frame through which is often presented, it seems clear that young parents rely on the material and moral support of their own parents, as well as siblings. It is called 'bonding capital' (Ipsos Mori 2013: 33), a term which actually does not help to understand what is going on in terms of the social relations that parents in precarious work establish in their daily lives. Bonding capital obscures the simple fact that parents do not simply adapt to precarious circumstances but are instead active in strengthening bonds around love, family and friendship (Giannini 2012) and they do so outside the logic of the market, which we have seen in the previous section that it is a logic which commodifies labour and commodifies human relations in general. In other words, the concept of bonding capital does not help to illuminate what may constitute the dignified aspects of parents' lives in precarious work.

Similarly, Pugh conceptualises 'commitment heroism' (2015: 202) when analysing the struggle for emotional, material and symbolic security of mothers in precarious employment. Commitment heroism refers to the fact that mothers, despite being in insecure employment with meagre salaries and despite being pressed to find time for work, for their children and for their personal needs, sacrifice themselves and work hard to ensure care for their immediate relatives. With this 'immense' commitment, Pugh says that mothers are trying to erect a moral wall between the world of paid employment and the world of intimate relationships.

'Doing security' and struggle

From the above subsection we have an interpretation of mothers' work as those who 'struggle to care' amid rampant insecurity. This interpretation for the American context finds its match in the Italian context, where the literature individuates a 'child-centred culture' for couples with young children, where parents sacrifice themselves in similar terms as their American counterparts (Bertolini *et al.* 2007: 126). However, on closer analysis, using the interpretation of 'commitment heroism' and self-sacrifice, in order to understand parents' everyday strategies, implies an acceptance of the logic of the market. The logic of the exchange that was discussed in the first section implicitly enters in the considerations around 'commitment' and 'sacrifice' because something (the affection and love of mothers) is given in return of nothing (the children cannot repay immediately this affection and care). Mothers sacrifice themselves because they are selfless and they accept that, given the insecure conditions their families are in, there is nothing else they can do. This reading underestimates the level of struggles that mothers and parents are able to sustain in their everyday lives.

The correct emphasis should be placed on the broader concept of struggle: parents (and especially mothers) struggle to get the basic needs for their families and also struggle for decent standards of life. This broader idea of struggle is captured by Cooper's (2014) concept of 'doing security'.

Doing security may seem an awkward expression, but with this formulation Cooper points to the daily struggles of mothers, struggles oriented to override an economic logic that sees them as purely pieces of 'labour force' to be used only when convenient for the employer. It is perhaps the most fascinating side of this area of research: understanding how parents, even when at the margin of the labour market, show an active role in the face of economic adversity. It is so because precarious employment does not simply determine precarious living conditions for families. Doing security means struggling through precarious work; in that sense, precarity does not enter into family life from the outside but from the inside, because adaptation to precarious life is never passive and struggling for a decent standard of life is always linked to a degree of resistance.

Concluding, it is possible to assess from the specialised literature around parents in precarious employment that there is an agency, a spontaneous way of organising social and intimate relationships from their part, which emerges through the form of insecure work. Through this form, parents are still able to form meaningful social relations and forge the basis for intimate life, although in conditions not of their choosing. The next session will link these social relations to dignity as self-defined standards of life of parents in insecure jobs. The concept of dignity will finally allow a discussion on everyday social justice as instigated by parents themselves.

Dignity and social justice

How do we arrive at the concept of dignity from the discussion of insecure jobs and parenthood? One term used to investigate what parents (and especially mothers) do when they are in job insecurity is 'entrepreneurialism'. The concept 'entrepreneurialism' helps us in investigating the inner workings of parents' and mothers' lives in precarious employment, as it emphasises the 'active' side of parents in shaping their destiny. To be sure, this term is not used in the sense of celebrating parents happily mobilising themselves and their own resources, recurring to the market instead of the welfare state (Wilson and Yochim 2015). These studies tell us that the internalisation of the faith in the market produces ways of relating to each other as well as adaptation (Fumagalli 2011; Wilson and Yochim 2015). Entrepreneurialism indicates how precarious conditions are often privatised and interiorised and how the attempt of getting out of them is redefined through the free market ideals: 'become your own entrepreneur!'

Mothers as 'entrepreneurs'

In their study, Wilson and Yochim (2015) examine mothers in insecure jobs and ask how this situation might create 'mothering through precarity'; that is, how do mothers manage to care for children and families while being in insecure jobs or in unemployment? This is a pressing issue as, very often, even in rich countries as the USA, families need to rely on two wages, or at least one full-time plus a part-time wage. Wilson and Yochim observe that the free market ideal of becoming self-employed is embraced by many mothers. In other words, they find that the insistence on personal responsibility and the privatisation of social relations in the world of work make mothers in precarious work inclined to feel personally responsible for their own employment status. Thus, their answer to precarity is 'becoming mamapreneurial' (Wilson and Yochim 2015: 669).

Importantly becoming mamapreneurial is seen in an ambivalent way: mothers are active in exploring options and operating within their social environment, but the final outcome seems that they adapt to the precarious status quo. This uneven contrast of adaptation and resistance to precarious employment is important, because it means nothing less than the creation of social life for a new generation and, at the same time, the reproduction of the fundamental conditions for personal life (Wilson and Yochim 2015: 673).

These studies (see also Fumagalli 2011) tell that the difficult adaptation to precarity is the result of the daily struggles of mothers, who have to ensure stability in the face of economic insecurity. It is important to challenge the idea that 'adaptation' may be a simple category, as adaptation is tightly connected with ideals of family life and with ideals relating to a decent standard of living (Wilson and Yochim 2015: 679). In turn, these ideals may be connected to traditional expectations around gender roles in the household (Giannini 2016; Murgia 2010; Pugh 2015; Wilson and Yochim 2015), however we are in the presence of an active process of doing everyday family life. As in the other studies examined above, adaptation to precarity is not a passive state for mothers, who struggle to reinvent family life in adverse economic circumstances.

Insecurity culture

There are not many studies, in English or Italian, that consider the contrasts and the hidden links between parents' everyday lives, struggles through job insecurity, and dignity. An approach that considers the meaning of working and caring in an age of insecurity at the everyday level is Pugh's *The Tumbleweed Society* (2015). In the face of job insecurity, Pugh (2015) maintains that parents adopt a number of psychological 'stances'. She analyses a number of them: the 'independence' stance, the stance of 'moral duty first' and the 'pragmatic' stance. According to Pugh, these psychological approaches constitute a culture around precarity, which she calls 'insecurity culture' (2015: 76).

Seemingly these 'stances' originate from parents in a spontaneous way, but the author continuously observes how the logic of the 'economic' constitutes an overwhelming force in orienting actions for the individuals in question. In Pugh's study, the intimate lives of families in precarious employment, despite their sophisticated psychological defences, are desperately intertwined with the economic value people give to things and to relationships. Contrary to other approaches (like Giannini 2012; Cooper 2014; Wilson and Yochim 2015), concepts like 'insecurity culture' do not help to understand the complexities of adaptation, as they base their analysis on a complete severance between the economic structure and the sphere of personal life. Indeed, observations such as parents 'adapt to insecurity culture with independence' (Pugh 2015: 76) are profoundly contradictory and accept that there may be a fundamental split between a supposedly objective structure (insecurity culture) and the sphere of personal action (independence).

Rather, one of the main features emerging from studies on children and families in precarious employment is exactly the tension between adaptation and resistance (Ba' forthcoming). Other researches (Armano 2010; Giannini 2016; Murgia and Armano 2014) suggest that struggling *through* the conditions of precarious employment means also resisting complete subordination to the needs of the market. In these researches, the theme of dignity is highlighted in various ways. Let's see how.

Dignity

In Giannini's studies (2012, 2016), the difficult adaptation to precarity is the result of daily struggles of mothers, who have to ensure stability in the face of economic insecurity. This struggle is linked to dignity. Dignity is an element of vital importance for families in precarious employment conditions and this concept is usually taken as self-defined by parents participating to these researches (Giannini 2012, Murgia and Armano 2014; Tyler 2013). Mothers are at the centre of this struggle: given precarious forms of employment, the stability of family life is no longer a 'given' (if it ever was) and its very existence relies on mothers' deployment of care and emotional support for their families (Wilson and Yochim 2015: 674).

For parents in insecure jobs, dignity is connected to the 'temporality of life' (Giannini 2012, 2016); that is: everyday life is seen as something specific to a family unit, something that parents are able to construct or preserve for their private life. This temporality is contrasted to the temporality of (precarious) labour (Giannini 2012, 2016; Giannini and Orientale Caputo 2011). For mothers and fathers in job insecurity, these two different aspects of life are becoming ever more blurred, with the danger of the temporality of life collapsing into the temporality of (precarious) labour (Giannini 2012, 2016). However, these studies (Giannini's in particular) highlight the resistance from the part of couples to this 'economic' tendency. Couples continuously attempt to arrange personal lives outside the crude logic of market economy and the commodification of labour, hence their dignity. Their resistance is productive of daily social and familial order.

Following Holloway (1998), we take dignity as a 'class concept', not a mere, vague human rights concept, more or less formalised in international charts. This is important because 'precarious parents' very often arrange their lives and their limited resources in a way that goes beyond the frame of the precarious employment in which they are confined. If we take dignity as 'the negation of humiliation, the struggle against subordination' (Holloway, 1998: 182), then this concept helps us to understand the daily realities of parents in precarious employment.

Parents in precarious work and dignity

The specialised literature observes that the class of people in job insecurity constitutes a recognisable group which is characterised by changes in or threats to their employment status (Gallie *et al.* 2017; Standing 2011; Toscano 2007). In the first section, we saw the class of people in insecure jobs is formed through a precise form of capitalist labour relation: their 'labour force', their labour skills, become goods that need to be traded in the labour market, because if they are not sold, they cannot get a wage in return. For parents exposed to this type of contractual weakness, it is now as it was at the beginning of the Industrial Revolution, whereby the bargaining power position of the employer is immensely superior to that of the perspective employee (Marx 1997 [1844]: 17).

However, this class in precarious work is not a homogeneous class. To be sure, there are 'relations of subordination', which can be linked to forms of exploitation (fixed-term contract labour is cheaper than indefinite-term contract labour), but what is more apparent in the case of families in precarious labour relations, it is that they struggle against those relations, as we have seen in the previous sections. For those in precarious employment, the market represents something more than a temporary passage. One of the most common experiences of parents in the precarious labour force is the humiliation of continuously having to look for insecure work opportunities. Precarious parents have to go through that, and to an extent they have to accept their commodification, as imposed by the logic of the market (Murgia and Armano 2014), but they also struggle against this logic, on a daily basis. It is this daily struggle against subordination that is linked to dignity (Giannini 2012: 220).

Thus, families in precarious employment do not simply fit in an existing social order; they struggle against it and in doing so they produce new social relations, which more often than not places them in disadvantaged positions. In the midst of these transformations, families in precarious employment struggle over ideals of family life (Cooper 2014), which in some cases were the product the twentieth-century social and economic landscape (Hochschild 2013), in the sense that these socio-economic arrangements facilitated a certain type of family life (the nuclear family: the father as the provider, the mother as the nurturing member of the unit etc.). However, these are not marginal dreams that are empty of meaning just because the material basis (e.g. secure jobs) for realising them is simply not there. In the social sciences, there is the tendency to criticise parents' views of normal family life, as this normality often hides (normative) assumptions, often discriminatory, around the role of women. Nonetheless the negation of these ideals is often the task of the market economy, which demands 'zero drag' from parents and their availability and commitment to 'the job' (Hochschild 2013). Dignity against the negation of these ideals is then to be linked with the class experiences and the class aspirations of 'precarious parents', in the sense that these experiences and aspirations prefigure the overcoming of class division (Ba' forthcoming).

Conclusion on everyday social justice

In this chapter, the social justice element is considered through accounts of parents about their struggle to accomplish what they would consider minimal levels of dignity in family daily life and their resilience to face the adversities of insecure times (Giannini 2012; Murgia and Armano 2014; Wilson and Yochim 2015). In that sense, the concept of social justice is not considered in abstract, through political theories, but linked to parents' daily life and their self-definition of dignity. It would be easy to formulate it through positive ideals, which are substantiated by research on these families. Parents' accounts around positive ideals can be quite explicit and simple; for instance, 'happy families live in well kept homes, possess nice things, have fun together and never worry about money' (Wilson and Yochim 2015: 681). However, these authors themselves make it clear that these ideals are clichés and real aspirations at the same time, underpinning the longing for dignity. Thus, what is emerging from the most progressive literature, it is a concept of social justice in 'negative', so to speak, meaning that precarious parents consider their personal and social conditions to be unfortunate circumstances placing them below their standards of dignity and that this social and economic order is a class based order, rather than a just one. Their daily struggles are aiming at a social justice 'in negative', in the sense that ideals about social justice are not here, yet they still have to be substantiated in social reality.

Social justice as dignity here is then linked to the fact that the call for dignity from families in precarious conditions refers to an existing class-divided society based on precarious employment which necessarily negates their dignity. In that sense, dignity is an everyday life concept, rather than a principle that can be as generic as meaningless. Dignity is linked to the daily struggles of families to secure decent level of living in the face of an obsolete economic form crudely based on the exchange of their lives into money. That private life may not be marked by this form is ultimately dependent on their level of struggle.

Notes

1 Economic recession and cuts to social services in Britain seem linked to a rise in death rate and suicide rates (especially among those who suffer from so-called mental health problems) – see *The Canary*, 16 February 2016 (www.thecanary.co/2016/02/16/official-tory-cuts-social-services-lead-biggest-rise-death-rates-since-war, accessed 12 December 2016).

2 Austerity is a form of politics which restricts public spending in order to regulate the state's finance, in order to stimulate private investment; however, one direct consequence of this move is the squeezing of wages, the reduction of public employment and the attempt to mobilise part of the 'inactive' population into paid employment (Radice 2011).

3 See http://touchstoneblog.org.uk/2015/02/uk-household-debt-still-amongst-the-highest-in-the-world (accessed 12 December 2016).

References

Adorno, T.W. (2005 [1951]). *Minima Moralia*. London: Verso.

Armano, E. (2010). *Precarietá e Innovazione nel Post-Fordismo*. Bologna: Emil.

Ba', S. (forthcoming). Parents with young children in precarious employment, the case of central Italy. *Rivista Italiana di Sociologia*.

Bellofiore, R. (2012). *La Crisi Capitalistica, la Barbarie che Avanza*. Trieste: Asterios.

Benzer, M. (2011). *The Sociology of Theodor Adorno*. Cambridge: Cambridge University Press.

Bertolini, S., Luciano, A. and Naldini, N. (2007). 'Quando la flessibilitá é donna', in S. Piccone Stella (ed.) *Tra un Lavoro e l'Altro. Vita di Coppia nell'Italia Postfordista*. Rome: Carocci.

Bonefeld, W. (2014). *Critical Theory and the Critique of Political Economy*. London: Bloomsbury.

Callinicos, A. (2010). *Bonfire of Illusions*. Cambridge: Polity.

Cingolani, P. (1986). *L'Exil du Précaire. Récit de Vies en Marge du Travail*. Paris: Méridiens Klincksieck.

Cingolani, P. (2005). *La Précarité*. Paris: PUF.

Clark, T. and Heath, A. (2015). *Hard Times – Inequality, Recession, Aftermath*. London: Yale University Press.

Cooper, M. (2014). *Cut Adrift – Families in Insecure Times*. California: University of California Press.

Family and Childcare Trust (2013). *Living Precariously – Families in an Age of Austerity*. London: Family and Childcare Trust.

Foster, J.B. and Magdoff, F. (2009). *The Great Financial Crisis*. New York, NY: Monthly Review Press.

Fumagalli, A. (2011). 'La condizione precaria come paradigma bio-politico', in F. Chicchi and E. Leonardi (eds) *Lavoro in Frantumi. Condizione Precaria, Nuovi Conflitti e Regime Neoliberista*. Verona: Ombre Corte.

Gallie, D. Felstead, A. Green, F. and Inanc, H. (2017). The hidden face of job insecurity. *Work, Employment and Society, 31*(1): 36–53.

Giacché, V. (2012). *Titanic Europa*. Rome: Aliberti.

Giannini, M. (2012). 'Las trampas de los trabajos flexibles', in A. Giglia and A. Miranda (eds) *Precariedad Urbana y Lazos Sociales. Una Mirada Comparativa entre Mexico y Italia*, Iztapalapa: Juan Pablos & Universidad Autónoma Metropolitana-Iztapalapa, pp. 217–44.

Giannini, M. (2016). Epistemologia della condizione precaria: oltre il declino del lavoro salariato. *Quaderni di Teoria Sociale, 16*(2): 97–124.

Giannini, M. and Orientale Caputo, G. (2011). 'Introduzione', in M. Giannini and G. Orientale Caputo (eds) *Casa, Lavoro, Futuro*. Naples: Liguori.

Hardgrove, A., McDowell, L. and Rootham, R. (2015). Precarious lives, precarious labour: family support and young men's transitions to work in the UK. *Journal of Youth Studies, 18*(8): 1057–76.

Harvey, D. (2011). *The Enigma of Capital and the Crises of Capitalism*. London: Profile.

Hochschild, A. (2013). *The Outsourced Self, So How's the Family?* Los Angeles and Berkeley, CA: University of California Press.

Holloway, J. (2010). *Crack Capitalism*. New York, NY: Pluto.

Holloway, J. (1998). 'Dignity's revolt', in J. Holloway and E. Peláez (eds) *Zapatista! Reinventing Revolution in Mexico*. London: Pluto.

Illouz, E. (2008). *Saving the Modern Soul: Therapy, Emotions, and the Culture of Self-Help*. Berkeley, CA: University of California Press.

Ipsos Mori (2013). *Family Matters – Understanding Families in an Age of Austerity*. London: Ipsos Mori. Online. Available at www.ipsos-mori.com/DownloadPublication/1554_sri-family-matters-2013.pdf.

Marx, K. (1997 [1844]). *Economic and Philosophic Manuscripts of 1844*. London: Lawrence & Wishart.

Morini C. (2012). La cognizione dell'impermanenza. Il lavoro a tempo indeterminato paradigma della precarietà contemporanea. *Quaderni di San Precario, 3*: 175–96.

Murgia A. (2010). *Dalla Precarietà Lavorativa alla Precarietà Sociale*. Bologna: Emil.

Murgia, A. and Armano, E. (2014). 'Generazione precaria, nuovi lavorie processi di soggettivazione', in E. Armano and A. Murgia (eds) *Generazione Precaria*. Bologna: Emil.

O'Hara, M. (2015). *Austerity Bites: A Journey to the Sharp End of Cuts in the UK*. Bristol: Policy.

Piccone Stella, S. (ed.). (2007). *Tra un Lavoro e l'Altro. Vita di Coppia nell'Italia Post-fordista*. Rome: Carocci.

Pugh, A.J. (2015). *The Tumbleweed Society: Working and Caring in an Age of Insecurity*. Oxford: Oxford University Press.

Radice, H. (2011). Cutting government deficits: Economic science or class war? *Capital & Class, 35*(1): 125–37.

Standing, G. (2011). *The Precariat – The New Dangerous Class*. London: Bloomsbury.

Tischler, S. (2008). *Tiempo y Emancipación – M. Bajtín y W. Benjamin en la Selva Lacandona*. Guatemala City: F&G.

Toscano M.A. (ed.). (2007). *Homo Instabilis. Sociologia della Precarietà*. Milan: Jaca.

Tyler, I. (2013). *Revolting Subjects: Social Abjection and Resistance in Neoliberal Britain*. London: Zed.

Wilson, J.A. and Yochim, E.C. (2015). Mothering through Precarity. *Cultural Studies, 29*(5–6): 669–86.

9 Neo-liberalism and the family

Pam Jarvis

Introduction

This chapter will consider the ways in which the culture of British family life has changed over the past four decades, proposing that the impact upon parenting and, in particular, the construction of the role of the mother has been considerable. It is proposed that, within this process, feminism has to a great extent been hijacked by the contemporary mainstream (or 'malestream') dominant neo-liberal culture, and that this has had a negative impact upon the sociocultural position of socio-economically deprived families. In particular, the chapter will outline the problems that this process has created for mothers. McRobbie (2013: 128) claims that 'previous historical affiliations between social democracy and feminism which aimed to support women as mothers were dismantled and discredited [resulting in the] present day demonisation of welfare'. The chapter will discuss this issue from a social justice perspective.

The second oldest profession

Motherhood has a very long history but scant documentation, given that the daily lives of women and their children were not constructed by human societies as having the same level of importance as that of rulers and battles. While human life changed quite radically after 9000 BCE, as the Earth emerged from an ice age that had lasted approximately 15,000 years, one constant that remained was the care and education of children within their families, principally by mothers and grandmothers (Sterns 2011). In the new agricultural societies there was a dependent infancy until around the age of seven, by which time children were expected to have learned enough to be able to engage in simple domestic chores if they were female or apprenticed to begin learning about agriculture or a trade if they were male. By the end of the seventeenth century, in England, young children between three and eight routinely began to attend local 'dame schools', so named because they were usually run by elderly women, often in a room in their own house. Here children would learn the rudiments of reading, counting and possibly writing; girls were also taught to knit and sew (Cunningham 2006: 78). Philosopher John Amos Comenius (1592–1670) proposed that education should be differently structured for boys and girls: 'we are not advising that women be educated in such a way that their tendency to curiosity shall be developed [but] chiefly in those things that enables her … to promote the welfare of her husband and family' (in Cunningham 2006: 89–90). With the exception of the education provided for a few very privileged women, for example the daughters of Henry VIII, the philosophy of female education orienting in the direction of a 'care provider' adulthood held sway until the mid-twentieth century.

Following the Industrial Revolution, which began in England at the end of the eighteenth century, industrial workers were required to attain a higher standard of general education than had been necessary to work in an agricultural economy. This led to a growing interest in children and childhood, and the social construction of children as objects of investment, not only for their family but for the nation as a whole. There was a consequent expansion of state provision for children, not only with respect to education but in initiatives relating to the role of the family. While mothers were still expected to be the main source of early socialisation, they were increasingly provided with a barrage of 'parenting' advice from wider society. Paula Fass (2016) explores how this process unfolded, documenting the steady transformation of pamphlet-based health advice offered to mothers during the latter part of the nineteenth century simply to help them keep their children alive and healthy, into the 'pop' child psychology advisory media that first arose in the early part of the mid-twentieth century and was carried by new mass-circulation magazines and 'kitchen shelf' advice books:

> the battles fought on behalf of … children by the old-fashioned (even spinsterish) women of the turn of the century … were succeeded by male advisors [who] spoke to the private concerns of twentieth century women eager to make sure that little Johnny or Jane … became 'normal' and 'well-adjusted'.
>
> (p. 103)

Fass comments that the burgeoning of the parenting advice industry led to a society which 'determine[s] the fate of children under the careful supervision of experts' (p. 121); this issue will be further explored below.

The 'old-fashioned women' advisers of the turn of the nineteenth century were, in effect, the heirs to the elderly women who had presided over dame schools; however, they began to offer a range of public challenges to the mainstream (malestream) culture dominated by men, from the perspective of an overarching 'social maternalism' (Brebony 2009: 191), focused upon the well-being of young children, particularly those from socio-economically deprived backgrounds. This was a gender divide that typically crossed social class and party political differences. For example, in early twentieth-century Britain, highly diverse characters such as fiery Christian socialist Margaret McMillan (1860–1931), Queen Mary (1867–1963) and the first two women to sit in the House of Commons, the aristocratic Conservative Nancy (Lady) Astor (1879–1964) and earnest Liberal reformer Margaret Winteringham (1879–1955) worked tirelessly together over a long period of time in order to put the case for state-funded nursery schools on the national agenda (Jarvis and Liebovich 2015). However, it should be emphasised here that, as Fass (2016) points out, their voices were soon replaced by those of more 'learned' men, for example John Bowlby and Donald Winnicott in the UK and Benjamin Spock in the US, carrying messages more effectively aligned with those of the malestream sociopolitical agenda of the era.

Jarvis (2016) details the history of policy for children and families in England throughout the twentieth century in which state-funded provision for infants waxed and waned depending upon whether women were required by the national situation to replace men in the workforce; an issue that arose during both World Wars.

She outlines her analysis:

> A maternalist initiative is only likely to succeed when it is in harmony with similar malestream policy. It can further be argued that we have not moved on significantly from this position, even a century later … by the early twenty-first century, although the child and his/ her parents continued to be constructed through malestream economic policy, the underlying milieu had changed. The population of England now found themselves within a highly technological *post*-industrial society, where adults were not only defined as units of production, but all human beings, both adults and children, were constructed as participants within a complex wheel of demand-led consumption.
>
> (2016: 40)

While the mother who carried out paid work outside the home became normalised by sociopolitical changes in the years leading up to the turn of the twentieth century, women, particularly those from the lower socio-economic echelons of society, still faced a formidable level of social control from a 'malestream' establishment. The remainder of this chapter will document how this situation unfolded, and how it continues to impact on social justice for families, mothers in particular, within the contemporary UK.

The rise of neo-liberalism

In 1980, British Prime Minister Margaret Thatcher and her American contemporary Ronald Regan began to introduce a range of cultural changes into Anglo-American society, heralding the rise of a political philosophy which became widely known as neo-liberalism. In an interview with the *Sunday Times* in May 1981, Thatcher commented:

> it isn't that I set out on economic policies; it's that I set out really to change the approach, and changing the economics is the means of changing that approach. If you change the approach you really are after the heart and soul of the nation. Economics are the method; the object is to change the heart and soul.
>
> (Margaret Thatcher Foundation, n.d., online)

The philosophy at the core of neo-liberalism is that all adults should be compliant, uncritical consumer/workers within the national economy in order to stimulate national and international money markets to the maximum extent. At the political level, neo-liberalism is a theory of society that presumes that the best way forward for all societies is one of extreme individual choice, and a deregulated economic market where there are as few constraints upon free trading as possible. In such a construction, a human adult becomes only valued to the extent that s/he is able to work and consume, and a child becomes valued only to the extent of his/her potential to work and consume in adult life. This change in societal values created a great change in family life. Barbara Tizard, a psychologist who worked with children in the period following World War II, remembers:

> Soon after the end of the Second World War … there was a big movement to get women, in many ways liberated by their wartime work experiences, to stay at home. Professional women like myself … became worried that they would damage their children by returning to work even on a part-time basis, and those who worked full-time were widely criticised.
>
> (Tizard 2009: 902)

However, this 'malestream' position, supported by the maternal deprivation theories of John Bowlby (1952), changed rapidly with the advent of Thatcherism. Figure 9.1 below depicts a significant rise in female employment levels in the

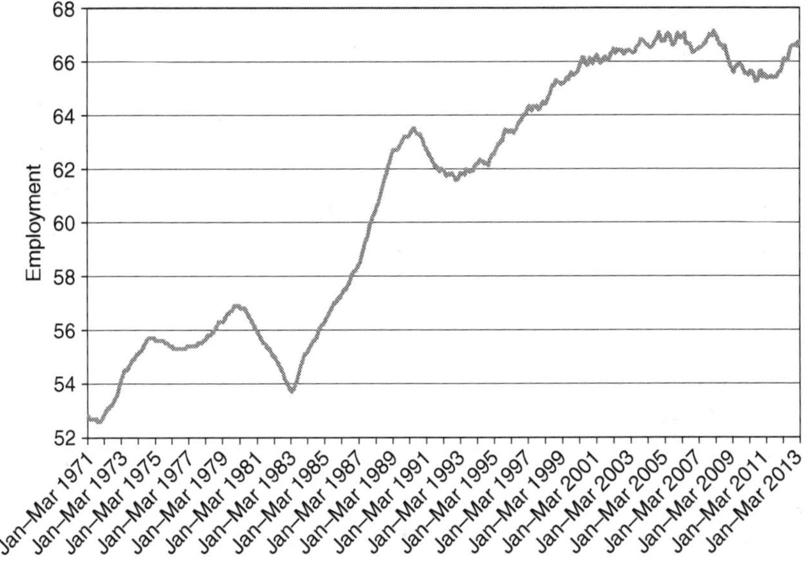

Figure 9.1 UK female employment 1971–2013.

Source: Jarvis *et al.* (2016: 244); data drawn from Office for National Statistics 2013.

ten years between 1985 and 1995, with an upward trajectory continuing into the twenty-first century.

Whereas mothers were expected to stay at home with their children until the last quarter of the twentieth century, mothers of the early twenty-first century are instead expected to engage in economic exchange with others (most typically other women) to take care of their children while they engage in paid labour, thus creating two workers within the economy. In this way, both children and adults can become units of economic capital.

> More women in the workforce boosts GDP, increases income from taxes, and reduces welfare costs.... An increasingly competitive, knowledge-based global economy is [also] helping to convince both governments and parents that pre-school education is an investment in future academic success and employment prospects.
>
> (UNICEF 2008: 4)

Leite (2013: 1) commented upon the 'voracious power Neo-Liberalism has over all types of policy making and opportunistic advancement of certain political strategies', and this can certainly be demonstrated in the great change in the rates of female employment over the past forty years. How this has impacted upon mothers, children and families is intricately bound up with socio-economic status; this will be considered in the section below.

Parenting in the neo-liberal age

In a recent review of the academic literature on parenting in the UK, I entered a surprisingly dystopian culture in which 'intensive parenting' had become an intrinsic part of the overarching neo-liberal culture and in which the primary role of parents has become ensuring that their children become school- and thereafter, employment market-ready. However, mothers are also required to play an onerous dual role, not only as child socialisers but also as wage earners in the culture that arose following the Thatcher government's reworking of the economy. So how is this situation experienced at the level of the individual family?

The construction of contemporary parenting that emerges from the literature depicts parents, mothers in particular, feeling torn between paid labour and parenting, worried that they did not have enough time to do a good job in either role and being constantly weighed down by the prospect of being negatively evaluated by others through performance targets at work and external evaluations of their parenting competence. A vast array of electronically networked modern media carries exacting messages to parents about the 'ideal' family, in which the skill and diligence of the mother is seen as the main determinant of everyone's fate, particularly that of the children.

Jensen (2013: 51) reflects that modern parents voraciously 'consume parent pedagogies'. In the media-saturated twenty-first century, which includes interactive electronic socialisation, this becomes a voyeuristic process in which individuals continually engage in interactions which lead them to compare themselves to those unfortunate enough to be publicly presented in ways that elicit mass censure and/or ridicule. While this may make the viewer feel temporarily better about him or herself, Hoffman (2013: 239) reflects 'what is so ironic is that in the end the power struggles are ... between parents themselves'. The state does not need to act directly, as people enthusiastically sanction and condemn each other in an interactive fashion, with all participants in the process developing a deep, private concern about becoming the next social media pariah.

In this way, neo-liberal values carried by relentless public and social media feeds condition individuals to police both themselves and others, 'creating and sustaining a power relation independent of the person who exercises it ... in which all become "prisoners of experts" [whose power is] everywhere and also inside us' (Henderson *et al.* 2010: 236). This is a process that Michel Foucault first illustrated in his concept of a 'Panopticon' (1979), in which prisoners are held in an area where they are aware that they are constantly under surveillance. In the contemporary 'socially mediated' world, however, 'there are no guards and no prisoners in Facebook's virtual Panopticon. We are both guards and prisoners, watching and implicitly judging one another' (Rayner 2012, online). Leite (2013: 10) proposes that 'contemporary hegemonic discourses ... intensify the external surveillance over parents'. This process is clearly problematic from a social justice perspective, with parents, mothers in particular, being squeezed from both sides, expected to 'perform' both in paid work and as a parent, under the ongoing threat of public censure for not meeting the exacting expectations of an anonymous, omnipresent collective 'other'.

Faircloth *et al.* (2013: 121) commented that 'the word parent has shifted from a noun denoting a relationship with a child (something you *are*) to a verb (something you *do*)'. The focus of governments in neo-liberal Western democracies is squarely upon the parental function of 'successfully' socialising the child, making 'modern motherhood [something that] is "done" rather than experienced', hence parenting, and mothering in particular, becomes 'not only a politicised issue but a profoundly moral issue, too' (Hinton *et al.* 2013: 73). Burman (2012: 426) comments that 'child-centred discourses of "sensitive mothering" and "authoritative parenting" not only socialize children (in gender-normative ways), they also regulate mothers'. Politicians have been quick to disseminate moral panic to legitimate greater state surveillance of the family; for example, Alan Johnson MP proposed in 2007: 'traditionally parenting has been a no go area for governments – but now it is an essential area for us to focus on' (Vincent *et al.* 2010: 124).

The emphasis in neo-liberal societies is upon freedom of choice, with society depicted as a meritocracy in which each individual has the power to determine his or her fate through 'entrepreneurship'. The overwhelming cultural message is that citizens are expected above all to become 'strivers' (McRobbie 2013: 120). However, a problem arising from such a culture is the emergent possibility that the social order may be disrupted by *over*competitive cheating, for example in the famous case of early 2000s bankers illegally gambling with clients' money in order to maximise their own profits (*The Economist* 2013). Therefore, Conroy (2010) proposes that modern neo-liberal governments advocating extreme individual freedom nevertheless place a huge responsibility upon parents to maintain the social order by placing trainee citizens on the 'right' path at the very beginning, creating 'an inescapable tension internal to Neo-Liberalism' (p. 326).

> It is no easy task [for neo-liberal governments] to balance the competing claims of the individual to freedom of expression and personal choice with the needs of the state to secure the collective well being of its citizens and offer protection to its most vulnerable members.
>
> (Conroy 2010: 325)

Such a balance requires covert management of individuals within an overtly laissez-faire culture. This concept is consequently deeply diffused within the sea of media in which contemporary Western societies are immersed, a depth and breadth of remote superintendence of parenting that twentieth-century child development experts could never have imagined.

> The knowledge bases for child-centered policies have created positions for 'experts', such as psychiatrics and psychologists, while parents and children are made to fit into these experts' representational and normalizing discourses.… These discursive formations reflect ideas about the welfare and best interests of all children and reinforce notions of Eurocentric middle class ideals that, in turn, negatively affect the lives of children and parents who do not fit these ideals.
>
> (Hennum 2014: 442)

Neo-liberal societies are therefore premised upon 'overt prescription [which] moves over time to become covert normalisation … those who do not fit the norms are rendered deficient or pathological' (Burman 2012: 431). Where families cannot meet such ideals, there is consequently a price to pay, and it is extracted from the most vulnerable in society.

Yummy and slummy mummies

McRobbie (2013: 121) proposes that 'female labour power is far too important to the post-industrial economy for anyone to be an advocate of long term stay at home wives and mothers'. This puts modern mothers at the heart of a neo-liberal dichotomy in which they are not only required to be 'supermothers' but also 'superworkers'. The literature suggests that it is families from the lower socio-economic echelons, mothers in particular, who are most disempowered by these expectations. For example, Vincent *et al.* (2010) described the momentous struggles of seventy mothers living on two council estates in inner London to work long hours for low pay and to simultaneously engage in the intensive parenting stipulated by government propaganda. In essence, they could not find the psychological and emotional space to reconcile the requirement to be a good mother with the requirement to be a good worker: 'the impossible tensions that these discourses articulate for working class mothers … an unstable mix of support, exhortation and the threat of punitive action' (Vincent *et al.* 2010: 124).

Mothers who were on benefits rather than in paid work fared no better, feeling deeply censured by the state, the media and society in general for 'sponging'. Whether they were in or out of work, all of Vincent *et al.*'s participants were consumed with worry about being able to provide for their families on very low incomes. The researchers concluded: 'the women did not take any of this lightly and were left to deal with the ambivalences and sense of guilt that are generated by contradictory discourses and the "perfection codes" upon which such discourses and policy trade' (Vincent *et al.* 2010: 135). In this way, it can be demonstrated that contemporary mothers are cast as 'guarantors of the social order [through a] commodification of maternity under Neo-Liberalism' (Orgad and De Benedictis 2015: 419–410) in which the mother is compelled to straddle two essentially competing roles: the mother/carer and the labourer/consumer.

In an article entitled 'Re-engineering Motherhood', Hey and Bradford (2006: 53) propose that the neo-liberal establishment 'has mapped a terrain upon which mothers' identities have been positioned in various discourses'. They list key features of neo-liberal policies for families including a focus on social exclusion, a vocabulary of risk and, above all, new welfare/social engineering processes aimed at reducing dependency. The element of feeling under surveillance with respect to mothering skills can be added to the pressure experienced by working-class mothers in terms of working long hours for low pay in order to avoid being labelled as a scrounger:

> Invocations of 'social inclusion' that are so over reliant on labour market participation have real and worrying implications for mothers … in the sense of mothers' guilt about not giving their children enough time, but at the same time, about being a feckless, state-sponging parent 'who couldn't care less'.
>
> (Conroy 2010: 61)

On Monday 11 January 2016, Prime Minister David Cameron gave a speech in which he vowed to extend the provision of parenting classes to improve the (apparently inadequate) standard of British parenting. Imelda Redmond, Chief Executive of the charity 4Children subsequently commented that 'families are telling us that despite their best intentions, long working hours and financial pressures are having a detrimental impact on family relationships' (Nursery World 2016, online).

Sime and Sheridan (2014) carried out a study focusing on working-class parents' relationships with their child's early years setting in Scotland. They found parental involvement to be 'a catch all term' (p. 328), based upon a cultural deficit model, with inevitable associated attempts from the establishment 'to impose middle class values' (p. 329). The parents themselves voiced concerns that the areas and communities that they lived within were potentially problematic for the child's future; a point that can be further analysed in a Foucauldian manner to suggest that the parents had been socially conditioned by the culture in which they are immersed to judge their own lives and those of their neighbours as deficient. Hennum (2014: 191) claims that, in this way, neo-liberal policy 'pathologis[es] the poor,' a process that Smith (2010) claims constitutes 'soft totalitarianism'.

It is interesting to note that while the term 'parenting' is gender-neutral, the research indicates that those who are most oppressed by the neo-liberal societal order are mothers, the socio-economically deprived in particular, who are set the impossible task of managing a relentless double shift of paid labour and child care on insufficient resources. From a feminist point of view, Tyler (2008) comments that given that only abundant financial resources can enable women to fully comply with what is required from them within neo-liberal societies, the culture subsequently 'not only mocks poor … mothers but also challenges middle-class women to face their "reproductive responsibilities"' (p. 30), an issue that remains psychosocially buried in the individual, hence consequently unchallenged by the mainstream collective. McRobbie (2013) alleges that liberal feminism, which pursued equal employment rights for women throughout the mid-twentieth century has, through this process, morphed into 'a gendered dimension to the mantra of individualism, the market and competition' (p. 121), resulting in 'feminist complicity' (p. 120) with the ideals of neo-liberalism.

Indeed, the mainstream popular media has recently created the stereotypes of the 'yummy' (prosperous, well groomed, hard-working, successful) 'mummy' and her antithesis, the 'slummy' (poor, shabby, work-shy, failing) 'mummy' (Bradford 2013). This narrative has been further extended through the mantra of 'hard-working families' much loved by neo-liberal politicians, most recently in Prime Minister Theresa May's construct of 'Jams' (just about managing families) (Sodha 2016). McRobbie (2013) proposes that the setting up of such cultural icons has brought about a 'mediated maternalism' in which prosperous middle-class 'yummy' mummies are marshalled through a range of media to voice disapproval of the perceived lack of enterprise shown by socio-economically deprived, apparently shiftless 'slummy' mummies. McRobbie (2013: 120) proposes that via this process liberal feminism has been hijacked 'as an aspect of the ambitious reach of Neo-Liberalism … at a time when the political left has been crushed'. This is a clear illustration of a Foucauldian control system in which the government is aided and abetted in its coercive oppression through a judgemental surveillance system enacted upon one group of mothers by another.

Consequently, McRobbie proposes, the underpinning culture of the contemporary UK constructs the condition of the socio-economically deprived mother as feckless and dangerous rather than unfortunate and vulnerable, placed in her situation through personal failings and poor life planning rather than misfortune: 'the rise of new binaries of good and bad motherhood' (p. 126). Tyler

(2008: 31) proposes that this process has become entrenched in mainstream culture to the extent that contemporary media commentary 'doesn't pretend to be sociological, there is no ethnography, no gathering of knowledge about the poor, no charity, no reaching out to touch, and no liberal guilt; there is nothing but disgust and pleasure.' In her article 'Chav Mum, Chav Scum', she details incidences in contemporary mass media in which socio-economically deprived women are collectively mocked for comedic purposes, detailing the example of the fictional character Vicky Pollard, the creation of two upper-class, middle-aged male comedians: an 'incurably sub-literate, sexually promiscuous, pregnant, teenage chavette' (pp. 27–8). This point was previously made by journalist Johann Hari, who in 2005 commented that *Little Britain*, the television programme in which Vicky Pollard appeared was 'a sadistic, unfunny piece of spite', concluding that 'it's hard to escape the conclusion this is … woman-hatred with a laughter track' (Hari 2005, online).

McRobbie (2013) concludes that the British welfare state needs extensive rethinking, from the perspective that it was initially created to work on the basis of a male breadwinner, a societal construction that has now been wholly rejected by the neo-liberal consensus between centre-left, centre-right and liberal feminists, making the stay-at-home mother a figure of the past. Without such recognition of significant societal change, she argues that women will inevitably continue to be placed in the eye of the resulting storm, relentlessly driven to become mythical 'superwomen' who can somehow magically negotiate home, children and paid work on insufficient resources. She proposes that benefit-dependent and struggling women with no hope of 'access to as many nannies as they need' (p. 126) are further alienated and stigmatised on an ongoing basis by media glamorisation of super rich families with allegedly 'busy, working' mothers, such as the Beckhams and (until recently) the Jolie-Pitts. Such articles in multi-media outlets such as the *Daily Mail Online* are frequently accompanied by advertising features from chain store clothing companies exhorting readers to 'get her look', further magnifying the relentless 'striving' expected of contemporary mothers: to look as slim, glossy and stylish as an airbrushed image of a multi-millionaire.

One example of fallout from this culture was recently poignantly demonstrated in the BBC's high-profile dramatisation *The Moorside*, which narrated the story of uber-slummy mummy Karen Matthews, 'twice diagnosed by psychologists as having a borderline learning disability and described in the report as "emotionally vulnerable"' (Williams 2010 online), who staged the kidnapping of one of her children in order to launch a public appeal for money after consuming media that glamorised a professional, middle-class couple whose daughter had allegedly been abducted, resulting in a multi-million pound response to a public appeal. Recent analysis of Matthews's actions construct them as a desperate, dysfunctional attempt to escape from the punitive, all-encompassing panopticon in which she had been placed by the prevailing culture.

McRobbie comments that the construction of the downtrodden, shabby working-class mother is now viewed not as she would have been in the past, as a person of potential strength and dignity, respected for doing her best for her children against the odds, but as an icon of failure only worthy of scorn and censure. McRobbie concludes: 'new forms of consumer hedonism ... reinstate new norms of middle class hegemony against which less advantaged families can only feel themselves to be inferior or inadequate or else judging themselves as not having tried hard enough' (2013: 136). The fact that many mothers in Britain currently live under such psychosocially oppressive conditions is clearly a social justice issue, and one that urgently requires a remedy.

Conclusion

The brief overview of history and contemporary events within this chapter suggests that family life, and mothers in particular, are defined by dominant malestream ideologies on an ongoing basis. This situation can be tracked through the past century from the 'private family' ideology, in which women were placed on a narrow determinist track to becoming mothers and housewives, to the advent of the 'mediated public family', which depends upon the overburdened mother/carer/worker/consumer to provide the platform upon which neo-liberalism is orchestrated. The impetus to move parents of both genders into the workplace has resulted in a relentless psychosocial assault on socio-economically deprived mothers, marginalising and discrediting those who fail to manage the onerous role of the mother/carer/worker/consumer in the monolithically decreed fashion, regardless of the impossibility of acquiring sufficient financial resources. This places many women on a relentless 'hiding to nothing' in which they cannot escape the double bind of constant fatigue through overwork, alongside an abiding guilt that they are not doing enough to be considered a 'good mother'. McRobbie comments that this insoluble problem is dismissed by the malestream establishment with 'banal phrases like the work-life balance [and the absence of] a sustained debate about how motherhood and work could be realistically combined' (2013: 128). Tyler (2008: 26) comments that 'whilst young unwed working-class mothers have always been a target of social stigma, hatred, and anxiety, the fetishisation of the chav mum within popular culture has a contemporary specificity and marks a new outpouring of sexist class disgust'.

In conclusion, this is clearly an issue that urgently needs addressing through a newly constructed maternalist–feminist critique. Trevarthen (1998) proposed that, for human beings, culture becomes as invisible as water may be to fish and air may be to birds; a medium of vital and inescapable immersion which makes it difficult to initially perceive the enabling elements of an unjust, dysfunctional dominant ideology. Davies (1999) suggests a feminist strategy to increase 'visibility': a comparison of the cultural milieu not to water but to a clear pane of glass that can subsequently be metaphorically 'broken', allowing it to become visible, thence accessible to exploration, deconstruction and challenge. It is suggested that this strategy may be of use to a newly formatted critical maternalist feminism in the pursuit of a solution to the impasse faced by many contemporary working mothers.

This chapter has argued that the incorporation of liberal feminism within the dominant 'malestream' culture of neo-liberalism has trapped women within a culture which sustains an ongoing socio-psychological assault, most recently extending into the socially networked environment, upon the most vulnerable sector of the female population. It is suggested that we must now construct a new feminist approach which critically reviews the maternal situation for women within neo-liberal societies, with the intention of reviving 'the values of the social democratic tradition … through the pursuit of a genuine equality and collective provision for families as a public good' (McRobbie 2013: 135).

Reflection points

- What experience do you have of the 'yummy and slummy mummy' social construction?
- How do you feel about the shaming of individuals on social media? Has this gone too far in general? If so, how might we deal with it?
- How should society deal with families in poverty? How do you think the role of the parent and the state should be rebalanced?
- Have you experienced the neo-liberal 'striving' culture? What benefits and drawbacks do you see as associated with this?
- How do you think parents might most successfully balance work and family life, and how might the government help them to do this?
- Do you agree that there is a need for a new type of feminism to help women deal with contemporary societal expectations? What suggestions can you make relating to the initiation of such a movement?

References

Bowlby, J. (1952). *Maternal Care and Mental Health*. Geneva: World Health Organization. Online. Available at http://apps.who.int/iris/bitstream/10665/40724/1/WHO_MONO_2_(part1).pdf (accessed 16 April 2017).

Bradford (2013). Yummy, slummy, WAGs and suck-ups… which mum are you? *The Huffington Post*. Online. Available at www.huffingtonpost.co.uk/2013/07/23/yummy-slummy-wags-and-suck-ups-which-mum-are-you_n_7385480.html.

Brebony, K. (2009). Lady Astor's campaign for nursery schools in Britain 1930–1939: attempting to valorize cultural capital in a male-dominated field. *History of Education Quarterly*, *49*(2): 196–210.

Burman, E. (2012). Deconstructing neoliberal childhood: Towards a feminist antipsychological approach. *Childhood*, *19*: 423–30. doi:10.1177/0907568211430767.

Conroy, J. (2010). The state, parenting, and the populist energies of anxiety. *Educational Theory*, *60*(3): 325–40.

Cunningham, H. (2006). *The Invention of Childhood*. London: BBC Books.

Davies, B. (1999). *A Body of Writing*. Walnut Creek, CA: AltaMira.

Faircloth, C., Hoffman, D. and Layne, L. (2013). *Parenting in Global Perspective*. Abingdon: Routledge.

Fass, P. (2016). *The End of American Childhood: A History of Parenting from Life on the Frontier to the Managed Child*. Princeton, NJ: Princeton University Press.

Foucault, M. (1979). *Discipline and Punish: The Birth of the Prison*. New York, NY: Vintage.

Hari, J (2005). Why I hate Little Britain. *The Independent*, 22 November. Online. Available at www.independent.co.uk/voices/commentators/johann-hari/johann-hari-why-i-hate-little-britain-516388.html (accessed on 14 April 2017).

Henderson, A., Harmon, S. and Houser, J. (2010). A new state of surveillance? An application of Michel Foucault to modern motherhood. *Surveillance & Society*, *7*(3/4): 231–47.

Hennum, N. (2014). Developing child-centred social policies. When professionalism takes over. *Social Sciences*, *3*: 441–59.

Hey, V. and Bradford, S. (2006). Re-engineering motherhood? Sure Start in the community. *Contemporary Issues in Early Childhood*, *7*(1): 68–79.

Hinton, D., Laverty, L. and Robinson, J. (2013). 'Negotiating (un)healthy lifestyles in an era of "intensive" parenting: ethnographic case studies from north-west England, UK', in C. Faircloth, D. Hoffman and L. Layne (eds) *Parenting in Global Perspective*. Abingdon: Routledge, pp. 71–85.

Hoffman, D. (2013). 'Power struggles: the paradoxes of emotion and control among child-centred mothers in privileged America', in C. Faircloth, D. Hoffman and L. Layne (eds) *Parenting in Global Perspective*. Abingdon: Routledge.

Jarvis, P. (2016). Critical maternalism: a window on the 21st century. *Early Years Educator*, *18*(2): 38–44.

Jarvis, P., George, J., Holland, W. and Doherty, J. (2016). *The Complete Companion for Teaching and Leading Practice in the Early Years*. Abingdon: Routledge.

Jarvis, P. and Liebovich, B. (2015). British nurseries, head and heart: McMillan, Owen and the genesis of the education/care dichotomy. *Women's History Review*, *24*(6): 917–37. Online. Available at www.tandfonline.com/doi/pdf/10.1080/09612025.2015.1025662. doi:10.1080/09612025.2015.1025662.

Jensen, T. (2013). 'Creating distinction: middle-class viewers of Supernanny in the UK', in C. Faircloth, D. Hoffman and L. Layne (eds) *Parenting in Global Perspective*. Abingdon: Routledge.

Leite, M. (2013). (M)othering: Feminist motherhood, neoliberal discourses and the 'other'. *Studies in the Maternal*, *5*(2). Online. Available at www.mamsie.bbk.ac.uk (accessed 14 April 2017).

McRobbie, A. (2013). Feminism, the family and the new 'mediated' maternalism. *New Formations*, *80*(80): 119–37.

Margaret Thatcher Foundation (n.d.). *Interview for Sunday Times 3rd May 1981*. Online. Available at www.margaretthatcher.org/document/104475 (accessed 14 April 2017).

Nursery World (2016). Cameron pledges to make parenting classes the norm. *Nursery World*. Online. Available at www.nurseryworld.co.uk/nursery-world/news/1155498/cameron-pledges-to-make-parenting-classes-the-norm (accessed 16 January 2016).

Orgad, S. and De Benedictis, S. (2015). The 'stay-at-home' mother, postfeminism and neo-liberalism: content analysis of UK news coverage. *European Journal of Communication*, *30*(4): 418–36.

Rayner, T. (2012). Foucault and social media: life in a virtual panopticon. *Philosophy for Change*. Online. Available at https://philosophyforchange.wordpress.com/2012/06/21/foucault-and-social-media-life-in-a-virtual-panopticon.

Sime, D. and Sheridan, M. (2014). You want the best for your kids. *Educational Research*, *56*(3): 327–42.

Smith, R. (2010). Total parenting. *Educational Theory*, *60*(3): 357–69.

Sodha, S. (2016). Will Theresa May's 'just about managing families' fall for the rhetoric? *Guardian*, 21 November. Online. Available at www.theguardian.com/commentisfree/2016/nov/21/theresa-may-jams-rhetoric-just-managing-families-autumn-statement (accessed 15 April 2017).

Sterns, P. (2011). *Childhood in World History* (2nd Ed.). Abingdon: Routledge.

The Economist (2013). Why have so few bankers gone to jail? *The Economist*. Online. Available at www.economist.com/blogs/economist-explains/2013/05/economist-explains-why-few-bankers-gone-to-jail. (accessed 13 January 2016).

Tizard, B. (2009). Looking back: the making and breaking of attachment theory. *The Psychologist*. Online. Available at https://thepsychologist.bps.org.uk/volume-22/edition-10/looking-back-making-and-breaking-attachment-theory.

Trevarthen, C. (1998). 'The child's need to learn a culture', in M. Woodhead, D. Faulkner and K. Littleton (eds) *Cultural Worlds of Early Childhood*. London: Routledge.

Tyler, I. (2008). Chav mum chav scum. *Feminist Media Studies*, *8*(1): 17–34. doi:10.1080/14680770701824779.

UNICEF (2008). *The Child Care Transition: A League Table of Early Childhood Education and Care in Economically Advanced Countries*. Online. Available at www.unicef-irc.org/publications/pdf/rc8_eng.pdf (accessed 28 May 2015).

Vincent, C., Ball, S. and Brown, A. (2010). Between the estate and the state: struggling to be a good mother. *British Journal of Sociology of Education*, *31*(2): 123–38.

Williams, R. (2010). Karen Matthews's chaotic lifestyle left her children frequently at risk. *Guardian*. Online. Available at www.theguardian.com/uk/2010/jun/16/shannon-matthews-family-life (accessed 14 April 2017).

10 Developing socially just citizenship education in divided contexts

The freedom to self-define and not define

Helen Hanna

This chapter considers the challenge of developing a socially just conception of citizenship education in ethno-nationally divided societies, where citizenship and understandings of the conflict-affected past are contested issues. Drawing from qualitative research conducted by the author in Israel and Northern Ireland, it focuses on the relationship between a socially just citizenship education and two interrelated ideas: the freedom to have an identity and the freedom to define it. Ultimately, it proposes that, in order to encourage a socially just citizenship education, educators need to go beyond their own, sometimes narrowly defined understandings of identity and allow students the freedom to develop their own, multiple, emergent and even seemingly contradictory identities – but also allow them the freedom to not openly define themselves. In this way, it supports the thrust of this book, which is that citizenship and social justice may be – and should be permitted to be – perceived differently by different people across varying contexts, spaces and history, informed by personal experience.

Introduction: citizenship education and identity in a divided society

Society attests to the centrality of identity as a source of meaning for human beings (Castells 2010). Although it is widely held that education is a tool in socialisation (Podeh 2000), its role in helping develop certain identities is disputed, particularly within ethnically, sociopolitically, culturally or religiously divided societies (Bush and Saltarelli 2000; Gallagher 2004). Education holds the potential to promote social justice through challenging inequality and power (North 2006). At the same time, however, it may also work against social justice if it reproduces attitudes and identities that have played a role in social conflict (Buckland 2005). Citizenship education may be found within schools across the world, but it is most contested in so-called divided societies that have experienced violent conflict, such as Israel and Northern Ireland, as there understandings of citizenship, identity and national belonging are varied, and so ethno-national divisions are highly complex and persistent. Such divisions are also reflected in the segregated schooling systems in these two jurisdictions, where most young people attend school alongside primarily those of the same ethnicity or religion (McGlynn *et al.* 2009; Agbaria and Pinson 2013).

On a national level, citizenship education (CE) curricula vary widely in terms of the kind of 'citizen' they aim to create. In Israel, citizen identity may be seen as being tightly defined and even exclusive, particularly for Palestinian young people who may not consider themselves to be 'Israeli'. In contrast, in Northern Ireland, CE defines identity very loosely, with no reference to national identity/ies in its aims. Both approaches have their supporters and detractors (Ichilov 2008; Niens *et al.* 2013).

Moving out from the national, there is also the international sphere, in which can be found human rights law and bespoke children's rights law such as that found within the United Nations Convention on the Rights of the Child 1989, significant parts of which relate to identity and education. This chapter will propose that such laws codify not only the child's and young person's right to identity but also their right to define that identity (or those identities) for themselves. It will support the concept of identity as 'multiple, nested, and overlapping' (Kymlicka, 2004: xiv). It will also go further to suggest that this approach is entirely compatible with a social justice conception of CE that focuses on the 'recognition' of an individual and all aspects of their identities that they may wish to be recognised (see Honneth, in Fraser and Honneth 2003; Taylor 1994). This proposal will be supported by drawing on qualitative research conducted among secondary school students and teachers of CE in Israel and Northern Ireland, particularly those from the historically and/or currently less dominant ethno-national groups: 'Catholic' in Northern Ireland and 'Palestinian' in Israel.

The chapter will begin with an introduction to identity, citizenship and human rights, outlining a number of debates relating to citizenship identity and the rights both to have an identity and to define it. Then it will move on to focus on the two case countries, looking at citizenship and citizenship education, as well as responses from students and teachers gathered during fieldwork. The primary research will then lead to the climax of the chapter, which is the development of a tentative conception of a socially just approach to identity in citizenship education in a divided, conflict-affected society.

Identity, citizenship and human rights: having and defining

As mentioned earlier, identity is viewed as highly important to individuals. Castells (2010: 6) suggests that 'Identity is people's source of meaning and experience'. But it is also constructed within a context of power relations (North 2006), and, given that power is a central concept within social justice frameworks, it is unsurprising to find discussions of identity within social justice literature. Identity is also not a monolith; if we understand it to be constructed, it is then inevitable that there are multiple constructions, and multiple aspects of identity (Hall 1991, 1996; Kymlicka 1995, 2004). In other words, an individual may define themselves in myriad ways, in terms of their ethnicity, race, culture, religion, gender, marital status, age, profession, ability, health, personality … the list is potentially endless. And identity also changes and develops over time; psychologists (well-known among them include Erikson (1959) and Marcia (1966)) would point to specific stages in a child's life as they grow towards adulthood, where identity shifts, faces a 'crisis' and in some ways solidifies, but also, within education, scholars such as Banks (2004) have outlined how they view the kind of development of cultural identity that educators should enable students to follow in order to achieve a socially just education.

In terms of citizenship education, one of the debates that often arises relates to the definition of citizenship or a 'citizen identity' – whether 'citizenship' should be tightly defined and then transmitted through the curriculum or whether it should be kept open to interpretation by individuals. Citizenship is a complex and contested concept which gives rise to a wide range of interpretations, leading to an equally wide range of citizenship education programmes (Kerr 1999; Torney-Purta *et al.* 2001). It is a concept that dates back to ancient Greece and Rome and has been evolving and morphing ever since (Knight Abowitz and Harnish 2006). Unsurprisingly, this complexity may be transferred over into citizenship education, when a state or educational department is deciding what approach to take to the subject. Roth and Burbules (2007: 1) claim that understandings of citizenship education differ between states 'due to differences in social, cultural, economic, political and religious terms', with the governmental interest in the subject partly due to the belief that it can address social divisions (Morris 1997) and also shape and reshape collective identities (Pinson 2007). Ichilov (1998: 11) proposes that modern citizenship curricula have stressed the 'affinity and identity dimensions of citizenship', and this seems to be apparent, in different ways, in Israel and Northern Ireland.

In ethno-nationally divided societies that have experienced violent conflict from within the country, often of enormous concern is developing and maintaining social cohesion and peace. UNICEF (2014) defines social cohesion as

> the quality of coexistence between the multiple groups that operate within a society … along with the dimensions of mutual respect and trust, shared values and social participation, life satisfaction and happiness as well as structural equity and social justice.

Tightly defining 'citizenship' and relaying the ideal citizen identity through the education system is viewed as one way of encouraging this. Thus, it may be seen by some as risky to leave these definitions and identities open to students to decide for themselves, perhaps especially youth from minority or less advantaged backgrounds (see Hanna (2016) for more on this). However, the question arises whether it is essential to define or not define a citizen (or, for us here, student-citizen) in terms of national identity, thus compelling a student to equate this with being a member of the country where they are learning, in order to achieve a sense of social cohesion.

A related issue that emerges particularly in societies that have experienced conflict along ethno-national lines is the focus on binary identities – in the case of Northern Ireland, this would be the Catholic/Protestant binary, and in Israel it would be the Jewish/Palestinian, with corresponding expected binary feelings of belonging to different nations. Such binaries will be discussed later in relation to the concrete examples of the two case countries.

One of the tools at our disposal when analysing identity is that of international human rights law. Within qualitative approaches to social science, it is commonly held that human rights laws are socially constructed, brief and essentialised (Merry 2013). It is also of note that, contrary to popular belief, international law as codified is not a monolithic entity with one finite and decisive understanding. In fact, part of the international legal 'world' is the need for interpretation and reinterpretation of law, subject to the context of a particular society and even individual cases (Freeman 2011). Nevertheless, I agree with Davies (2005) when she says that they do, at the very least, offer a 'least worst' framework for rights across the world. Therefore, this chapter will take such rights as the foundation for much of the discussion here.

Looking at the two case countries, Northern Ireland (as a constituent part of the UK) and Israel are state parties to a number of international treaties. This includes the United Nations Convention on the Rights of the Child (1989). Therefore, they are bound to respect, protect and fulfil a long list of rights, a number of which are particularly significant to the current discussion around identity and choice: the right to be registered and to acquire nationality (Article 7, UNCRC); the right to respect for their identity in terms of nationality, name and family relations (Article 8); the right to express their views and for those to be given 'due weight' in issues that affect them (Articles 12 and 13); the right to freedom of thought, conscience and religion (Article 14); the right to education, and one which helps them develop respect for their cultural identity, language and values, the values of their country of residence, and for other people (Articles 29 and 30); and the right of a child from a minority or indigenous culture to enjoy that culture, language and religion (Article 28) (see Hodgson (1993) for a more detailed outline). Many of these laws reflect the aspects of identity already discussed earlier.

This list illustrates two points that here in brief, and later in full, I will argue are key to understanding a social justice approach to identity in citizenship education. The first is that children and young people have the right to *have* an identity. This is directly referred to in Articles 7, 8 and 28, where the emphasis is on particular aspects of a child's 'background' such as nationality, name, culture, religion and language. However, there is also a more subtle second point, and that is the right to *define* and *choose* identity/ies for themselves. This may be inferred from Articles 12 and 13, which prescribe a child's right to express their views (which could include those relating to their identity/ies) and for those to be given due weight, and from Article 14, which ensures freedom of conscience and religion, again tying in with the idea of choice over defining one's identity. Although the full text of these articles includes some mention of parental involvement, the child's identity is not necessarily tied to that of their parents or guardians; in UNCRC, there is a significant emphasis on treating the young person as an individual in their own right, independent of their families or their 'background'.

From a legal perspective, Ronen (2004) writes convincingly about how the child's right to identity should be redefined. She suggests that, rather than simply understanding it as a child having the right to identity (Ronen interprets it as a child's 'ties'), we should respect a child's wishes regarding their ties and regard each child as an 'individualized identity', rather than simply part of predetermined groups. As Ronen claims, when a number of articles, including Articles 12 and 13, are taken together, the UNCRC implicitly 'reaffirms commitment to a dynamic child-constructed identity' (p. 147) which acknowledges the multiplicity of culture as it is 'uniquely experienced by the individual child' (p. 158). These are issues on which writers such as Ronen and those active in the area of citizenship and children converge. Within the latter, there are those who argue that, rather than considering children as only part of a group or as a 'possession' of their parents – as 'passive objects of socialisation' (Bacon and Frankel 2013: 2) or as 'citizens-in-waiting' (Verhellen 2000) who are incapable of making rational choices about their own lives (Roche 1999) – children should be considered as endowed with rights 'on the same basis as adults' (Starkey 2006: 58) and as 'citizens of now'.

Related to such ideas of identity and choice is that of 'recognition', a concept which features in identity theory, politics, conflict studies and social justice. After the discussion of citizenship education in Northern Ireland and Israel, which follows, the chapter will return to this link with social justice, bringing together the threads of the argument for a social justice approach to identity in citizenship education.

Citizenship and citizenship education in Northern Ireland and Israel

Context and curriculum

Northern Ireland and Israel show some key similarities that offer a helpful basis for comparison when considering identity and social justice. Some of these will become clear in this section, where the background context and the CE curriculum will be explained.

The difference of views on national belonging in Northern Ireland (NI) originates in the British Protestant colonial settlement of the north of Ireland, the partition of the island in the early twentieth century, and real and perceived inequalities between Catholics and Protestants (favouring the latter) in terms of representation in government and access to employment and housing (Cochrane 2013). Following decades of violent conflict among local sectarian paramilitaries and the British armed forces, changes in equality legislation and new political structures were instigated by the Good Friday Agreement in 1998 (Mitchell

2015). However, even today, in much more peaceful times, most schools remain separated along ethno-national lines; in other words, most young people go to either a majority-Protestant or a majority-Catholic school, with 'integrated' (Catholics and Protestants together) and other schools making up a minority (Byrne and Donnelly 2006).

The population of NI is approximately 1.8 million (Northern Ireland Statistics and Research Agency 2012: 12), and identity and citizenship are understood in a variety of ways. The majority of Protestants in the region affiliate themselves with the UK (unionists, in political terms), and the majority of Catholics with the Republic of Ireland (nationalists), and it is this dichotomy that lies at the heart of the conflict within the jurisdiction. Currently, 43.9 per cent of the population identify as from a Catholic background, and 53.1 per cent describe themselves as Protestant (NISRA 2012: 19). Furthermore, four principal national identity markers are used: 'British', 'Irish', 'Northern Irish' and 'Ulster' (Northern Ireland Life and Times Survey 2012). Thus, as Arlow (2002: 40) has claimed, in the NI context 'there is no agreed concept of a "citizen" ', and this context has been reflected in the CE curriculum.

Citizenship education in NI is compulsory up to age sixteen, although it is not mandatorily examined and there is no compulsory textbook (CCEA 2009, 2013). It aims to 'help ... young people learn how to participate positively in society, to influence democratic processes and to make informed and responsible decisions as local and global citizens throughout their lives'. It looks at four themes: 'diversity and inclusion', 'human rights and social responsibility', 'equality and social justice' and 'democracy and active participation' (Partnership Management Board 2007: 20). Particularly pertinent to this chapter is the 'diversity and inclusion' theme, which is to include opportunities for pupils to 'consider the range and extent of diversity in societies locally and globally and to identify the challenges and opportunities which diversity and inclusion present in local, national, European and global contexts'. Within this strand, students are to be given the opportunity to investigate, among other aspects, factors that influence individual and group identity, ways in which identity is expressed and how and why conflict, prejudice, stereotyping, sectarianism and racism may arise. Students are to be taught critical thinking skills, be given opportunities to 'explore and express their own values and attitudes about current issues' and be 'challenged to develop an appreciation of the needs and perspectives of others' (PMB 2007: 21). It is notable that, within CE, citizenship in terms of the national, ethnic and religious identities mentioned earlier is not defined in the curriculum.

In Israel, the dichotomy of views on national belonging between Jewish and Palestinian citizens of the state originates in Jewish immigration to the majority-Arab region in the late nineteenth and early twentieth century, and the division of land that followed the establishment of the state of Israel as a Jewish state in 1948 (Ministry of Foreign Affairs 1948; Segev 2000). There has been protracted violent conflict both within and outside the Israel's borders, and Jewish/Palestinian divisions within Israeli society. The many Israel–Palestine peace initiatives have ultimately failed to bring about a permanent solution to the contentious issues of land, security and peace (Smith 2013). This is in contrast to the relatively stable situation of NI, particularly following the Good Friday Agreement of 1998. Although there is Palestinian representation at the Ministry of Education, and formal equality between Jewish and Palestinian citizens of Israel (as there is between Catholics and Protestants in NI), in Israel there are also widely reported inequalities between Jews and Palestinians in terms of government representation, educational resources and social and economic outcomes (Ichilov 2008; Rouhana and Ghanem 1998). Ben-Nun (2013: 2) has written that

> while Northern Ireland has recognized and is struggling to make amends for inherent inequality and discriminatory policies that shaped Catholic and Protestant relations, in Israel, formal and informal discrimination towards the Arab community is not being addressed in most cases.

However, similar to NI, the schooling system is separated into different strands, with most Jewish or Palestinian young people studying only with those from their own ethno-national group.

The population of Israel is 7.6 million, with 5.7 million (75.5 per cent) Jews and 1.5 million (20.3 per cent) Arabs (Palestinians) (Central Bureau of Statistics, Israel 2010). Jewish and Palestinian citizens largely differ with regard to language, religion and culture (Jabareen and Agbaria 2010). Palestinian citizens exhibit much lower levels of pride in their Israeli citizenship than Jewish citizens (Arad and Alon 2006), and some suggest this is because Israel is an 'ethnocracy' that reflects specifically Jewish values and culture (Yiftachel 2002). There is a wide range of Palestinian identities, with one study (Lowrance 2006) claiming seven: 'Palestinian in Israel', 'Israeli Arab', 'Palestinian Arab', 'Israeli Palestinian', 'Arab', 'Israeli' and 'Palestinian'. This confirms that the concepts of national identity and citizenship are just as complex in Israel as they are in NI.

Citizenship education ('civics') is compulsory in Israel's schools. A compulsory textbook is used and it is examined in the matriculation exams at the end of upper secondary school (Tatar 2004; Cohen 2013). The official goals of civics lessons include 'to inculcate a common Israeli civic identity, together with the development of distinct national identities', to teach tolerance and respect for those who are different from them, and to help them become critical thinkers with independent opinions (Ministry of Education 1994, cited in Ichilov *et al.* 2005: 40). Some of the themes in civics include the Jewish and democratic values inherent in the state, key debates relating to cultural diversity and minorities, citizenship, and civil and human rights. Students are to study and critically analyse a range of opinions from a variety of sources (Ministry of Education 1994, cited in Cohen 2013).

Thus, despite some similarities in terms of statutory content, the CE curriculum in Israel departs from that in NI insofar as it arguably seeks to define the citizenship which students are expected to adopt in relation to a specific state or national identity – 'Israeli' – which many would associate with being 'Jewish'

(Yiftachel 2002). In contrast, NI avoids any definition in relation to religious or ethno-national identity.

Student and teacher views

In the context of both the background to citizenship education and the key ideas of the right to identity and the right to define identity, this section will present responses of students and teachers of CE in Northern Ireland and Israel that relate to the concern of this chapter to develop a social justice approach to identity within citizenship education in divided societies. It will focus in particular on responses from the so-called 'Catholic' and 'Arab' (Palestinian) education sectors, as these would be regarded as currently or historically less dominant groups, a distinction which is relevant to discussions within a social justice framework. Semi-structured interviews with teachers and focus groups with students were conducted in 2011–12 and were analysed together with policy and curriculum documents as part of my doctoral research.

When one considers 'Catholic' and 'Palestinian' respondents, one of the striking differences relates to representation of their community's 'story' in the curriculum. I have written about this at length elsewhere (Hanna 2016) but it is worth reiterating, in the context of the discussion here, that students and teachers in NI appeared to feel that students' religious, cultural or ethno-national identities were, if not extensively represented, then at least not *mis*represented in CE. Teachers were keen that students' communities' identities be part of the curriculum, that they should be 'looking at local identity, looking at local communities' historical experience and why identity has emerged in the way it has' (Nicola, teacher, Catholic school). However, some teachers were also very concerned that students begin to think in a different way to that of their families or communities; the same teacher continues: 'we mustn't allow a previous generation's limited thinking to copper fasten that thinking onto their children'. This latter quote appears to point towards the desire for new understandings of identities to emerge among students.

In contrast, in Israel, Palestinian teachers highlighted that there was insufficient opportunity to look at Palestinian identity, owing to the dominance of the Jewish perspective in the compulsory textbook: 'This book is the Jewish version, we [Palestinians] don't believe in the same things that they wrote in this book, we believe in other things' (Layla, teacher, Arab school). Thus, the right to identity as recognised in the curriculum appears to be denied in this instance. Inevitably, here, given the context of the conversation around CE, the teacher highlights the 'national' aspects of being a Palestinian which 'we' don't believe in, and there is an unspoken assumption about the unity of Palestinian identity (Shafir and Peled 2002). This lack of recognition of Palestinian identity/ies may have led to a lack of desire to challenge young Palestinians' views and identities as well, unlike in the examples from NI, where recognition seemed to be at a higher level. Perhaps only when the right to identity is assured does it feel 'safe' to diversify in terms of allowing a variety of (non-traditional) identities.

Students in both jurisdictions appeared to want the freedom to discuss their own identities more in class – but not necessarily in the terms that their teachers wished. Many felt that they did not get enough opportunity to discuss what was happening in their local area that affected both of the main communities, including conflicts that related to ethno-national identity. For example, in the Catholic school in NI:

INTERVIEWER: Do yous get to talk about that [Protestants and Catholics] a lot in school?

HANNAH: Not a lot.

CAITLÍN: Not a lot because there's not like loads of stuff that we're allowed to bring up about all the Troubles [the most violent period of the ethno-national conflict in NI] and all …

HANNAH: You just learn about how it was back then, you don't learn about it now.

INTERVIEWER: Yeah. Is that something yous would maybe like to feel that you could talk about a wee bit more in class?

ALL STUDENTS: Yeah.

…

CAITLÍN: Protestants and Catholics have so much history, so like we're all sort of on the same page, we all know what's going on.

In this dialogue, there was clearly appreciation of the Catholic/Protestant binary, but there was also a wish to discuss the common Catholic–Protestant history. Identity may have been narrowly defined on behalf of these students; there was clearly attention paid to their 'Catholic' identity in their Catholic school, but less attention was paid to those over-arching and uniting identities that may spring from a consideration of Catholic and Protestant culture as a whole (potentially, a 'Northern Ireland' identity or a 'Belfast' identity or, differently, simply a 'teenager' or 'female' identity, and so on).

Among students in Israel, too, understandings of identity proved more complex than might initially be assumed. In the conversation below, students seek to go beyond the stereotypical view of them as 'Arab' by the rest of the world, towards a more complex and less politicised view:

RANYA: Most of the world … think that Arabs are terrorists.

JAMILA: But we're not.

…

BASIM: Yeah we're goofy, we're funny.

MALIK: We are from the name 'Islam', 'Islam' means 'peace', and we want peace, making peace with other countries.

BASIM: We're not that serious about everything, we laugh, we joke.

In the above dialogue, we see the desire for recognition as *people* – in terms of a multitude of personal characteristics and values rather than simply national or ethnic group identities and stereotypes. A desire for self-definition arises again and again.

Thus, what emerge in both jurisdictions, and particularly among students, are the two strands of this chapter: the right to (and desire for) identity and its recognition and also the right to define that identity rather than have it defined for them. The key points from the findings in relation to recognition-as-social-justice are unpacked in the following, final section.

Towards a socially just citizenship education in a divided society: recognition and identity

This closing section will draw out what the research presented in this chapter may mean for a socially just approach to identities within citizenship education, and will seek to build on what has been established by the other authors of the volume in terms of the principles of social justice when working with children, young people and vulnerable adults.

The centrepiece of this chapter has been the proposal that, in so-called divided societies, as elsewhere, young people should be considered as 'individualized identities' (Ronen 2004), holding their own right to identities of their choosing. Earlier, this idea was linked to the concept of recognition, which it was explained arises often in discussions of identity and social justice in ethno-national conflict-affected societies. This is particularly in relation to the recognition of minority or less dominant groups in society, who may be perceived as possessing, in practice, fewer rights, freedoms and opportunities. Among scholars, Taylor (1994) has published highly influential work on the politics of recognition and Young (1989) has written extensively on group differentiated rights, whereby the minority is assured recognition and equality with the majority. But Young has also unpacked the definition of a social group, destabilising it so that it becomes a 'flowing process' (Young 1990: 172). And, within the area of education in conflict-affected societies, Ben-Nun (2013) highlights the importance of recognition of the minority. Most significant for this book is that, although as Fook (2014: 160) has attested, 'social justice is a contested idea, with multiple, varied and possibly contradictory interpretations', recognition is a key concept in some understandings of social justice. Among social justice theorists, Honneth (in Fraser and Honneth 2003) is a prominent advocate of recognition approaches, viewing recognition by one individual of another as essential to flourishing as a human being, and locating 'the core of all experiences of injustice in the withdrawal of social recognition, in the phenomena of humiliation and disrespect' (p. 134). North (2006: 513) expands on Honneth's work by suggesting that 'individuals and groups who cannot or choose not to play by the rules of those in power often face exclusion, marginalization, or silencing'. Reich (2002: 8) suggests that Rawls's principles of justice should ensure an education system where all children 'are provided an education that fosters their autonomy'.

Taking the concept of recognition further, I contend, as mentioned earlier, that this recognition is not simply of a fixed or predetermined identity (the right to *have* an identity) but as the right to determine one's own identity using the categories of one's choice. The desire of students in Israel and NI for recognition of their identities – and not necessarily those identities that their ethno-nationally divided school systems or groups would ascribe to them – was clear. On paper, Israel's curriculum appears to define identity so tightly that Palestinians felt at a distance from it. However, in NI, although freedom from definition was offered, the 'light touch' approach may have meant that even options or alternatives for identities were not discussed. If one understands the concept of identity as 'multiple, nested, and overlapping' (Kymlicka 2004: xiv; see also Hall 1991) and as transient and even contradictory, a social justice approach to citizenship education may be one that assures recognition (and, indeed, equality, in all its various outworkings) to children and young people no matter which identities they choose for themselves. Thus, although these young people come from jurisdictions with a history of a binary approach to identity, they appear to be seeking out a poststructural, multifaceted identity for their own lives that is perhaps more evocative of the idea of a 'global' or 'cosmopolitan' citizen (see Osler and Starkey 2003).

The contentious side of such a proposal in relation to divided societies lies in the fact that children and young people's chosen identities may differ from those of the adults in their lives, especially those who may have experienced first-hand the 'troubled' past in a conflict-affected society. A socially just citizenship education, in the view of this chapter, allows young people to define their own identities, recognising that young people are the adults and therefore decision-makers of the future. It allows young people to move away from the 'copper-fastened' thinking of the past in order to create new, and sometimes even seemingly conflicting identities rather than simply adhering to those categories that adults have defined. But it also allows them to not ascribe to any national identity – or to keep silent about it. Part of learning to have the freedom to choose one's identity lies in the opportunity to be exposed to different types of identities. As Lynch and Baker (2005) suggest, as far as possible, students and teachers should have multiple opportunities to experience diverse perspectives and people; similarly, for Agarwal *et al.* (2009), the key markers of teaching for social justice include curricula with multiple perspectives, which question dominant narratives and are inclusive of racial, ethnic and linguistic diversity. However, as citizenship education scholars such as Banks (2004) acknowledge, the task of balancing this diversity with the need for some sense of unity, belonging and social cohesion in a multicultural society remains – but invites our continual re-engagement.

Questions to consider

1 This chapter considers the development of a socially just approach to identity in citizenship education specifically within ethno-nationally divided societies. Which identities might be 'contested' or accepted in England, Wales or Scotland? Think, perhaps, about 'bricolage' identities such as 'Brasian' (British Asian).

2 Do you think that young people should *always* have the freedom to choose their own identities?
3 To what extent should education be teaching young people what it means to be a citizen in their particular country, and therefore how to 'fit in'? Or, conversely, to what extent should it be preparing them to *challenge* what the state has decided is a 'good citizen'?

References

Agarwal, R., Epstein, S., Oppenheim, R., Oyler, C. and Sonu, D. (2009). From ideal to practice and back again: beginning teachers teaching for social justice. *Journal of Teacher Education, 61*(3): 237–47.

Agbaria, A. and Pinson, H. (2013). When shortage coexists with surplus of teachers: the case of Arab teachers in Israel. *Diaspora, Indigenous, and Minority Education: Studies of Migration, Integration, Equity, and Cultural Survival, 7*(2): 69–83.

Arad, U. and Alon, G. (2006). *Patriotism and Israel's National Security: Working Paper. Herzliya: Herzliya Patriotism Survey*. Available at www.herzliyaconference.org/Eng/_Uploads/1388Pat_e.pdf.

Arlow, M. (2002). 'The challenges of social inclusion in Northern Ireland: Citizenship and life skills', in S. Tawil (ed.) *Curriculum Change and Social Inclusion: Perspectives from the Baltic and Scandanavian countries*, Final Report of the Regional Seminar Held in Vilnius, Lithuania, 5–8 December 2001. Geneva: UNESCO International Bureau of Education.

Bacon, K. and Frankel, S. (2013). Rethinking children's citizenship: negotiating structure, shaping meanings. *International Journal of Children's Rights, 21*: pp. 1–20.

Banks, J. (2004). Teaching for social justice, diversity, and citizenship in a global world. *The Educational Forum, 68* (Summer): 289–98.

Ben-Nun, M. (2013). The 3Rs of integration: respect, recognition and reconciliation; concepts and practices of integrated schools in Israel and Northern Ireland. *Journal of Peace Education, 10*(1): 1–20.

Buckland, P. (2005). *Reshaping the Future: Education and Postconflict Reconstruction.* Washington, DC: World Bank Publications.

Bush, K.D. and Saltarelli, D. (2000). *The Two Faces of Education in Ethnic Conflict.* Florence: UNICEF Innocenti Insight.

Byrne, G. and Donnelly, C. (2006). 'The education system in Northern Ireland', in C. Donnelly, B. Osborne and P. McKeown (eds) *Devolution and Pluralism in Education in Northern Ireland.* Manchester: Manchester University Press.

Castells, M. (2010). *The Power of Identity* (2nd Ed.). Chichester: Wiley-Blackwell.

Cochrane, F. (2013). *Northern Ireland: The Reluctant Peace*. Newhaven, CT: Yale University Press.

Cohen, A. (2013). *Conceptions of Citizenship and Civic Education: Lessons from Three Israeli Civics Classrooms*. Unpublished PhD thesis. New York, NY: Columbia University Academic Commons.

Council for Curriculum, Examinations and Assessment (CCEA). (2009). *Learning for Life and Work: Implementation Matters*. Available at www.nicurriculum.org.uk/docs/learning_for_life_and_work/training/LLW_Implementation_Matters.pdf.

Council for Curriculum, Examinations and Assessment (CCEA) (2013). *Learning for Life and Work.* Available at www.nicurriculum.org.uk/key_stage_3/areas_of_learning/learning_for_life_and_work.

Davies, L. (2005). Teaching about conflict through citizenship education. *International Journal of Citizenship and Teacher Education, 1*(2): 17–34.

Erikson, E.H. (1959). *Identity and the Life Cycle*. New York, NY: International Universities Press.

Fraser, N. and Honneth, A. (2003). *Redistribution Or Recognition?: A Political-Philosophical Exchange*. London: Verso.

Fook, J. (2014). 'Social justice and critical theory', in M. Reisch (Ed.) *The Routledge International Handbook of Social Justice*. Abingdon: Routledge.

Freeman, M.A. (2011). *Human Rights: An Interdisciplinary Approach*. Cambridge: Polity.

Gallagher, T. (2004). *Education in Divided Societies*. Basingstoke: Palgrave Macmillan.

Hall, S. (1991). 'Old and new ethnicities, old and new identities', in A. King (ed.) *Culture, Globalization and the World System*. London: Macmillan, pp. 41–68.

Hall, S. (1996). 'Who needs identity?', in S. Hall and P. du Gay (eds) *Questions of Cultural Identity*. London: Sage.

Hanna, H. (2016). 'Everyone has to find themselves in the story': exploring minority group representation in the citizenship curriculum in Northern Ireland and Israel. *Diaspora, Indigenous and Minority Education, 10*(2): 84–97.

Hodgson, D. (1993). The international legal protection of the child's right to a legal identity and the problem of statelessness. *International Journal of Law, Policy and the Family, 7*: 255–70.

Ichilov, O. (2008). 'Citizenship education in Israel: a contested terrain', in J. Arther, I. Davies and C. Hahn (eds) *The SAGE Handbook of Education for Citizenship and Democracy*. London: Sage.

Ichilov, O. (1998). *Citizenship and Citizenship Education in a Changing World*. London: Woburn.

Ichilov, O., Salomon, G. and Inbar, D. (2005). Citizenship education in Israel – a Jewish-democratic state. *Israel Affairs, 11*(2): 303–23.

Jabareen, Y.T. and Agbaria, A. (2010). *Education on Hold: Israeli Government Policy and Civil Society Initiatives to Improve Arab Education in Israel (English Executive Summary)*. Haifa: Arab Center for Law and Policy, Arab Minority Rights Clinic and Faculty of Law, University of Haifa.

Kerr, D. (1999). Citizenship education in the curriculum: An international review. *School Field, 10*(3/4): 5–32.

Knight Abowitz, K. and Harnish, J. (2006). Contemporary discourses of citizenship. *Review of Educational Research, 76*(4): 653–90.

Kymlicka, W. (1995). *Multicultural Citizenship: A Liberal Theory of Minority Rights*. Cambridge: Cambridge University Press.

Kymlicka, W. (2004). 'Foreword', in J.A. Banks (ed.) *Diversity and Citizenship Education: Global Perspectives*. San Francisco, CA: Jossey-Bass.

Lowrance, S. (2006). Identity, grievances, and political action: Recent evidence from the Palestinian community in Israel. *International Political Science Review, 27*(2): 167.

Lynch, K., and Baker, J. (2005). Equality in education: An equality of condition perspective. *Theory and Research in Education, 3*(2): 131–64.

Marcia, J.E. (1966). Development and validation of ego-identity status. *Journal of Personality and Social Psychology, 3*(5): 551.

McGlynn, C., Lamarre, P., Laperrière, A. and Montgomery, A. (2009). Journeys of interaction: shared schooling in Quebec and Northern Ireland. *Diaspora, Indigenous, and Minority Education: Studies of Migration, Integration, Equity, and Cultural Survival, 3*(4): 209–25.

Merry, S.E. (2013). 'Monitoring and the question of indicators', in M. Goodale (ed.) *Human Rights at the Crossroads*. New York, NY: Oxford University Press.

Ministry of Foreign Affairs (Israel) (1948). *Declaration of Establishment of the State of Israel*. Available at www.mfa.gov.il/MFA/Peace+Process/Guide+to+the+Peace+Process/Declaration+of+Establishment+of+State+of+Israel.htm.

Mitchell, D. (2015). *Politics and Peace in Northern Ireland: Political Parties and the Implementation of the 1998 Agreement*. Manchester: Manchester University Press.

Morris, P. (1997). 'Civics and citizenship education in Hong Kong', in K. Kennedy (ed.) *Citizenship Education and the Modern State*. London: Falmer.

Niens, U., O'Connor, U. and Smith, A. (2013). Citizenship education in divided societies: Teachers' perspectives in Northern Ireland. *Citizenship Studies, iFirst Article, 17*(1): 1–14.

Northern Ireland Life and Times Survey (NILTS). (2012). *Which of These Best Describes the Way You Think of Yourself?* Belfast: ARK.

Northern Ireland Statistics and Research Agency (NISRA) (2012). *Census 2011: Key Statistics for Northern Ireland*. London: National Statistics.

North, C. (2006). More than words? Delving into the substantive meaning(s) of 'social justice' in education. *Review of Educational Research, 76*(4): 507–35.

Osler, A. and Starkey, H. (2003). Learning for cosmopolitan citizenship: theoretical debates and young people's experiences. *Educational Review, 55*(3): 243–54.

Partnership Management Board (2007). *Learning for Life and Work for Key Stage Three*. Belfast: CCEA.

Pinson, H. (2007). At the boundaries of citizenship: Palestinian Israeli citizens and the civic education curriculum. *Oxford Review of Education, 29*(2): 331–48.

Podeh, E. (2000). History and memory in the Israeli educational system: The portrayal of the Arab-Israeli conflict in history textbooks (1948–2000). *History and Memory, 12*(1): 65–100.

Reich, R. (2002). *Bridging Liberalism and Multiculturalism in American Education*. Chicago, IL: University of Chicago Press.

Roche, J. (1999). Children: rights, participation and citizenship. *Childhood, 6*(4): 475–93.

Ronen, Y. (2004). Redefining the child's right to identity. *International Journal of Law, Policy and the Family, 18*(2): 147–77.

Roth, K. and Burbules, N.C. (2007). 'Understanding the meaning of citizenship education', in K. Roth and N.C. Burbules (eds) *Changing Notions of Citizenship Education in Contemporary Nation-States*. Rotterdam/Taipei: Sense.

Rouhana, N. and Ghanem, A. (1998). The crisis of minorities in ethnic states: The case of Palestinian citizens in Israel. *International Journal of Middle East Studies, 30*: 321–46.

Segev, T. (2000). *One Palestine, Complete: Jews and Arabs Under the British Mandate*. New York, NY: Little, Brown.

Shafir, G. and Peled, Y. (2002). *Being Israeli: The Dynamics of Multiple Citizenship*. Cambridge: Cambridge University Press.

Smith, C. (2013). 'The Arab-Israeli conflict', in L. Fawcett (ed.) *International Relations of the Middle East*. Oxford: Oxford University Press, pp. 245–67.

Starkey, H. (2006). 'Intercultural understanding and human rights education: where are we now and where are we heading for?', in S.-M. Lee and J. Encabo (eds) *Intercultural Understanding and Human Rights Education in the Era of Globalization*. Seoul, South Korea: Asia-Pacific Center of Education for International Understanding.

Tatar, M. (2004). 'Diversity and citizenship education in Israel', in J. Banks (ed.) *Diversity and Citizenship Education: Global Perspectives*. San Francisco, CA: Jossey-Bass.

Taylor, C. (1994). 'The Politics of Recognition', in A. Gutmann (ed.) *Multiculturalism: Examining the Politics of Recognition.* Princeton, NJ: Princeton University Press, pp. 25–73.

Torney-Purta, J., Lehman, R., Oswald, H., and Schulz, W. (2001). *Citizenship and education in twenty-eight countries. Civic knowledge and engagement at age fourteen.* Amsterdam: IEA.

UNICEF (2014). *Learning for peace.* New York, NY: UNICEF. Available at http://learningforpeace.unicef.org/cat-about/key-peacebuilding-concepts-and-terminology.

United Nations General Assembly (20 November 1989). *Convention on the Rights of the Child.* United Nations, Treaty Series, vol. 1577: 3.

Verhellen, E. (2000). 'Children's rights and education', in A. Osler (ed.) *Citizenship and Democracy in Schools: Diversity, Identity, Equality.* Stoke-on-Trent: Trentham.

Young, I.M. (1989). Polity and group difference: A critique of the ideal of universal citizenship. *Ethics, 99*(2), 250–74.

Young, I.M. (1990). Justice and the politics of difference. Princeton, NJ: Princeton University Press.

Yiftachel, O. (2002). The shrinking space of citizenship. *Middle East Report*, 233. Available at www.merip.org/mer/mer223/shrinking-space-citizenship?ip_login_no_cache=e6c51150e8cc28cc984b9d980cf25a2e.

11 Social justice in local government

A delicate balance

Sue Elmer

Introduction

This chapter concerns the application of social justice principles to the delivery of services for vulnerable adults by local authorities (who administer local government). Many such adults tend to live socially isolated lives, marginalised from their families and their wider community. They often lack the social capital necessary for adequate care and social support or the financial resources to be able to make choices which would change or improve their lives (Burchardt *et al.* 2015). In addition they may lack the cognitive or mental capacity to make informed decisions which are in their best interests, even when these decisions have the potential to negatively impact on their health and well-being. A further group of adults, particularly but not exclusively women, are made vulnerable through the experiences of domestic abuse, human trafficking or modern human slavery. These adults often share a common experience of coercive control, which results in social isolation, degrading treatment and disempowerment. They can be physically and emotionally entrapped in what they believe to be a relationship (Stark 2007; Mullender 2009; Elmer 2013). These adults do not have the personal resources to exercise personal choice and are disempowered as a result. These themes will be discussed again later in this chapter.

It is the responsibility of health and social care agencies, coordinated by local authorities, to protect the rights and freedoms and the ability of vulnerable adults to be able to make their own decisions and to live independent fulfilled lives. Where this is either challenging or not possible for vulnerable adults, who for example have dementia, are experiencing psychosis or have severe learning disability, local authorities have a statutory responsibility to ensure the provision of adequate social and health care to engage in 'adult safeguarding' in order to meet their needs and ensure they are kept safe from significant harm (Cree and Wallace 2009; Hollomotz 2011). This necessitates a delicate balance between the needs of the vulnerable adult to self-advocate and their family members, or local authority practitioners advocating on their behalf and responsible for planning their care or acting to keep them safe. Their decisions impact directly on individuals and their families in both the short and long term and need to be taken with family members rather than about them. This balance is particularly important in decisions concerning issues of health and social care service provision. The power imbalance between the vulnerable adults in need of care and support and the providers of services is something providers need to be constantly mindful of, given that power inevitably lies with providers (O'Sullivan 2010; Torn, 2017).

In this chapter, the reader will be encouraged to consider the social justice issues associated with gender, ethnicity, disability, culture and diversity and how these are reflected in social policy and associated practice for vulnerable adults by local authorities, working together with other agencies. Social justice was adopted by the UK government in 2012 in anticipation that this would be adopted by local authorities (to read more about this, see links at the end of this chapter in the further reading section).

Social justice has been defined in a range of ways, however key aspects of these definitions include: taking personal and moral responsibility, both individually and collectively to improve the lives of all others, ensuring that they are treated with dignity and respect, ensuring fair, equal and impartial treatment and access to services and actively responding to inequality. The UK government recently suggested that social justice concerns a set of principles, including:

- prevention and early intervention
- recovery and independence
- unconditional support to those who are severely disabled
- recognising that solutions can often be designed and delivered at local level
- ensuring a fair deal for the tax payer.

(Duncan Smith 2012: 8)

Aspects of these principles are now being adopted by local authorities. For example, Leeds City Council has introduced a wide-ranging strategy which focuses on social justice and restorative practice.

Local authorities employ a wide range of practitioners including adult social workers (the name given to social workers who specialise in working with vulnerable adults, including mental health and learning disability), social care support workers, housing advisers, personal care workers, welfare benefits advisers, health practitioners and specialist domestic abuse support workers. They also employ service commissioners who work with independent-sector housing providers and adult health and social care service providers to agree service contracts for vulnerable adults. This wide-ranging group of practitioners work together with vulnerable adults and their families to provide integrated support which counters the effects of marginalisation through social class, gender or cultural factors, and maximises their social inclusion, through anti-oppressive and ethical approaches to assessing and meeting their needs (Adams *et al.* 2009; Hatton 2008).

Vulnerable adults, marginalised through social class, gender and culture, can have particular difficulties in accessing services when they have additional health and social care needs, struggling to access services. Local authority practitioners are trained to focus on working to empower vulnerable adults. Barry understands the dilemmas that this can raise for social workers, where they 'operate at the interface of, and hence mediate between advantage and disadvantage, self-determination and dependency, integration and marginalisation' (Barry 1998: 7). It is in this interface that the practitioners must ensure that a balance is maintained. Self-determination, as a matter of social justice, is being given increasing emphasis and this is reflected in the direct payments made by local authorities to individual adults and their families to sustain them in their own homes as well as residential care to ensure they have choice and control of the services they need to meet their needs (Wittenberg *et al.* 2017).

Local authorities have begun to recognise the importance of social justice and the need to apply this in the fair and equitable delivery of services to meet the care and support needs of vulnerable adults. The Human Rights Act and the Equality Act 2010 support this by ensuring that local authorities monitor their activities, providing evidence that they are complying with the equality guidance.

The legislative and policy context regarding vulnerable adults

Successive UK governments since the 1990s have identified the need to ensure adequate care and protection for vulnerable adults through statutory regulation and practice guidance. In 2000 the government published the advisory document *No Secrets* (Department of Health 2000) to provide practice guidance on developing and implementing multi-agency policies and procedures to protect vulnerable adults from abuse. The intention was that this should be an interim step to future statutory regulation, similar to that in place for safeguarding children. The No Secrets policy defined a vulnerable person as one:

> who is or may be in need of community care services by reason of mental or other disability, age or illness; and who is or may be unable to take care of him or herself, or unable to protect him or herself against significant harm or exploitation.
>
> (DoH 2000: 8)

The Care Act 2014 finally introduced statutory regulation of services for vulnerable adults in England and Wales. This redefined the vulnerable adult as one who:

(a) has needs for care and support (whether or not the authority is meeting any of those needs),
(b) is experiencing, or is at risk of, abuse or neglect, and
(c) as result of those needs is unable to protect himself or herself against the abuse or neglect or the risk of it.

(Section 42)

Examples of adults who may be vulnerable, defined above, include:

- frail elderly adults, particularly those who have developed dementia and who lack mental capacity;
- adults with mental health issues;
- adults with learning disabilities;
- adult survivors of physical abuse, sexual abuse, emotional abuse, neglect and/or financial abuse;
- Adult survivors of coercive control and domestic abuse (this may be from intimate partner abuse, by family members or, in some instances of frail elderly adults, by care home or hospital staff) (Torn 2017);
- Adults who have been subject to human trafficking, are in forced labour or are modern human slaves.

In each case the vulnerable adults described above may be socially isolated and may lack the confidence or have the ability to seek help. Adults with complex health and social care needs are likely to be vulnerable because they have a combination of the factors listed above. They may also have drug and/or alcohol dependency issues. Such adults can be made more vulnerable when English is a second language, particularly if they are recently arrived in the UK and their immigration status influences whether they will have recourse to public funds and associated service provision or indeed whether they are willing to ask for help by local authorities (Equality and Human Rights Commission 2016). They may be unaware of the health and social care services they are entitled to receive. They may also be fearful that any request for help may impact on their entitlement to stay in the UK. A particular vulnerability for women who are asylum seekers is that they may be dependent on their husbands' asylum applications.

When vulnerable adults have poor health or disability, such as those described above, they may not be able to articulate their wishes and feelings or they may lack the capacity to make decisions (Hollomotz 2011). It is in such circumstances that practitioners must make every effort to ensure that their needs and wishes are understood and careful reflection is required to ensure the best possible outcomes.

In the circumstances how are their human rights to be protected? The European Convention on Human Rights ensures that public authorities have a duty to ensure that they do not commit human rights abuses; this applies to their treatment of vulnerable adults (Age UK 2011). In addition, the Mental Capacity Act (MCA) 2005 and subsequent MCA code of practice (Department of Health 2016) provides guidance to both carers and professionals responsible for vulnerable adults whose decision-making capacity is impaired and they cannot make decisions for themselves. Local authority practitioners in adult social care, welfare and housing support, including adult social workers, are trained to assume that such adults have mental capacity and with support can be empowered to make their own decisions concerning the services they are entitled to receive. For example, they may have support needs and have a number of options concerning service providers. Empowering vulnerable adults to make decisions about their own needs is an important opportunity to recognise their strengths, their right to self-determination and is intended to promote their social inclusion (Hollomotz 2011).

The following scenario is typical of elderly vulnerable adults.

Jack, aged 83, lives on his own and is becoming increasingly confused. His son and daughter, who live 20 and 100 miles away, respectively, are pressing for him to go into a residential care home, because they cannot easily meet his needs. Jack wants very much to maintain his independence, and health and social care practitioners have determined that, given daily support, he will be able to do so for now. One key point is that they will arrange transport for him so he can continue to attend a bi-weekly lunch club with other local elderly people he has known since his school days, as one issue strongly raised by his daughter was that Jack once lost his way when he walked to the venue and she was contacted by the police, who found him wandering and distressed. Practitioners have to consider how they will sensitively negotiate with the family to ensure that, on the one hand, Jack is empowered to make this decision but, on the other, his adult children are reassured that he will be safe, cared for and his condition regularly reviewed.

Despite the many policies and procedures that ensure partnership and cooperation for everyone involved in the care of vulnerable adults, it can still prove hard to define whether an adult has the capacity to consent, for example, to health and social care assessments and to ensure that they can make informed decisions. It can also prove challenging for professionals to ensure that they are working in an effective partnership with family members and professionals who may be involved in providing care, support and safeguarding from significant harm, particularly when the decisions of family members are not judged by professionals to be in the vulnerable adult's best interest or where family members are an adult safeguarding risk.

Work with vulnerable adults is informed by a legal and policy framework, including the Equality Act 2010. This has been important, particularly for disabled people because it enshrined duties and responsibilities that public bodies, including local authorities, must actively consider in their work with vulnerable adults. Evidence of progress is regularly reviewed by the Equality and Human Rights Commission. A recent report, *Is England Fairer?* (2016) reviews progress against ten domains: education; standard of living; productive and valued activities; health; life; physical security; legal security; individual, family and social life; identity, expression and self-respect; and participation, influence and voice. In considering England's most disadvantaged groups, the authors argue:

> Some people in our society are being left further behind because they face particular barriers in accessing important public services and are locked out of opportunities. There are several factors that may contribute to this, including socio-economic deprivation, social invisibility, poor internal organisation of the group, distinctive service needs that are currently not

> met, cultural barriers, stigma and stereotyping, small group size, and very importantly, a lack of evidence which limits us in our ability to assess the multiple disadvantages these people face.
>
> (p. 106)

Vulnerable adults face multiple and cumulative disadvantages and local authorities focus on acting to counter such disadvantage.

The dignity policy

In the debate about vulnerable adults, new areas of theory, policy and practice have been introduced, including the introduction of the 'dignity agenda' (SCIE 2013). The application of the social justice principles, described earlier in this chapter, is evident in this policy. The policy guidance requires health and social care providers to focus on maintaining personal dignity and self-respect in all aspects of health and social care, including ensuring that the vulnerable adult has personal choice and control, that communication with them is respectful and that, just as importantly, equality of access to services and treatment is ensured, including access to advocacy to represent their views (Anderberg *et al.* 2007). Social justice principles continue to inform each aspect of policy and practice development. Typical of local authority responses to the requirement to introduce the dignity agenda is that of Derbyshire County Council, which provides the following information for its '10 point Dignity challenge for practitioners':

> Before the Dignity in Care campaign launched, numerous focus groups took place around the country to find out what Dignity in Care meant to people. The issues raised at these events resulted in the development of the 10 Point Dignity Challenge (now the 10 Dignity Dos). The challenge describes values and actions that high quality services that respect people's dignity should:
>
> 1 Have a zero tolerance of all forms of abuse
> 2 Support people with the same respect you would want for yourself or a member of your family
> 3 Treat each person as an individual by offering a personalised service
> 4 Enable people to maintain the maximum possible level of independence, choice and control
> 5 Listen and support people to express their needs and wants
> 6 Respect people's right to privacy
> 7 Ensure people feel able to complain without fear of retribution
> 8 Engage with family members and carers as care partners
> 9 Assist people to maintain confidence and positive self-esteem
> 10 Act to alleviate people's loneliness and isolation.
>
> (Derbyshire.gov.uk n.d.: 1, online)

Local authority responsibilities to safeguard and protect vulnerable adults from significant harm

The Care Act 2014 recognises the potential risks to vulnerable adults. These are compounded when the vulnerable adult is, in addition, socially marginalised and unable to express their wishes and needs or has someone who is willing to advocate for them. One of the most important duties that local authorities have is the duty to investigate and safeguard such risks to adults. Cree and Wallace (2009), in reflecting on adult exposure to risk of significant harm, maintained that:

> The care of 'vulnerable adults' has experienced a great deal of public attention in recent years ... and over the past decade steps have been taken, throughout the UK, by way of Government legislation, policy and practice guidance for health and caring agencies to bring practice in line with measures to protect children.
>
> (p. 45)

Health and social care practice for vulnerable adults follows a similar set of procedures to that for children, not least because adults can be vulnerable to abuse in many of the same ways as children, e.g. physical, sexual, emotional and neglect, and additionally financial abuse. Consequently, local authority-led multi-agency safeguarding practice to protect vulnerable adults from harm is modelled on best practice processes in safeguarding children. The Local Government Association (2013) recently updated its safeguarding advice to better protect vulnerable adults (see ADASS website, www.adass.org.uk). Safeguarding was identified as one of the highest priorities for local governments. The Care and Support White Paper ('Safeguarding is Everybody's Business') argued that high-quality service must keep people safe from harm (Department of Health 2013).

A further consideration is that some vulnerable adults are also parents who have both their own care needs and parental responsibilities towards their children. It can be a difficult balance for practitioners to maintain the rights and independence of the vulnerable adult while at the same time ensuring adequate care and well-being of their children, who in many cases are also acting as their primary carers.

Adults can be particularly vulnerable to domestic abuse where there are issues of social exclusion, mental health, disability and/or substance addiction. Cleaver *et al.* (2007) maintain that:

> One of the first questions to address is how prevalent is parental mental illness, learning disability, drug or alcohol misuse and domestic violence in families with dependent children.
>
> (p. 34)

Vulnerable adult women (particularly those who are disabled or are from an ethnic minority culture), and those who experience domestic abuse, worry about disclosing the reality and severity of their experiences. In particular they worry that the perpetrators of the violence might find out that they have sought help from local authorities. They may also be censured by their community for seeking help from outside the community. They need a high level of sustained support from local practitioners, to develop sufficient trust and rapport to be able to disclose their experiences. This requires practitioners to work with skill, empathy and cultural understanding with the different perspectives and values of members of the family and social network as a means of ensuring their long-term protection (Thompson 2006).

This is illustrated in the following account from a narrative study of women who were survivors of sustained domestic abuse:

> In reviewing detailed case records and comparing each interviewee's narrative, it became apparent that there were some disparities between what women had said to the Police and what they disclosed during the narrative interviews. In particular it was apparent that *women routinely minimised and normalised the seriousness of domestic violence to the Police as a means of both seeking immediate help and managing events following their departure to ensure that the perpetrator did not further escalate the violence on his return to the family home*. Where the Police recorded an incident of verbal abuse as the reason for initial contact in each of the case studies, in our subsequent interviews the women described physical, sexual and psychological abuse by their partner or ex partner and in some cases, other family members of the partner.
>
> (Elmer 2013: 35)

The following case illustrates some of the challenges of maintaining socially just and ethical practice in working with families who face multiple challenges, including abuse and coercion. Local authority practitioners need to ensure effective safeguarding from harm. In this case, Jenny and her mother need to be empowered to re-establish personal control and autonomy to be able to self-advocate to meet their immediate needs. It can be tempting for practitioners to assume power and authority when this may have an adverse effect.

Case example

Jenny is an eighteen-year-old young woman with a moderate learning difficulty. She lives at home with her mother, Sarah, and her mother's partner of five years, Steven. Her mother has long-term mental health difficulties. Sarah and Steven both have a history of alcohol abuse. Steven ensures that he takes all of the decisions concerning their day to day lives. He had sometimes been emotionally and physically abusive towards Sarah, and Jenny has witnessed this. Steven was previously prosecuted for domestic abuse towards his former partner. Sarah is not aware of this. The family lives in social housing and in many cases struggles to access services that would meet Jenny's needs. Jenny attends a day-care service twice each week to encourage social inclusion and to engage in meaningful activities with other young adults at the centre. Jenny's attendance has become increasingly erratic and her mood, appearance and anxiety levels have all deteriorated. Her key worker, Rachel, and the day-care team are increasingly concerned. Then Jenny calls Rachel to say her mother has been admitted to hospital following an overdose, and that she thinks it is all her fault. An adult care social worker (Ruth) is asked to visit Jenny and discovers that Jenny has been coerced into sexual activity with Steven. Jenny is not sure whether her mother is aware of this and in Ruth's view Jenny lacks the cognitive capacity to understand that this is harming her. Jenny also confirms that both she and her mother are frightened of Steven because he sometimes slaps them. They are not allowed to leave the house unless Steven is with them. However, he is happy for Jenny to attend the day-care service.

Ruth consults her manager concerning adult abuse concerns and together they agree the need to call an adult safeguarding strategy meeting. This meeting includes police, adult social care services and health care to ensure that Jenny is safeguarded from further harm. The situations of vulnerable adults such as Jenny highlight some of the social justice issues that can arise, particularly concerning exploitation. Jenny is unable to articulate the distress she experiences in Steven's use of coercive control and physical abuse, either of her mother or herself. Neither does Jenny see herself as being at risk. Jenny and Sarah live socially marginalised lives and lack the emotional or financial resources to make significant changes, including ending the relationship with Steven. They have only a limited support network because Steven had largely succeeded in socially isolating Sarah and Jenny from their extended family.

Ruth and her colleagues are trained to use a social model of disability. This model focuses on 'social process when explaining disabled people's disadvantages' (Hollomotz 2011: 14), recognising that adjustments may need to be made that are specific to Jenny's specific social situation, rather than Jenny needing to fit with the more formulaic processes and procedures that already exist at the day-care centre. As a social care team, Ruth and her colleagues aim to work with Jenny to be confident and independent. They help Sarah to focus on Jenny's strengths, making the assumption that, with guidance and support, Jenny can make decisions in her best interest, giving careful consideration to her needs and ensuring her safety and protection. They recognise that Jenny must be helped to make decisions in the context of her cognitive impairment and her ability to interpret and understand the risk she faces from Steven. The need to respect Sarah's wish to remain with Steven have to be balanced with the need to protect Jenny. The social care team share the ethical dilemmas this presents with each other and with Jenny and her mother. The team will be aware that the recent *Is England Fairer* (2016) report found that:

> Learning-disabled people in residential and inpatient care were admitted for disproportionately long spells, in inappropriate settings, often a very long distance away from family and home.
>
> (p. 105)

Consequently the team will recognise how important it is that Jenny is able to sustain a relationship with her mother, the day-care centre and the social network available to them.

Local authority responsibilities: modern human slavery, forced labour and human trafficking

Local authorities have specific duty, under Section 52 of the Modern Slavery Act 2015, to notify the Home Office where they identify people who are modern human slaves, who are subject to forced labour or have been subject to human trafficking. This duty also applies to 'the police, local authorities, the National Crime Agency, the Gangmasters Licensing Authority and UK Visas and Immigration, Immigration Enforcement and Border Force staff'. The Modern Slavery Act 2015 establishes that:

> A person commits an offence if—
>
> a the person holds another person in slavery or servitude and the circumstances are such that the person knows or ought to know that the other person is held in slavery or servitude, or
>
> b the person requires another person to perform forced or compulsory labour and the circumstances are such that the person knows or ought to know that the other person is being required to perform forced or compulsory labour.
>
> (p. 7)

Criminal prosecutions for modern human slavery are now taking place. The first concerned:

> Mohammed Rafiq, a factory owner who employed large numbers of Hungarians as a 'slave workforce' in his multi-million pound bed manufacturing business has today been sentenced to 27 months imprisonment for conspiracy to traffic.... The case came to light after two Hungarians, Janos Orsos and Ferenc Illes, were arrested and subsequently convicted of human trafficking charges.
>
> (CPS 2016)

Many retail companies supplying these beds would not have been aware that a slave workforce produced them. The entire supply chain is now required to ensure that they have made adequate checks concerning the employment status of workers who manufacture any goods supplied to them.

Vulnerable adults are perhaps the most vulnerable to slavery, forced labour and human trafficking, and local authority adult safeguarding practice guidance has been revised to take this into account. Nevertheless, it is a hidden problem for many vulnerable adults. However, in a recent review of progress to date, Townsend (2016) reports that:

> Efforts to eradicate modern slavery in the UK are failing, with the number of potential victims being trafficked into Britain rising by 245% over the last five years, according to official figures.... Police and other authorities identified 3,266 people last year thought to have been the victims of modern slavery compared with 946 in 2011, a rise that has prompted disquiet among MPs and charities.
>
> (2016, online)

It may be the case that practitioners are not recognising when vulnerable adults are experiencing forced labour or modern human slavery. However, it is much more likely that adults who become entrapped in slavery or forced labour are hidden in plain sight from practitioners who are in a position to take action to free them and meet their needs for protection. Recent examples of this include the case of 'Mary', described by Cheshire Police. Mary was persuaded to come to the UK from Nigeria with the promise of a job but was forced to work as a sex worker, kept as a modern human slave and attacked when she became pregnant (Cheshire Police 2017). A midwife visiting Mary concerning her pregnancy might understand that she is a sex worker but may not be aware that she has been trafficked unless Mary herself disclosed this.

There was global recognition of the need to agree an internationally recognised definition of human trafficking because this is an activity which crosses international borders (Dominelli 2010). The UN Convention against Transnational Organised Crime, known as 'The Palermo Protocol', was ratified in in UK law in 2006 and defines human trafficking. Article 3 of the convention defines human trafficking as:

> Trafficking in persons shall mean the recruitment, transportation, transfer, harbouring or receipt of persons, by means of the threat or use of force or other forms of coercion, of abduction, of fraud, of deception, of abuse of power or of a position of vulnerability or of the giving or receiving of payments or benefits to achieve the consent of a person having control of another person, for the purpose of exploitation. Exploitation shall include, at a minimum, the exploitation of the prostitution of others or other forms of sexual exploitation, forced labour or services, slavery or practices similar to slavery, servitude or removal of organs.
>
> (Palermo Protocol, online)

Local authorities' safeguarding practice guidance aims to identify potential victims who may be vulnerable to adult abuse. For example, Salford Local Adult Safeguarding Board suggests that practitioners need to consider that service users may be trafficked vulnerable adults when they are:

- people facing poverty in their countries of origin;
- people who are already victims of abuse in their countries of origin and believe this behaviour of abuse, power and control to be 'normal' and for some an improvement in their living conditions;

- learning disabled adults or children;
- orphaned children with no family support networks;
- minority groups;
- people of little or no education and unable to read or write in English and/or in their mother tongue;
- socially excluded;
- living in dysfunctional families;
- 'those who won't be missed'.

Local authorities recognise that one of the indicators listed by Salford may not in isolation be sufficient to become a victim of human trafficking or modern slavery; it is when these factors combine that vulnerable adults are at increased risk. Vulnerable adults are often socially excluded, living on the margins of society, and in many cases they have transient lifestyles. It is these factors that make them additionally vulnerable to those who wish to induce them into forced labour, trafficking and in some cases modern human slavery and it is a matter of social justice that society must seek to actively protect them.

Case example

Aisha typifies young adults who can become subject to human trafficking and forced labour. She is aged eighteen and has lost her whole family in her nation's civil war. She comes to England on a forged student visa arranged by a trafficker, who pretends to be her uncle. She knows that she is not going to study but become a domestic worker. However, when she arrives she finds she is to sleep in a large cupboard in a basement room in a large house; she is not given any money or allowed to go out, and she is expected to work sixteen-hour days cooking, cleaning and laundering for transient crews of agricultural workers. When some of the men sexually assault her, her complaints are not listened to and she is told to 'stop whining'. She does not speak or write English, and has been told that she must not under any circumstances contact the police or any other authorities, as they will immediately arrest her – she is a criminal who knew all along that she was not coming to England to study. When she is around eight months pregnant, her boss takes her to the hospital, proposing that she is his wife who has just arrived in England. The midwife who treats her is not able to understand the little that Aisha says, but it is clear that something is not quite right and, most of all, that Aisha is very frightened. The midwife calls an interpreter and encourages Aisha to tell her story, ensuring that this cannot be overheard by Aisha's 'husband'. It is at this point that Aisha asks for help.

Chapter summary

This chapter considered some of the key responsibilities and issues that local authorities must manage in terms of the care and protection of vulnerable adults. Social justice is a significant factor in their coordination and delivery of services to vulnerable adults, including the commissioning of services by third-sector providers, who must complete impact assessments, based on equality, as part of service-level agreements.

Adults can be or become vulnerable for a wide range of reasons, and in many cases they have complex health and social care needs and need a care package which reflects this. Local authorities must coordinate individual care packages based on sensitive practice and reflecting social justice principles of user empowerment, which avoids oppression and is ethical and fair.

Practitioners need to consistently manage the careful balance of power, personal autonomy and dignity needed in their partnership work with adult service users. The capacity to make informed decisions and maintain human rights are just as important to vulnerable adults as they are to the reader. The 'delicate balance' to ensure social justice principles are adhered to involves a capacity to assess the service users' abilities to make informed decisions in a way which does not deny their dignity or autonomy. Finally, we considered how domestic abuse, human trafficking and modern human slavery share aspects of coercive control which leave vulnerable adults without the capacity to change or improve their lives. Local authority practitioners play a key role in improving the lives of vulnerable adults in both the immediate and the long term, allowing them to lead full and independent lives. The role of local authorities, and the practitioners they employ, is vital in ensuring social justice is met through their own professional capacities to balance the dignity of service users with the skilful communication of relevant information, and the supportive context for decision-making which they are able to provide. Social justice in local authority settings for vulnerable adults, while being clear in principle, involves sensitive application of professional and interpersonal skills to be achieved in practice.

References

Adams, R., Dominelli, L. and Payne, M. (2009). Towards a critical understanding of social work. *Social Work: Themes, Issues and Critical Debates, 3*: 1–9.

ADASS (2013). *Safeguarding Adults: Advice and Guidance to Directors of Adult Social Services*, Advice Note 4. Online. Available at www.adass.org.uk/AdassMedia/stories/Policy%20Networks/Safeguarding_Adults/Key_Documents/LGA%20ADASS_SafeguardingAdviceAndGuidanceToDASS_Mar13.pdf (accessed 16 February 2017).

Age UK (2011). *Older People and Human Rights: a Reference Guide for Professionals Working with Older People*. Online. Available at www.ageuk.org.uk/documents/en-gb/for-professionals/equality-and-human rights/older_people_human_rights__expert_series_pro.pdf?dtrk=true. (accessed 4 April 2017).

Anderberg, P., Lepp, M., Berglund, A-L. and Segesten, K. (2007). Preserving dignity in caring for older adults: a concept analysis. *Journal of Advanced Nursing, 59*: 635–43. doi:10.1111/j.1365-2648.2007.04375.

Barry, M. (1998). 'Social exclusion and social work: an introduction', in Hallett (eds), *Social Work Theory and Social Work: Issues of Theory, Policy and Practice*. Lyme Regis: Russel House.

Burchardt, T., Obolenskaya, P. and Vizard, P. (2015). *The Coalition's Record on Adult Social Care: Policy, Spending and Outcomes 2010–2015*, Social Policy in Cold

Climate Working Paper No. 17. Online. Available at http://sticerd.lse.ac.uk/dps/case/spcc/WP17.pdf (accessed 15 February 2017).

Cheshire Police (2017). *Modern Slavery and Human Trafficking Case Studies*. Online. Available at www.cheshire.police.uk/advice-and-support/modern-slavery-and-human-trafficking/modern-slavery-and-human-trafficking-case-studies (accessed 11 May 2017).

Cleaver, H., Nicholson, D., Tarr, S. and Cleaver, D. (2007). *Child Protection, Domestic Violence and Parental Substance Misuse: Family Experiences and Effective Practice*. London: Jessica Kingsley.

Commission for Social Care Inspection (2008). *Safeguarding Adults. A Study of the Effectiveness of Arrangements to Safeguard Adults from Abuse*. Online. Available at www.cqc.org.uk (accessed 15 March 2017).

Cree, V.E. and Wallace, S. (2009). 'Risk and Protection', in R. Adams, L. Dominelli and M. Payne (eds) *Practicing Social Work in a Complex World* (2nd Ed.). London: Palgrave Macmillan.

Crown Prosecution Service (CPS). (2016). *Mohammed Rafiq Prosecution*. Online. Available at www.cps.gov.uk/news/latest_news/bed_manufacturer_jailed_for_27_months_for_conspiracy_to_traffic_people/index.html (accessed 13 April 2017).

Department of Health (March 2000). *No Secrets: Guidance on Developing and Implementing Multi-agency Policies and Procedures to Protect Vulnerable Adults from Abuse*. Online. Available at www.dh.gov.uk/prod_consum_dh/groups/dh_digitalassets/@dh/@en/documents/digitalasset/dh_4074540.pdf (accessed 16 February 2017).

Department of Health (2005). Mental Capacity Act. Online. Available at www.legislation.gov.uk/ukpga/2005/9/pdfs/ukpga_20050009_en.pdf (accessed 4 April 2017).

Department of Health (2014). Care Act 2014. Online. Available at www.legislation.gov.uk/ukpga/2014/23/contents/enacted/data.htm (accessed 16 February 2017).

Department of Health (2015). *Care and Support Policy Guidance*. Online. Available at www.gov.uk/government/publications/care-and-support-whats-changing/care-and-support-whats-changing (accessed 17 February 2017).

Department of Health (2016). *Mental Capacity Act Code of Practice*. Online. Available at www.gov.uk/government/publications/mental-capacity-act-code-of-practice (accessed 13 April 2017).

Derbyshire.gov.uk (n.d.) *10 Point Dignity Challenge*. Online. Available at www.derbyshire.gov.uk/social_health/care_and_health_service_providers/dignity_respect/default.asp (accessed 11 April 2017).

Dignity in Care (n.d.) www.scie.org.uk/publications/guides/guide15/factors/index.asp (accessed 4 April 2017).

Dominelli, L. (1 Sept 2010). Globalisation, contemporary challenges and social work practice. *International Social Work*, *53*(5): 599–612.

Duncan Smith, I. (2012). *Social Justice: Transforming Lives*. Online. Available at www.gov.uk/government/speeches/social-justice-transforming-lives (accessed 10 May 2017).

Elmer, S. (Winter 2013). Marginalised children in marginalised communities: the challenges for early years and parenting support services where there is domestic violence. *North East Branch Newsletter*. British Psychological Society.

Equality and Human Rights Commission (2016). *Is England Fairer? The State of Equality and Human Rights 2016*. Online. Available at www.equalityhumanrights (accessed 4 April 2017).

Hatton, K. (2008). *New Direction in Social Work Practice*. Exeter: Learning Matters.

Hollomotz, A. (2011). *Learning Difficulties and Sexual Vulnerability*. London: Jessica Kingsley.

Home Office (2015). Modern Slavery Act 2015. Online. Available at www.legislation.gov.uk/ukpga/2015/30/pdfs/ukpga_20150030_en.pdf (accessed 13 April 2017).

Local Government Association *Care Act Statutory Guidance*. Online. Available at www.local.gov.uk/care-support-reform/-/journal_content/56/10180/7740017/ARTICLE (accessed 17 February 2017).

Mullender, A. (2009). *Children Exposed to Domestic Violence and the Challenges Ahead.* Online. Available at http://journals.sagepub.com/doi/abs/10.1177/1468017309350663 (accessed 11 April 2017).

O'Sullivan, T. (2010). *Decision Making in Social Work* (2nd Ed.). Houndslow: Palgrave Macmillan.

Torn, A. (2017). 'Nursing the adult', in A. Torn and P. Greasley (eds) *Psychology for Nursing*. Cambridge: Polity.

Transnational Organised Crime (Palermo Protocol). *International Definition of Human Trafficking*. Online. Available at http://palermoprotocol.com (accessed 13 April 2017).

SCIE (2013). *Dignity in Care*. Online. Available at www.scie.org.uk/publications/guides/guide15 (accessed 4 April 2017).

Salford Local Adult Safeguarding Board *Trafficking Guidance*. Online. Available at www.partnersinsalford.org/asg-trafficking.htm (accessed 13 April 2017).

Stark, E. (2007). *Re-presenting Battered Women: Coercive Control and the Defence of Liberty*. Online. Available at www.stopvaw.org/uploads/evan_stark_article_final_100812.pdf (accessed 10 May 2017).

Townsend, M. (2016). Modern slavery and human trafficking on the rise in the UK. *Guardian*, 10 July 2016. Online. Available at www.theguardian.com/law/2016/jul/10/modern-slavery-on-rise-in-uk (accessed 5 April 2017).

Thompson, N. (2006). *Anti-discriminatory Practice*. Basingstoke: Palgrave Macmillan.

Wittenberg, R., Ettelt, S., Williams, L., Damant, J., Lombard, D., Perkins, M. and Mays, N. (2017). *Evaluation of Direct Payments in Residential Care Trailblazers*, Policy Research Innovation Unit Final Report.

Further reading

Derbyshire Dignity Challenge: www.dignityincare.org.uk/About/The_10_Point_Dignity_Challenge.

Equality and Human Rights Act (2010): www.equalityhumanrights.com/en/equality-act/equality-act-2010.

Modern human slavery: www.gov.uk/government/news/home-office-to-be-notified-on-modern-slavery-cases; www.lancashire.police.uk/news/2017/march/three-men-jailed-for-human-trafficking-in-victimless-prosecution.

Palermo Protocol: www.unodc.org/documents/treaties/UNTOC/Publications/TOC%20Convention/TOCebook-e.pdf.

Social justice and restorative practice: www.leeds.gov.uk/docs/Civic%20enterprise%20in%20action.pdf.

Social justice policy: www.gov.uk/government/uploads/system/uploads/attachment_data/file/49515/social-justice-transforming-lives.pdf.

Safeguarding adults: www.gov.uk/government/uploads/system/uploads/attachment_data/file/197402/Statement_of_Gov_Policy.pdf.

SCIE publications: www.scie.org.uk/publications/guides/guide15/dignitychallenge/index.asp.

12 Children, young people and sport

Graham Turner

Introduction

Participation in sport is advocated as a means to foster mutually beneficial relations and to introduce young people to shared values and norms of behaviour (Griffiths and Armour 2013). In the UK, the nature and focus of sporting provision are differentiated according to participation or performance orientation, hence the young person's sporting experience is shaped according to their context of enactment. This has led to the creation of alternative environments where practice is constructed according to the expectations and priorities of society. This chapter discusses participation in each context, specifically drawing upon the young person's view of participation in the talent development environment to invoke consideration of interaction between the adult and the young person in this distinct social context.

Sport and participation

In the UK sporting context, social justice is typically considered in relation to the principle of inclusion and so where differential opportunity to participate has the potential to disadvantage the concept of equity has been brought into focus (Elling and Claringbould 2005). This concept is now embedded within the National Coaching Framework and the vision of the National Coaching Foundation signifies that inclusion is a key underpinning principle: 'The vision of the UK Coaching Framework is to create a cohesive, ethical, inclusive and valued coaching system where skilled coaches support children, players and athletes at all stages of their development' (Sportscoach UK 2009: 3).

In the UK, the government's belief in the value of sports participation to the nation's young people is reinforced through policy specifically designed to 'raise the proportion of 14 to 25 year olds who play sport' (Sport England 2012: 3). This comes on the back of empirical research that has estimated that levels of physical activity begin to decline during childhood by about 7 per cent and that this decline continues through adolescence for both boys and girls (Brooke *et al.* 2014). Neuroscience explains how during adolescence the young person's brain changes through interaction with the social and physical environment and is then moulded through experience and relationship to enable the individual to develop an understanding of self and become autonomous (Laursen 2009).

Critical exploration of young people's engagement in society has sought to interrogate the boundary between child and adulthood and participative research has emerged to reflect a discourse attending to power and agency (Holland *et al.* 2010; Nutbrown and Clough 2009). As the conditions of contemporary childhood have changed, critics have claimed that we should not assume that children and young people are dependent on adults but instead recognise their ability both to influence and give meaning to interaction (Christensen and Prout 2002; Semi 2011). Conceptions of the young person should not therefore be determined in accordance with connection to or membership of a social group, but childhood and adolescence should instead be recognised as a product of generational rather than structural processes and regarded as a phenomenon that is subject to multiple 'generational orderings' (Prout 2011). The concept of generational ordering depicts an open-ended process of influence that accounts for how different versions of child or adult may interact to produce different versions of child or adult. This concept does not assume that the process of generational ordering must persist with a natural order and, likewise, does not assume that childhood should proceed at a particular pace. Instead it is premised on the belief that the capacity of the child to act and influence is determined by his or her individual circumstances, experience and knowledge. In this conception, capacity is not correlated with age and instead autonomy is supported by a mix of maturity and experience which develops to allow the young person to form an opinion and then think through the consequences of their actions (Burke 2010).

In the UK, sports policy has been developed to target the time at which the young person begins to exert greater control over the nature of their engagement and government strategy now articulates 'an increased focus on youth sport' (Sport England, Strategy Outline, DCMS 2012). This strategy supports divergent pathways of participation and context of enactment now places emphasis upon the creation of a sporting system that relies upon the provision of quality coaches and the creation of bespoke environments designed to cater to the wants and needs of sporting participants within distinct populations (Sportscoach UK 2009).

Nomenclature

In the UK, the nature and focus of sporting provision for children and young people represent the transmission of socially constructed conventions where participation is now subject to differentiation according to context of enactment. This is a notion that is reinforced by the names given to the different areas of research and scholarly activity in the published literature in sport known as participant development and talent development. The choice of a particular word or term that is used within a scientific discipline or specialist field is defined as nomenclature. Nomenclature is significant to treatment of the phenomenon because in practice it informs understanding, supports accurate decision-making and determines intervention. In medicine, for example, analysis has demonstrated that current nomenclature is often derived from historical understanding and treatment is enacted according to traditional conception (Larson *et al.* 2005). In the medical field, research enquiry has revealed the potential of scientific endeavour to produce new knowledge, identify limitation and expose gaps in understanding to challenge current nomenclature. When this has happened, treatment has been reviewed, intervention has been modified and outcomes have been improved (Larson *et al.* 2005). Interrogation of nomenclature is therefore important to consideration of how treatment of the young person in sport may be orchestrated according to the design of a specific context and how particular types of interaction may have distinct implications for the experience of the young person: 'The conditions of the living context result from interaction between an individual and the structures of society' (Jakobsson *et al.* 2014: 208).

In the sporting context, nomenclature appears to represent a simple and obvious distinction where the words 'participant' and 'talent' have been chosen to represent different types of population and the construction of each term is the result of a practicable exercise. Viewed from a social perspective, however, it appears that nomenclature in sport reflects a distinction in the way that the interests of society are prioritised in relation to the interests of young people according to the context of participation. From an alternative view, this difference represents a social perspective, a perspective that reflects the commitments that were made to the child in the Geneva Declaration (United Nations 1924), where the conception is determined according to consideration of what society can offer the child or young person balanced against what the young person might be able to give back. It is therefore important to consider if in sport nomenclature reflects a difference in context that is represented by the way that society treats the young person compared to the young person with talent.

The Rights of the Child

In 1924 the League of Nations published the Geneva Declaration of the Rights of the Child in recognition of the obligation of mankind to provide the child with 'the best that it has to give' (United Nations 1924: 1). The League of Nations came into being after World War I and, although the primary function was to maintain peace through the brokering of agreement to resolve international dispute, it also worked to promote social equity (League of Nations n.d.). The Geneva Declaration represented an agreement between the forty-two original member nations and enshrined five commitments to the child:

1 The child must be given the means requisite for its normal development, both materially and spiritually;
2 The child that is hungry must be fed; the child that is sick must be nursed; the child that is backward must be helped; the delinquent child must be reclaimed; and the orphan and the waif must be sheltered and succoured;
3 The child must be the first to receive relief in times of distress;

4 The child must be put in a position to earn a livelihood, and must be protected against every form of exploitation;
5 The child must be brought up in the consciousness that its talents must be devoted to the service of fellow men.

(United Nations 1924: 1)

Created against the backdrop of war, these commitments served to represent a visionary agreement to provide for the contemporary needs of the world's children. World leaders recognised the need to secure protection and provision for children, but the child's right to participation had yet to be established (United Nations 2009). The 1924 declaration originated from a patriarchal society where children were subservient and discrimination by adults against children was the accepted norm (Shier 2012). In essence, this declaration represented governments' desire and intention to orientate childhood towards preparation for the needs of the labour market (Reynaert *et al.* 2012).

Sport and participant development

In a world where life chances are not equal, governments continue to pursue a common responsibility to promote the mental and physical well-being of all children and young people (Bhui *et al.* 2010). In sport, this mission has been supported across the globe by the International Olympic Movement, which promotes sports participation and the Olympic ideal, 'to create a way of life based on the joy of effort, the educational value of good example and respect for universal fundamental ethical principles' (IOC 2011: 3).

The modern Olympic movement was founded in France by Pierre de Coubertin. Coubertin was a prominent figure in French society during the second half of the nineteenth century. He had a particular interest in the way that society worked and he was concerned by the social problems of the time (Martínez-Gorroño and Hernández-Álvarez 2014). During this period, industrialisation had changed the structure of society, people were moving to live in newly created large urban centres and there became a need for new ways for people to meet and socialise; this need was termed 'la sociabilité'. Coubertin advocated the use of sports participation to effect social change and promoted Olympism and the Olympic ideal to pursue social reform (Light and Lémonie 2010). The Olympic movement was designed to support the pursuit of a better and more peaceful world through the education of youth to promote friendship, understanding, solidarity and fair play (Corral *et al.* 2010). This idea was based on educational practice that originated in male boarding schools in England, where sport was practised to promote moral and social development (Chatziefstathiou 2002). Coubertin pursued an ambition to make sport a main feature of the education of children and young people and saw Olympic competition as a way to provide an international perspective to the power of sport to educate the body and the mind (Lucas 1974). Coubertin's lasting contribution was to locate the values of humanism and universalism in the context of sport and education to emphasise 'equality, fairness, justice, respect, rationality, international understanding, peace, autonomy and excellence' (Chatziefstathiou 2002: 386).

More recently, belief in the far-reaching effect and influence of sport and sports participation on and within society has been reinforced by the European Commission White Paper on Sport (2007), which proposed sporting initiative to foster social inclusion, improve health, and enhance education. Publication of this policy underlined a move to support young people to expand their social networks to maximise the potential for social engagement to confer collective benefit (Kay and Bradbury 2009). In the UK, the use of sports-based intervention continues to reflect the belief that sports participation has the potential to improve the lives of young people through a process of connection, engagement and empowerment (Kay and Bradbury 2009). Sport in the community is regarded as a focus for social action (Griffiths and Armour 2013) and research suggests that sports participation has the potential to impact upon social and moral development, lifestyle choice and aspiration (Holroyd and Armour 2003). Sports-based interventions now draw from a growing evidence base that advocates participation in sport to educate children and young people about fairness and to help them learn how to build a respectful culture (Ladda 2014). Such intervention adheres to the principle of social justice for mutual benefit by attending to both the good of society – engaging young people through recognition of youth culture and allocation of resource to utilise sports participation as a means of social intervention – and the needs of the individual, by providing children and young people with the opportunity to strive to achieve their own personal potential (Ladda 2014).

Sport and talent development

The original Geneva Declaration made five commitments to the child (United Nations 1924). While the first four sought to establish the rights of the child through confirmation of society's responsibility for and to the child, the fifth commitment articulated the imposition of a demand, changing the emphasis from provision to obligation to impress upon the talented child the nature of their individual responsibility: '5. The child must be brought up in the consciousness that its talents must be devoted to the service of fellow men' (United Nations 1924: 1). This commitment reflects a conception of social justice where, although society may advocate a process of engagement that relies upon the principle of mutual obligation (Kamtekar 2001), in reality the essence of that obligation is inevitably determined by context of enactment that is constructed according to the wants and needs, and priorities and ambitions of a patriarchal society (Griggs and Biscomb 2010). Such situations shape the priority given to and status associated with the child or young person according to the context of their participation (Pot and van Hilvoorde 2013) and, in sport, transition to the talent development environment marks the point at which the dynamic of interaction between young person and adult begins to shape a different type of experience.

Within the context of sport, commodity status is conferred to children and young people by talent development programmes that stay loyal to ability but only commit to the young person for as long as their talent trajectory is maintained (UK Sport 2014). Allegiance to talent is a phenomenon that has been shared by academics and practitioners alike, who, when engaging in the process and practice of talent development in sport, have deferred the interests of the participant to prioritise the pursuit of evidence to improve sports performance (Bishop *et al.* 2006): 'Identifying talent in athletes and developing that ability to its fullest potential is a central concern of sport scientists, sports coaches and sports policy makers.' (www.routledge.com 2014).

From the social perspective, it may be contended that the time of talent identification demarcates a point at which societal interests diverge and, for the child with 'talent' a change in the emphasis of engagement becomes legitimised by interaction that changes to concentrate upon what the child can do. In a reality where talent is coveted this practice has come to represent a unique process of social exchange (Ribarsky 2013) whereby the adult's desire to associate with the talent phenomenon has acted to reinforce process and perpetuate social convention. Accordingly, the young person has become subject to a reality where treatment has a different emphasis and experience takes on a new meaning. It is therefore important to consider if orientation towards talent may have led the adult to emphasise an interest in context that has legitimised focus on process and outcome for sport rather than the interests and experience of the child or young person.

Equity

When a young person engages with an adult, adult perception of the ability of the child is the foremost barrier to the child's participation and adult self-interest will often orientate adult behaviour towards maintaining status in respect to the child (Lambert *et al.* 2011). 'The first inequality in life is that of child and adult' (Erikson 1981: 106). The concept of equity is concerned with equal treatment and outcome (Bessant 2008) and when consideration of the involvement of children in adult culture is examined through the lens of a human rights perspective social scientists confirm the need for recognition that children play an active role in construction, co-construction and reconstruction of not only their own lives but also the lives of the adults with whom they interact (Rajabi-Ardeshiri 2011). In practice, in order for a child to become a member of a democratic society the child must first experience democracy, for if when engaging with the child we automatically require them to learn what it is to defer to the adult then we reinforce the fact that they are not yet equal (Earnshaw 2014). This premise demands that the principle of equity be considered in relation to equality among children and in relation to the relationship between children and adults (Shier 2012) for, while in principle it is a fundamental right of the young person to be able to influence and to have his or her voice heard, in the talent development environment in sport this right is not routinely applied (Turner 2016). It is therefore pertinent to examine intersections of engagement in sport to consider the nature of this experience for young people who participate in the context of talent.

Authority

Once inducted into the talent development environment the participant becomes subject to the influence of authority and in return for the opportunity to participate each young person must accept greater accountability and reduced control (Turner 2016). Authority relates to the probability of a command being obeyed by a specific person or group of people and involves hierarchy, obedience and command (Coleman 1988). Empirical studies have proven that obedience is subject to situational influence and level of obedience can be determined by contextual factors (Auzolt 2015). Thus, talented young people become subject to pressure exerted by adults who try to influence them to act in accordance with their wishes. Here Eboni (a seventeen-year-old female participating in a netball talent development programme) provides an example of just such an interaction:

AUTHOR: Can you think of anything where you've gone along with things that you didn't necessarily think were the best way?

EBONI: Yeah, erm. We had a tournament, like a really small tournament a few weeks ago and they said, 'cause we lost one of the matches ... 'You have more of a chance of winning the whole thing, if we throw this match.'

AUTHOR: Oh, really?

EBONI: And I was like, well what would be the point, why would we not? 'Cause if we won the match we'd have to play the first of the next group. If we lost the match we'd have to play the second of the next group. So if we won the second we'd have more likely of a chance of going on, getting further on in the tournament. So a few of us were like, well no, 'cause it's just wrong.

AUTHOR: Yeah.

EBONI: And in the end I think, she kept, she ended up switching and because we kind of said to her, 'Well it's a bit wrong, we just want to play, we don't really mind about winning that much.' And she ended up switching all our positions, so we were all out of place. So it kind of ended up us throwing the match and not by our own choice in a way.

AUTHOR: Oh, okay. So you did lose it then?

EBONI: No, I think we ended up drawing. So we didn't end up going any further anyway. So it was kind of like karma.

This example shows how, in the context of talent, the authority of the coach may constitute a form of subordination where the subordinator assumes the right to influence the nature of the individual's sporting participation. Analysis of such interaction has demonstrated that the distribution of power among different social units can be viewed as interaction between controller and responder (Dahl 1957) and within this type of relation the controller demarcates a clear line to distinguish the position of domination. Young people's experiences reveal that the power dynamic within the talent development environment is such that when the objectives of the coach and participant do not align participation for the young person may feel more like compulsion, for within the talent development hierarchy adult status is secure and there is no requirement to justify to the subordinate (Lukes 2005). Steve (a sixteen-year-old male participating in a rugby union talent development programme) reveals just what this experience can be like for the young person:

AUTHOR: So how aware of your injury situation was #######?

STEVE: Yes he knew, he said to me before if it hurts don't do it but don't use it as an excuse not to do it and from that I took it well I'm going to have to do it then.

AUTHOR: So were you feeling it in the session?

STEVE: Yes, but I just kept running because of what he said. I probably made it worse.

AUTHOR: So from your perspective then, why is that?

STEVE: It is because if you want to impress the coach, then you do not want to say, 'Oh I'm injured can I drop out?' You just want to keep playing because you don't want to look silly not doing it.

Steve's example shows how in the context of talent the young person can be exposed to a situation where the wants and needs of the adult may relegate consideration of their best interests and when this happens, if the young person perceives that the influence of the adult is important they will not want to risk conveying a negative impression (Payne 2011). It is within such a power dynamic that the authority of the adult teaches the young person to accept the position of a subordinate (Holland *et al.* 2010) and George (a sixteen-year-old male athlete and also member of a rugby union talent development programme) explains why this is so:

GEORGE: You're pretty much talking to the guys that are gonna decide whether you're gonna become a professional player or not. So you don't want to say anything that's gonna put you in a bad spot with them really.

Coaches and young people

Within the talent development environment interaction relies upon an intersection of structure (institutional norms, rules and beliefs) and agency (the ability of the individual to act in their own best interests) to promote individual autonomy and effect positive change (Pettit 2012). New conceptions of the way that adults, children and young people interact now signify the principle of participation; however, participation alone does not constitute an end in itself, rather participation is essential to afford young people the opportunity to raise individual issues and to address personal challenges that are specific to their own lived experience of childhood (Fleming 2013). The essence of the young person's experience of participation within a talent development programme in sport resides within the social conditions of their lived reality and ultimately for each young person this experience is determined by the way they are treated by adults (Turner 2016). In this context, enactment of social justice is determined by the nature of engagement between young person and adult and legitimate interaction is dependent upon the development of symmetrical relations. Symmetrical relations require that an adult is willing and able to concede a position of power and learn to listen and accept the opinion of the young person.

STEVE: Yes, they are much better, much better coaches, yes.

AUTHOR: OK, so what makes you say that then?

STEVE: They have one on one conversations with you about things like what they want you to do next game or how the last game went and they seem like they care a bit more and they are actually happy that we have done well.

EBONI: I spoke to my coach recently and said 'Well I don't really the see the point in doing it anymore if I'm not going to get any further' so then we had a talk and she said I need to improve my fitness, which I did, and I needed to get to the next step and go through regional for another half a year, so I can get moved up to the next level which is RPA. So she has moved me up again, so I am half in regional and half in RPA.

AUTHOR: Do you think he [your Athletics Coach] stepped it up as well? You said, 'I'm serious.' And suddenly he's thought, oh right …

GEORGE: Yeah, definitely. Yeah as soon as he saw I was sort of making decisions to focus on it a lot more, he's given me a lot more time and he's given me a lot more focus.

The concept of empowerment comes from the Latin word *potere* which means 'to be able' (Grealish *et al.* 2013) and empowerment is defined as the process that enables an individual to make an informed decision, exercise their own choice and take charge of their life (Grealish *et al.* 2013). For the young person in the talent development environment, empowerment requires a sharing of power and when this is realised it can enhance both individual and collective capacity, support the development of self-efficacy and promote well-being (Lawson 2005). Empowerment for young people is therefore reliant upon the establishment of democratic relations where interaction is built upon communication and collaboration.

Conclusion

While sports participation has the potential to connect, engage and empower (Kay and Bradbury 2009), in the UK the young person's sporting experience is differentiated according to participation in a specific sporting context. Young people's accounts of engagement with adults in the talent development environment demonstrate that, in this context, in order to promote equity between young person and adult there remains a need for adults to become more conscious of how their interactions influence the young person's experience. Effective engagement in collective action therefore requires that the adult must better learn to listen to and engage with the young person's perspective.

References

Auzolt, L. (2015). Autonomy and resistance to authority. *Swiss Journal of Psychology, 74*(1): 49–53.

Bessant, J. (2008). Age and equity: a case for an intergenerational charter. *Journal of Australian Studies, 32*(3): 361–73.

Bhui, K.S. Admasachew, L.A. and Persaud, A. (2010). The promotion of children's health and wellbeing: the contributions of England's charity sector. *BMC Research Notes, 3*: 188–92.

Bishop, D. Burnett, A. Farrow, D. Gabbett, T. and Newton, R. (2006). Sports-science roundtable: does sports-science research influence practice? *International Journal of Sports Physiology & Performance, 1*(2): 161–8.

Brooke, H.L. Corder, K. Griffin, S.J. and Sluijs, E.M.F. (2014). Physical activity maintenance in the transition to adolescence: a longitudinal study of the roles of sport and lifestyle activities in British youth. *PLoS ONE, 9*(2): 1–8.

Burke, T. (2010). *Participation Works. The Children's Rights Alliance for England.* Online. Available at www.participationworks.org.uk (accessed 8 February 2014).

Chatziefstathiou, D. (2002). Olympic education and beyond: olympism and value legacies from the Olympic and Paralympic Games. *Educational Review, 64*(3): 385–400.

Christensen, P. and Prout, A. (2002). Working with ethical symmetry in social research with children. *Childhood, 9*(4): 477–97.

Coleman, J.A. (1988). Social capital in the creation of human capital. *The American Journal of Sociology, 94* (Supplement: Organizations and Institutions: Sociological and Economic Approaches to the Analysis of Social Structure): 95–120. Online. Available at www.jstor.org/stable/2780243 (accessed 26 March 2015).

Corral, C.D. Pérez-Turpin, J.A. Vidal, A.M. Padorno, C.M., Patiño, M.J.M. and Molina, A.G. (2010). Principles of the Olympic movement. *Journal of Human Sport & Exercise, 5*(1): 3–12.

Dahl, R.A. (1957). The concept of power. *Behavioural Science, 2*(3): 201–15.

Earnshaw, E. (2014). Learning to be a child: a conceptual analysis of youth empowerment. *Educational & Child Psychology, 31*(1): 13–21.

Elling, A. and Claringbould, I. (2005). Mechanisms of inclusion and exclusion in the Dutch sports landscape: who can and wants to belong? *Sociology of Sport Journal, 22*(4): 498–515.

Erikson, E.H. and Erikson, J. (1981). On generativity and identity: from a conversation with Erik and Joan Erikson. *Harvard Educational Review, 51*(2): 249–69.

European Commission White Paper on Sport (2007). Online. Available at http://eur-lex.europa.eu/legal-content/EN/TXT/?uri=CELEX%3A52007DC0391 (accessed 23 March 2014).

Fleming, J. (2013). Young people's participation – where next? *Children and Society, 27*: 484–95.

Grealish, A. Tai, S. Hunter, A. and Morrison, A.P. (2013). Qualitative exploration of empowerment from the perspective of young people with psychosis. *Clinical Psychology and Psychotherapy, 20*: 136–48.

Griffiths, M. and Armour, K. (2013). Physical education and youth sport in England: conceptual and practical foundations for an Olympic legacy? *International Journal of Sport Policy*, *5*(2): 213–27.

Griggs, G. and Biscomb, K. (2010). Theresa Bennett is 42 ... but what's new? *Soccer and Society*, *11*(5): 668–76.

Holland, S. Renold, E. Ross, N. and Hillman, A. (2010). Power, agency and participatory agendas: a critical exploration of young people's engagement in participative qualitative research. *Childhood*, *17*(3), 360–75.

Holroyd R.A. and Armour, K.M. (2003). *Re-engaging Disaffected Youth through Physical Activity Programs*. British Educational Research Association Annual Conference, Heriot-Watt University, Edinburgh, 11–13 September. Online. Available at www.leeds.ac.uk/educol/documents/00003304.htm (accessed 1 February 2014).

IOC (2011). When sport can change the world. *International Olympic Committee*. Online. Available at https://stillmed.olympic.org/Documents/Olympic_Museum/Education/DPHOPE/DP_Hope_EN_web.pdf (accessed 1 February 2015).

Jakobsson, B.T. Lundvull, S. and Redelius, K. (2014). Reasons to stay in club sport according to 19 year old Swedish participants: a salutogenic approach. *Sport Science Review*, *23*(5–6): 205–24.

Kamtekar, R. (2001). Social justice and happiness in the Republic: Plato's two principles. *History of Political Thought*, *22*(2): 189–220.

Kay, T. and Bradbury, S. (2009). Youth sport volunteering and the development of social capital in sport. *Education and Society*, *14*(1): 27–35.

Larson, E.E. Barrett, S.L. Battiston, B. Maloney, C.T. Jr, and Dellon, A.L. (2005). Accurate nomenclature for forefoot nerve entrapment: a historical perspective. *Journal of the American Podiatry Medical Association*, *95*(3): 298–306.

Ladda, S. (2014). Using sport for social change: theory into practice. *The Journal of Physical Education, Recreation & Dance*, *85*(6): 7–11.

Lambert, V. Glacken, M. and McCarron, M. (2011). Communication between children and health professionals in a child hospital setting: a child transitional communication model. *Journal of Advanced Nursing*, *67*(3): 569–82.

Laursen, E.K. (2009). Positive youth cultures and the developing brain. *Reclaiming Children & Youth*, *18*(2): 8–11.

Lawson, H.A. (2005). Empowering people, facilitating community development, and contributing to sustainable development: the social work of sport, exercise and physical education programs. *Sport Education and Society*, *10*(1): 135–60.

League of Nations Archives (n.d.). The United Nations Office at Geneva (UNOG). Online. Available at www.unog.ch/80256EE60057D930/(httpHomepages)/60249FAB9674BFA0C1256F560035AB55?OpenDocument (accessed 9 January 2013).

Light, R. and Lémonie, Y. (2010). A case study on children's reasons for joining and remaining in a French swimming club. *Asian Journal of Exercise & Sports Science*, *7*(1): 27–33.

Lucas, J.A. (1974). The modern Olympic games: fanfare and philosophy, 1896–1972. *Quest*, *22*(1), 6–18.

Lukes, S. (2005). *Power: a Radical View* (2nd Ed.). Basingstoke: Palgrave Macmillan.

Martínez-Gorroño, M.E. and Hernández-Álvarez, J.L. (2014). The free institute of education and Pierre De Coubertin: physical education to educate within liberty. *Revista Internacional de Medicina y Ciencias de la Actividad Física y del Deporte*, *14*(54): 243–63.

Nutbrown, C. and Clough, P. (2009). Citizenship and inclusion in the early years: understanding and responding to children's perspectives on 'belonging'. *International Journal of Early Years Education*, *17*(3): 191–206.

Payne, S.M. (2011). *Impression Management & Self-Presentation in Sport: Measurement, Process & Consequences*. Unpublished PhD thesis, Aberystwyth University.

Pettit, J. (2012). Empowerment and participation: bridging the gap between understanding and practice. *Institute of Development Studies*. Online. Available at www.un.org/esa/socdev/egms/docs/2012/JethroPettit.pdf (accessed 7 August 2015).

Pot, N. and Van Hilvoorde, I. (2013). Generalising the effects of school sports: comparing the cultural contexts of school sports in the Netherlands and the USA. *Sport in Society*, *16*(9): 1164–75.

Prout, A. (2011). Taking a step away from modernity: reconsidering the new sociology of childhood. *Global Studies of Childhood*, *1*(1): 4–14.

Rajabi-Ardeshiri, M. (2011). Children and conflict: exploring children's agency at UK mosque schools. *International Journal of Children's Rights*, *19*(4): 691–704.

Reynaert, D. Bie, M. and Vandevelde, S. (2012). Between 'believers' and 'opponents': critical discussions on children's rights. *International Journal of Children's Rights*, *20*(1): 155–68.

Ribarsky, E. (2013). Choose your own adventure: examining social exchange theory and relational choices. *Communication Teacher*, *27*(1): 29–32.

Semi, R. (2011). *Social Capital and Young People*, National Centre for Vocational Education Research. Online. Available at www.ncver.edu.au/__data/assets/file/0019/7660/lsay_briefingreport26_2400.pdf (accessed 23rd March 2015).

Shier, H. (2012). What does 'equality' mean for children in relation to adults? Addressing inequalities. The heart of the post-2015 development agenda and the future we want for all Global Thematic Consultation. Online. Available at www.worldwewant2015.org/file/284010/download/307867 (accessed 25 March 2015).

Sport England (2012). *Creating a Sporting Habit for Life*. London: Department for Culture Media and Sport. Online. Available at www.sportengland.org (accessed 30 November 2014).

Sportscoach UK (2009). *The UK Coaching Workforce 2009–2016. The National Coaching Foundation*. Online. Available at www.sportscoachuk.org/sites/default/files/pdm_user_guide_final_july_2009_790[1].pdf (accessed 4 September 2015).

Sportscoach UK (2015). *Participant Modelling*. Online. Available at www.sportscoachuk.org/resource/participant-modelling (accessed 14 October 2013).

Turner, G. (2016). *'Talent' Mentalities: Young People's Experience of Being in a Sports Talent Development Programme*. Unpublished PhD thesis, Liverpool John Moores University.

UK Sport (2014). *The UK's High Performance Sports Agency*. Online. Available at www.uksport.gov.uk (accessed 30 November 2014).

United Nations (1924). Geneva Declaration of the Rights of the Child of 1924. Online. Available at www.un-documents.net/gdrc1924.html (accessed 7 January 2013).

United Nations (2009). Convention on the Rights of the Child. Online. Available at www.coe.int/t/dg3/children/participation/CRC-C-GC-12.pdf (accessed 12 April 2013).

www.routledge.com (2014). *Talent Identification and Development in Sport*. Online. Available at www.routledge.com/books/details/9780415581615 (accessed 17 February 2015).

Part IV

Perspectives on education

13 Social justice in our schools

A need to reconceptualise ideas and classroom practice

Jonathan Doherty

Introduction

On 22 April 1993, black teenager Stephen Lawrence was fatally stabbed by a gang of white youths at a London bus stop. He was eighteen years old. Two men were subsequently found guilty of his murder and are currently serving prison sentences. The actual investigation into his death was confused with insecure evidence and allegations of police misconduct and led to two important changes in social justice legislation: the Race Relations Amendment Act 2000 and the Criminal Justice Act 2003. In 2016, further evidence came to light in the case. The road to justice for parents who have campaigned relentlessly for justice since their son's death has been long. Such was their belief in the need to educate, rather than punish, young people that they set up the Stephen Lawrence Education Trust to challenge racism in all areas and champion the transforming value of education. Speaking at Leeds Trinity University in November 2014, mother Doreen, now Baroness, Lawrence said, 'education is the most precious gift we can give our children. Understandably, without it we cannot achieve social justice'.

On 12 October 2012 in Aslamabad, Malala Yousafzai, a fourteen-year-old Pakistani girl, was shot and critically injured by a Taliban gunman on a school bus on her way home from school because of her public views on girls' education. Following her recovery she became a household name and an ardent campaigner for girls' rights to education. A year later, her speech to the United Nations contained these powerful words:

> let us wage, so let us wage a glorious struggle against illiteracy, poverty and terrorism, let us pick up our books and our pens, they are the most powerful weapons. One child, one teacher, one book and one pen can change the world. Education is the only solution. Education first.

Malala is now a strong voice in the global Education for All movement and the youngest person ever to win a Nobel Prize.

Have these two sad accounts changed our view of what education stands for? Can these lamentable incidents give us new hope for the transforming power of social justice in education? Arguably, one of the biggest challenges facing today's educators is how schools can work more equitably for all students in diverse classrooms (Kaur 2012). As teachers, we share a strong moral purpose to provide the best education for children and any system that advantages one child over another because of colour, social class, gender or language is discriminatory and inequitable. Yet, with the dominance of neo-liberalism that is undermining how teaching is perceived and indeed measured, that is a vision which is being eroded, leaving schools with very real challenges. Standardised testing, increasingly narrowed curricula and more teacher accountability with a focus on student outcomes (Zeichner 2010) has undermined responses to social justice and equity in schools. Young people everywhere, like Malala and Stephen in the opening vignettes, are entitled to an education experience that is fair to all, is respectful and develops their personality and abilities so they can flourish to the full. Social justice in education is not restricted to schools and their curricula. It is an imperative that extends beyond the school gates and is about promoting whole societies that are just, which value diversity and challenge injustices.

Social justice in education is far from an agreed term, to the extent it appears quite ambiguous (Gerwitz 1998). From a number of writers on social justice (e.g. Cochran-Smith 2004; Hackman 2005; Villegas and Lucas 2002; Zeichner 2003) it is possible to distil the main elements of social justice within education and simplify it to enhancing students' education and life experiences by challenging inequalities that exist in schools and the wider society. If we were to 'tag' this in common parlance today we could include words like 'inequity', 'democracy', 'reframing educational opportunities', 'redistributing resources', 'agency', 'social responsibility', 'participatory', 'power' and 'oppression'. Clearly then this goes beyond a definition of inclusion and a celebration of diversity and is more about recognising the potential of education as a tool for social transformation. There is a critical edge here that is important and demands a deeper engagement with issues of unjustness and the recognition of a voice that must be heard from both educators and students in order to effect social and political change.

Globalisation in education policy contexts

I open this chapter by stating that there exists a conflict of ideologies between education and social justice and this conflict is a global one. Such a relationship is flawed and unsustainable. Education in the twenty-first century is under attack from globalisation. The neo-liberal approach to education being adopted by jurisdictions worldwide, with competition at its centre, mitigates against curricula and school systems which strive to be inclusive and democratic. Market forces now dominate education policy and produce a climate where orientations towards social justice have been dismantled by political leaders in recent years (Peters and Beasley 2014). Against a backdrop of high-stakes testing, impossibly high targets for literacy and mathematics in schools and league tables that benchmark pupil performance internationally, education has bought into what Finnish educator Pasi Sahlberg refers to as the 'global education reform movement'

(Sahlberg 2011). This reform is sweeping education communities everywhere, not least in the richest and most successful nations of the Western world. It is this 'germ' that suffocates schools and stifles learning, reproducing systems of inequality and unequal opportunities for young people. Any system that truly values fairness and justice must be prepared to challenge this ideology of individualism and free market competitiveness.

Internationally recognised student performance indicators such as the Programme for International Student Assessment (PISA) provide a very public stage for countries to measure their academic attainment against. Rizvi and Lingard argue that international comparisons like PISA are grounded in a vison of children as potential workers and create pressures on local curricula to narrow to feed this neo-liberal agenda (2010: 3). The same point is echoed by Cochran-Smith (2004) when she describes how young people's preparation to live in a democratic society is more and more conceptualised as assimilation into mainstream values, language and knowledge to allow them to enter a nation's workforce and preserve power in a global economy. Outcomes of teacher and student learning and professional practice are linked to political agendas whereas social justice and equity are rarely included in such discussions. Commenting on the last round of PISA scores, American educationalist Linda Darling-Hammond (2011) equates the USA's low ranking to the inequality that exists there. The USA has more children living in poverty than any other industrialised nation and at the time of writing this was around 25 per cent. Darling-Hammond asserts that it will be the country's commitment to equity that will determine its future.

Closer to home, in the United Kingdom we find a similar pattern. Writing prior to the new (and much more inclusive) curriculum in Scotland, *Curriculum for Excellence*, Riddell (2009) argued that, although social justice was very much a part of education policy rhetoric, Scottish education was founded on the principles of meritocracy and universalism where categories such as social, emotional and behavioural difficulties were applied to children from socially disadvantaged areas, thereby as a group, bringing to the fore their marginalisation even more. In the peak times of the Troubles in Northern Ireland in the 1960s, there was much debate as to whether a divided school system exacerbated society's divide (Gallagher 2004). In Wales, a continuing picture of poverty impacts harshly on education achievement, such that 59 per cent of children from affluent homes achieve 'good' grades at GSCE, against 26 per cent of children who are from deprived home circumstances (Egan 2014). In England, there is extensive evidence that demonstrates the extent of inequality that exists. National achievement data produced annually identify groups of children who continue to underachieve compared with other groups. Broad themes are very evident in this and show how the system in England is failing different groups of learners in schools. For example:

- Many ethnic groups underachieve in comparison with white British pupils, especially black Caribbean pupils;
- Young people with disabilities have fewer qualifications and underachieve despite having similar aspirations to non-disabled peers;

- Boys underachieve in comparison with girls at all stages of the National Curriculum;
- The numbers of pupils with English as an additional language in UK schools are around one million with 360 different languages spoken. Their attainment is less than English-speaking peers and is lowest in the early years (ages 0–5);
- Compared to non-looked after children, attainment for who are looked after is much lower than those in Key Stage 1 (ages 5–7) and in Key Stage 2 (ages 7–11).

Inequalities are not only evident throughout the years of compulsory schooling; they continue into further and higher education. The evidence is that the education system in England as a whole is failing too many children. In the words of former Education Minister Michael Gove, this was to be envisaged by 'liberating individuals from ignorance, democratising access to knowledge, making opportunity more equal, giving every child an equal chance to succeed' (2014). Ironically, it was Gove himself who championed the kind of education system where high-stakes testing and public data comparisons were the very antithesis of an education system that is democratic and fair for all children.

Poverty and social inequality

Social class is the strongest predictor of educational achievement in the UK, where the social class gap for educational achievement is one of the most significant in the developed world (Perry and Francis 2010). Children in social deprivation anywhere do not achieve as well as their peers in more affluent circumstances. Poverty and social disadvantage blight the chances of young children even before they enter formal schooling. The 'gap' starts even before a child starts formal schooling with a range of factors that include home circumstances, maternal qualifications, neighbourhood, quality and provision for early learning in educational and care settings and so on. Pre-school achievement is a reliable predictor of academic success but there are social effects that impact on this in the school years. Policies to reduce inequality and increase pupil achievement after children reach primary school age mean that many children may struggle to achieve the successes wished for, owing to social class effects (Feinstein 2003). Early intervention is vital. Schools cannot close this gap for all children.

Children from socially disadvantaged backgrounds arrive at school less prepared for formal education and are frequently less equipped to build upon the rich environments for early learning in pre-school. They are less likely to achieve a good level of development at age five, to achieve well at school at age eleven and do well in their GCSEs at sixteen compared to children from affluent backgrounds (Doherty and Tobbell 2016). The relationship between poor educational outcomes and low family income is strongly correlated. Many children from poorer families leave our school system with low levels of educational attainment: a major contributing factor of social mobility and poverty (Goodman and Gregg 2010). Children in the UK from the poorest fifth of families are already a year behind those children from middle-income families in vocabulary tests by age five (Waldfogel and Washbrook 2010). Socially disadvantaged pupils are defined as those eligible for the pupil premium, meaning more funding received into schools for those children who have been eligible for free school meals at any point during the last six years. They come to formal education less equipped to take advantage of the curriculum and often lacking the social capital to succeed.

Education, inequalities and social justice

There is an unacceptable amount of inequality in all phases of education. England remains a divided society, with the strong association of low income and education underachievement discussed earlier in this chapter. It is a goal within Catholic education to provide quality education for all children that counters the inequalities in society and the marginalisation of communities. But this is accompanied by the realisation that such an aspiration has only been in part a success. To Cardinal Martino, working together to build a world of justice and peace is a task in which Catholic schools must play an integral part and believes that Catholic schools are unique places to do this (2010: 212). Writers Valadez and Mirci (2015) draw upon Catholic social teaching and tell us that creating educational experiences which offer full and equitable opportunities for all students is at the heart of a model of social justice in education. The same ethos is captured in one Catholic college in the north of England, where the following words are framed and displayed in the school entrance area:

> This College is proud to be a Catholic School building on universal Christian values of the dignity of each life, the equality of all people and aims to encourage all students to live out a vocation to love their neighbour as themselves and to serve the common good.

The Catholic Association for Racial Justice (CARJ), which celebrated its thirtieth anniversary in 2014, has produced *Stepping Stones to a More Equal Society* (2014), an excellent review of educational initiatives to support young people and families in marginalised communities and its messages strongly reflect this commitment to equality in educational settings.

The British Education Research Association (BERA), the leading voice for academics in this country, has produced an evidence-based policy manifesto on social justice (*Fair and Equal Education*), which eloquently informs this critical argument. In it the Association states:

- We need to raise all children and young people's educational attainment to high levels, while promoting and developing their non-cognitive outcomes, including health and wellbeing.

- We need to ensure children and young people have equal access to a stimulating and enriching curriculum that balances academic knowledge with opportunities to develop creative expression and practical skills.
- We need high quality schooling that is equitably distributed (both between and within institutions), and accessible to all.
- We need to recognise that children and young people's entitlement to good quality education extends beyond school to include early childhood, further education, higher education, work-based and vocational learning, informal learning and out-of-school activities.
- We need to encourage children and young people to form opinions about and participate in the decisions that affect them.
- We need institutions that are accountable to children, young people and the communities in which they live.
- We need to create a more equal, fairer and flourishing society where all children and young people feel included and have a sense of belonging in 21st century Britain.

(BERA 2015: 2)

Social justice in teacher education

Teacher education for social justice is 'a learning problem as well as a political one' according to American writer Marilyn Cochran-Smith (2004: 1). In her insightful book *Walking the Road* she says that concerns over social justice against the backdrop of underachievement in the USA have resulted in three things happening. First, educational equity is seen as opportunities for all students to be held accountable to the same high-stakes tests but without due resources or learning opportunities. Second, teacher preparation is more about training and testing so that teachers have adequate subject knowledge and technical skills and third, preparation to live in a democratic society has come to mean assimilation into mainstream values and language to enter the nation's workforce and make a contribution to the economy thus preserving the USA as a dominant global power. Her vision assertively challenges this view.

But is it possible to have high standards of student achievement and still offer a curriculum that teaches young people about values and equity? Yes indeed. Pantic and Florian (2015) call for teacher educators to become 'agents of change' and see them as playing a critical role as agents of social justice. This requires subject knowledge and knowledge of how to exercise this in the diverse classroom environments in which teachers and trainee teachers work but this is still much underdeveloped. In England, the recently revised Professional Teacher Standards (DfE 2013a) define the minimum levels of practice expected for teachers and trainee teachers. Clustered into eight groups, they require professionals to evidence how they teach and there is some application into equity and social justice. In Part One, Standard 1, for example, *Setting high standards which inspire, motivate and challenge pupils* requires teachers to establish a safe and stimulating environment for pupils, rooted in mutual respect. It further requires them to set goals that stretch and challenge pupils of all backgrounds, abilities and dispositions. Standard 5, *Adapt teaching to respond to the strengths and needs of all pupils*, requires teachers to demonstrate am awareness of the physical, social and intellectual development of pupils, and know how to adapt teaching to support pupils' education at different stages of development. In Part Two, *Personal and professional conduct*, teachers are expected to uphold public trust in the profession and maintain high standards of ethics. They must show tolerance of and respect for the rights of others. They must not undermine fundamental British values, including democracy, the rule of law, individual liberty and mutual respect, and tolerance of those with different faiths and beliefs. Research on social justice in teacher education has often focused on teachers in training at the start of their careers because it is here that their professional identities are formed. Boylan describes these 'social justice teachers' because of their particular beliefs and knowledge their willingness to engage with critical theory and criticality in relation to constructs like openness to change, self-awareness and reflexivity and the schools and its social role in society.

How can schools promote social justice?

Having the desire to teach for social justice isn't the same as actually delivering it but emerging school models offer an exciting way forward. Studio schools for fourteen- to nineteen-year-olds are government-funded and aim for academic excellence. Students study the National Curriculum through enquiry-based learning and enterprise projects and work with the local community. With the same age range, university technical colleges provide specialism in technical subjects and are sponsored by a university and local employers, giving students considerable time in work experience. Former Education Secretary Nicky Morgan has said that free schools are 'the modern engines of social justice' (Bloom 2015). The government has committed to opening 500 more free schools in the next five years, which will create 270,000 additional school places around the country, many of which are in areas of high deprivation. Citizen schools aim to promote a democratic culture throughout the whole school by fostering citizenship (more on this later) as part of the curriculum and their involvement with the local community. A report from the Institute for Public Policy Research investigating students as 'active citizens', involvement with the local community and efforts to renew the democratic instinct found the following shared features among free schools:

- They ensured citizenship was an integral element of the school's purpose;
- They created a democratic and participative culture of citizenship;
- They enabled learning through action;
- They connected citizenship education to the school's improvement strategy and work to raise overall educational standards.

(Audsley *et al.* 2013)

In Portstewart, in Northern Ireland, the Dominican College was recently awarded recognition as a school of sanctuary and the first school in Ireland to be recognised with this honour. A school of sanctuary is a school that helps its students, staff and the wider community understand what it means to seek sanctuary and extends a welcome to everyone as equal, valued members of that school community. The school actively campaigns for social justice. Its prospectus proudly announces that the search for justice and peace is fundamental to the Dominican ethos. It states that the school aims to empower pupils to appreciate their individual and collective responsibility in contributing to a more just society, at home and abroad. Justice, peace, reconciliation and mutual understanding will find clear expression first and foremost in the daily life of the school. It aims to educate students to be people of integrity and responsibility, as people whose potential has begun to be realised and who will use their gifts to contribute to a more just society (school prospectus: 8).

Whole-school approaches regardless of the type of school are effective ways to promote social justice. There is a tangible acceptance of the diversity that exists in society and the inequity that coexists. There is support in each class for the achievement of all groups of students to ensure that no child is marginalised or allowed to underachieve because of their race, religion, gender, class or ability. Teaching begins with respect for students alongside a curriculum that is rooted in students' own experiences stimulating them to learn and enquire. Learning is active and participatory where students are given first-hand experiences as much as possible. Project work, role play and discussions are typical learning strategies that work. The curriculum is a social justice one exploring the lives of everyone in society including those who have suffered from oppression and marginalisation. Students themselves are taught to be critical. They do not accept at face value. They question, seek other alternatives and other solutions. They themselves are encouraged to pose searching critical questions to their teachers and peers. They challenge and solve problems collaboratively.

Teachers in many curriculum subjects have found innovative ways to teach for equity and justice. Mathematics is a good example. Lecturer Peter Wright has formed the Teaching Mathematics for Social Justice Research Group of five teacher researchers with a commitment to social justice, working collaboratively to develop an alternative vision of mathematics education. Using participatory action research, maths classroom activities are designed, trialled and evaluated through open-ended and collaborative problem-solving approaches encouraging students to make decisions and take responsibility for their mathematical learning. Maths is used a means of enquiry to help students have a better understanding of, and help change, their own social, political, economic and cultural situations. They develop critical awareness of maths in the curriculum and its place in society.

In primary schools, an already-overcrowded curriculum and the relentless drive for higher standards in maths and literacy deliver challenges for teachers finding space to teach about justice and equity to younger children. That said, there are many good examples of citizenship education used effectively in primary schools to teach children about fairness and democracy. Most primary schools have school councils, which have become a very valuable part of school life. They provide an important forum for children's voices to be heard on decisions affecting the school and for becoming involved in campaigns relating to wider issues in society. Being twinned with a school in another country abroad is one such approach that effectively allows children from different cultures to learn more about each other and exchange ideas. Adopting a cross-curricular approach allows citizenship in the curriculum to be integrated into other lessons, such as speaking and listening in literacy, or in art and RE. It is now recognised that a thematic cross-curricular approach is the best medium to teach it (Kerr *et al.* 2007) through a whole-school ethos that I referred to earlier. Active citizenship is a powerful way of children learning about their local neighbourhood. A simple starter classroom activity to promote understanding here would be for a teacher to write on the whiteboard that 'Your life is a successful one when you do more for your community than your community does for you. Discuss this idea in groups'. Citizenship also develops understanding of wider societal issues and indeed global ones. The Global Citizen initiative is a whole-school approach that highlights social justice, an appreciation of diversity and the importance of sustainable development. It is best delivered in schools through a Learn–Think–Act process whereby students explore an issue by considering it from different viewpoints and trying to understand its causes and consequences. They then consider critically what can be done about the issue and act on it either as individuals or collectively. Such an approach is grounded in real-life scenarios. It demonstrates the inequities in the world, challenges misinformation and stereotyped views about majority world countries and encourages children to recognise responsibilities towards each other and to learn from each other.

Still something of a fledging subject, citizenship was introduced into the National Curriculum in schools in 2002 and has been a compulsory subject in secondary schools since then. It aims to foster pupils' awareness and understanding of democracy, government and law, develop skills and knowledge to explore political and social issues critically, weigh up evidence, debate and make reasoned arguments and prepare them to take their place in society as responsible citizens (KS 3&4 Programmes of Study Citizenship 2013). It is a key element in SMSC, which is spiritual, moral, social and cultural development. All schools in England must show how well their pupils develop in SMSC and an important part of this is the promotion of fundamental British values. This includes helping students to distinguish right from wrong, encouraging them to accept responsibility for their behaviour, to show initiative and to understand how they can contribute positively to the lives of those living and working in the locality of the school and to society more widely. It promotes tolerance and harmony between different cultural traditions by enabling students to acquire an appreciation of and respect for their own and other cultures. It encourages respect for other people and respect for democracy and support for participation in the democratic processes, including respect for the basis on which the law is made and applied in England. Citizenship education has moved up the political agendas of most countries in recent times, forcing traditional ideas about of citizenship to be reviewed. These revisions now no longer place it as a status but as an active practice, posing questions about the nature of identity, social and community cohesion and participation in today's societies. With this, the idea of it being a transforming agent that empowers students with the knowledge, skills and behaviours they will need to make active decisions in their lives is very plausible indeed. And long overdue.

Conclusion

As I move to the conclusion of this chapter I should like to offer a number of curriculum principles upon which teaching for social justice in schools might be based.

1. Central education policies must better support young people's confident sense of self-identity and belonging in twenty-first-century Britain. They must reflect a commitment to counter global neo-liberalism and elevate understanding of social justice as a key goal of education.
2. Teaching for equity is more than curriculum-based; it is about educators having understanding of its sociopolitical significance. Race, diversity and multicultural inequalities must be addressed in the classroom and in society as a whole.
3. Teacher training providers (universities and schools) should include social justice as a mandatory part of their core curriculum.
4. Roles for specialist teachers, national schemes of work and comprehensive training on citizenship education for all teachers are advocated.
5. Schools must see themselves as possessing powerful knowledge on behalf of society and take a lead on sharing this more widely.
6. Teachers who pause the roundabout of rhetoric for even higher standards and public high-stakes tests and reflect upon their own teaching and the curricula in their own schools are well placed to construct principled programmes of study that have democracy and equity at the core.
7. Such teachers must see themselves as agents of change and act with conviction as ambassadors of the social change agenda and champions of inclusive best practice.
8. Teaching must provide essential knowledge and skills for young people to challenge inequality and oppression, respect others and live their lives successfully as part of a democratic and pluralistic society.

I end by paraphrasing Nelson Mandela: education is our most powerful weapon with which to change the world.

Bibliography

Audsley, J., Chitty, C., O'Connell, J., Watson, D. and Wills, J. (2013). *Citizen Schools. Learning to Build Democracy*. London: Institute for Public Policy Research.

Bloom, A. (2015). Free schools are 'engines of social justice'. *Times Education Supplement*, May.

British Education Research Association (2015). *Fair and Equal Education*. London: BERA.

CARJ (2014). *Stepping Stones to a More Equal Society*. London: Catholic Association for Racial Justice.

Cochran-Smith, M. (2004). *Walking the Road. Race, Diversity and Social Justice in Teacher Education*. New York, NY: Teachers College Press, Columbia University.

Darling-Hammond, L. (2011). *The Flat World and Education: How America's Commitment to Equity Will Determine Our Future*. New York, NY: Teachers College Press, Columbia University.

Department for Education. (2013a). *Teachers' Standards. Guidance for School Leaders, School Staff and Governing Bodies*. London: DfE.

Department for Education (2013b). *National Curriculum in England: Citizenship Programmes of Study Key Stages 3 and 4*. London: DfE.

Department for Education (2014). *Promoting Fundamental British Values as Part of SMSC in Schools. Departmental Advice for Maintained Schools*. London: DfE.

Doherty, J. and Tobbell, C. (2016). 'The effects of poverty on early years attainment', in L. Trodd (ed.) *The Early Years Handbook for Students and Practitioners*. Abingdon: David Fulton.

Dominican College (2015). *School Brochure*. Portstewart: Dominican College.

Egan, D. (2014). A View from Wales. *Research Intelligence, 125* (Autumn).

Feinstein, L. (2003). Inequality in the early cognitive development of British children in the 1970 cohort. *Economica, 70*(277).

Gallagher, T. (2004). *Education in Divided Societies*. London: Palgrave Macmillan.

Gerwitz, S. (1998). 'Conceptualizing social justice in education', Mapping the territory. *Journal of Educational Policy, 13*(4): 469–84.

Goodman, A. and Gregg, P. (2010). *Poorer Children's Educational Attainment: How Important Are Attitudes and Behaviour?* York: Joseph Rowntree Foundation. Online. Available at www.jrf.org/uk/publications/educational-attainmentpoor-children.

Gove, M. (2014). *Speech at the Education Reform Summit*, London, July.

Hackman, H.W. (2005). Five Essential Components for Social Justice Education. *Equity & Excellence in Education, 38*: 103–109.

Kaur, B. (2012). Equity and social justice in teaching and teacher education. *Teaching and Teacher Education, 28*: 485–92.

Kerr, D., Keating, A. and Ireland, E. (2007). *Pupil Assessment in Citizenship Education: Purposes, Practices and Possibilities. Report of a CIDREE Collaborative Project*. Slough: NFER/CIDREE.

Lawrence, D. (2014). *Social Justice and Black History. Has Stephen's Death Changed Education*? Talk at Leeds Trinity University, Leeds, 13 November.

Martino, H.E.R.R. (2010). What Catholic schools can do to advance the cause of justice and peace in the world. *International Studies in Catholic Education, 2*(2): 212–16.

Pantic, N. and Florian. L. (2015). Developing teachers as agents of inclusion and social justice. *Education Inquiry, 6*(3): 333–51.

Perry, E. and Francis, B. (2010). *The Social Class Gap for Educational Achievement: A Review of the Literature*. London: RSA.

Peters, M. and Beasley, T. (2014). Children in crisis: child poverty and abuse in New Zealand. *Educational Philosophy and Theory, 46*(9): 962–88.

Riddell, S. (2009). Social justice, equality and inclusion in Scottish education. *Discourse, 30*(3): 283–97.

Rizvi, F. and Lingard, B. (2010). *Globalising Educational Policy*. London: Routledge.

Sahlberg, P. (2011). *Finnish Lessons – What Can the World Learn from Educational Change in Finland?* New York, NY: Teachers College Press, Columbia University.

Valadez, J.R. and Mirci, P.S. (2015). Educating for social justice: drawing from Catholic social teaching. *Journal of Catholic Education*, *19*(1), Article 8.

Villegas, A.M. and Lucas, T. (2002). *Educating Culturally Responsive Teachers*. Albany, NY: State University of New York Press.

Waldfogel, J. and Washbrook, E. (2010). *Low Income and Early Cognitive Development in the U.K.* London: Sutton Trust.

Yousafzai, M. (2013). *Speech to United Nations General Assembly*, 12 July.

Zeichner, K. (2003). 'Educating teachers to close the achievement gap: Issues of pedagogy, knowledge, and teacher preparation', in B. Williams (ed.) *Closing the Achievement Gap*. Alexandria, VA: ASCD.

Zeichner, K. (2010). Competition, economic rationalization, increased surveillance, and attacks on diversity: neo-liberalism and the transformation of teacher education in the U.S. *Teaching and Teacher Education*, *26*: 1544–52.

14 Developing a core compulsory module to teach principles of social justice and citizenship

Jan Fook, Jonathan Glazzard, Ann Marie Hayes, Ann Marie Mealey and Chris Rowley

Introduction

There is a plethora of current challenges which face the higher education sector in some Western countries. While economic concerns seem to dominate, with the related need to constantly measure achievements there is a body of literature which also calls for a vision of the mission of universities which transcends these relatively instrumental objectives (Maskell and Robinson 2002; Jones 2007). Put simply, the debate centres around whether the goals of higher education should be primarily for employability or also for citizenship. Some writers conceptualise this debate as the difference between 'educating to do' and 'educating to be' (DAll'Alba 2012) or developing 'knowledge-inquiry' as opposed to 'wisdom-inquiry' (Maxwell 2012). These distinctions polarise the separate tendencies to train the intellect ('educating to do') from the capacity to care ('educating to be'), in Dall'Alba's (2012) terms. In Maxwell's terms (2012) the polarisation is between a concern with purely scientific or technical knowledge and a concern with the more fundamental problems of living. In some instances, these conflicts may be conceptualised as trying to meet the demands of educating for professional practice, as opposed to a liberal arts agenda of exploring what it means to be fully human (Lederhouse 2014). At the university in question, it was assumed that these are not mutually exclusive aims, and that it was possible address both these educational aspirations.

Our university is a relatively new university (beginning in late 2012) founded on two former Roman Catholic teacher training colleges in a large city in the north of England. The originators of this module are the authors of this chapter. From the context of establishing a new university in such a climate, it was necessary to try to address students' potential employability in a significant way. In 1997, in a report investigating future demands for higher education in the UK, Dearing (1997) made the connection between employability and globalisation, noting the need for international competitiveness. At our university we have introduced innovations across all programmes, such as compulsory placements that serve to facilitate this. However, being founded on a Catholic tradition, the idea of social justice and citizenship is also important as a basis for education at our university. Therefore in 2015 we piloted a new compulsory module for new level 4 (first-year undergraduate) students, which was designed to introduce students to some of the broader ideals involved in citizenship. This took on many different forms, as the meaning of this evolved in our ongoing discussions, but broadly involved concepts of social justice and ethics, as well as critical thinking about ethical practice and behaviour. We were also interested in helping students to think in multidisciplinary ways.

In this chapter, we trace our experiences in piloting this module, the feedback received and the new developments which ensued. We believe that our efforts in trying to develop such a module in some ways capture the very real tensions and difficulties with which many contemporary British universities struggle on a broader level, in marrying current policy demands with more long-standing goals of higher education. In addition, there appears to be very little literature which provides details about the citizenship-related curriculum in current UK universities or indeed the early stages of translating the ideals which motivate a new programme into a specific curriculum (McCowan 2012). In this chapter, we aim to provide some of that detail.

Educating for citizenship

What guidance does the literature give us in relation to similar curriculum developments? It was difficult to conduct searches which located all the different and specific elements of the initiative, since this involved not just concepts of citizenship but also the related ideas of social justice, ethics, multidisciplinary perspectives and also the element of both core and compulsory curricula. It was even difficult to identify what keywords should be used, as terminology in relation to core curricula varied between country contexts. Nevertheless, several searches were conducted (using keywords such as the teaching of social justice, criticality, critical thinking, citizenship, and general and core curriculum). Articles were selected which included at least two of the foregoing themes (such as articles which focused on the teaching of citizenship in the core curriculum) as well as articles which also mentioned issues of interdisciplinarity.

From these it appeared that the bulk of the literature concerned developments in the USA, with a small portion from other countries (McCowan 2012). An obvious issue which arose was in defining the concept of 'citizenship', which may or may not include explicit notions of criticality, social justice or ethics. As McCowan (2012: 52) points out, there is a difference between focusing on the general effect universities have in the civic sphere and the more specific effect of endeavouring to 'make citizens'. This latter has a more explicitly activist aspect, as in motivating students to become actively engaged in their communities (McCowan 2012). Citizenship in this sense assumes teaching and learning of congruent values and skills (Gates 2006). These aspects may of course be addressed more specifically in some curricula through a focus on social justice issues, development of ethical stances, and the perspective and skills of criticality. There is of course a plethora of literature which focuses on these specific arenas without necessarily relating it to an overarching theme of citizenship. A prime example is the teaching of critical thinking (Behar-Horenstein and Nui 2011), which is commonly taught in specific programmes and is not necessarily linked to the teaching or learning of ethical or moral stances. Because of the extensive amount of literature involved in covering the teaching of citizenship as well as these more specific areas, the search prioritised articles which focused on the interplay of different aspects, such as critical thinking and multidisciplinarity (e.g. Jones 2007, 2009).

Initial searches also focused on both the compulsory and interdisciplinary nature of similar developments. These revealed that very few universities or colleges actually had the same module required across all programmes. Where the module was required across all programmes, this was normally in a more specialised college (Ardovini and Lopes 2009) and so was not broadly interdisciplinary. Alternatively, the module might only be required within a particular faculty, for example business (Nelson *et al.* 2014), and so was less interdisciplinary in nature than what we were attempting.

Within the literature the key terms used for this type of curriculum, which aims at a more generic education, are 'core curriculum' or 'general education' (Bourke *et al.* 2009). Citing Jones *et al.*, they state that 'general education is frequently taken to mean the collection of experiences crafted by the institution to provide students with a breadth of learning experiences and a broad knowledge base that sharpen students' problem- solving, interpersonal, and oral and written communication skills, as well as their cultural and linguistic literacy where does the quote end? (Bourke *et al.* 2009: 219) and later summarise this as 'students are expected to develop understandings of a breadth of topics, enhance their critical-thinking abilities, and become well-rounded, educated citizens' (Bourke *et al.* 2009: 221). Within general education, two main approaches are noted: 'core curriculum' and 'distribution requirement'. The former refers to a curriculum where specific core modules are compulsory. The latter refers to a situation where a range or stream of modules is available and students elect to take a particular number adding up to a certain amount of credits. Bourke *et al.* also note the importance of critical thinking in general education and that its teaching is not content-specific and may be taught through approaches such as problem-based learning (Bourke *et al.* 2009: 223–4). Jones (2007) argues however that understanding of critical thinking can vary significantly between different disciplines. She cites the examples of economics and history in which the former seems to conceptualise critical thinking defined in terms of the use of economic tools, whereas in history a range of perspectives is included. These types of findings have implications for needing a more in-depth understanding of different disciplinary approaches in general education, if we are to educate effectively for critical thinking which can be applied more generically.

Hall (2014) notes a different breakdown of five models of the core curriculum, ranging from a 'distribution requirement' through to 'required courses', 'correlated courses', 'combined courses' and 'integrated seminars' (focusing on life's 'bigger questions') (Hall 2014: 6). While the differences between models are not hugely significant, what is important is that the basic emphasis of all was problem-solving with a weighted focus on democratic group development (Hall 2014: 6).

Although many American doctoral granting institutions have a form of core curriculum, a feature of the USA is the liberal arts college, which focuses on providing a more general education upon which more specialist education can subsequently be built (Bourke *et al.* 2009). This latter type of institution of course does not feature so highly in the UK, so the context for offering such a curriculum is less well developed. This lack of context presents particular challenges for introducing such a curriculum in the UK context. These will be presented below.

In the next section, we provide more specific background to the development of the relevant core module and describe some detail of how the module was developed. The section following this then describes how it was actually implemented. A series of feedback sessions were conducted with both staff and students in order for us to learn from the pilot experience and we will outline the main themes from these, as well as discussing our further reflections. We end the paper with some broad conclusions about developing such a core curriculum.

Background and process of module development

The mission of our university is stated as:

> Guided by our Catholic identity and faith foundation. We provide an exceptional educational experience in a diverse community. We are committed to the promotion of dignity, respect, social justice and equality in order to deliver positive social and economic impacts.

The last sentence comprises the core values of the university (Strategic Plan).

In September 2015 the university's Learning, Teaching and Assessment Strategy (LTAS) was ratified. The overarching aim of this is to ensure that:

> A graduate of this university will be a confident individual, able to make a significant contribution to society. They will be comfortable with knowledge at the boundaries of their discipline, understand the connections between different disciplines and be able to collaborate across disciplines in professional contexts. Their professionalism will be underpinned by a clear understanding of ethical practice.
>
> (LTAS)

One of the specific strategies planned to meet this overarching aim was to:

> develop a single, university wide, module for all level 4 students that will deal with contemporary topics that raise significant ethical/moral issues. The module will be designed to also develop academic skills (academic writing, research, critical thinking, data presentation, information literacy etc.).
>
> (LTAS)

The university began restructuring in the second half of 2015, when disciplines such as sociology and criminology were added and some disciplines were integrated with others to create larger schools. However, when specific planning for the module began the university consisted of disciplines in the following areas: children, young people and families; teacher education; business and management; psychology; sport, health and nutrition; English, history, journalism and media.

In late 2014, planning for this new university-wide module began. A working group was formed of five to ten volunteers across all disciplines (attendance varied at each meeting) led by a member of the then Theology and Religious Studies Department. The leading member was interested primarily through her background in teaching ethics. The initial focus was on the teaching of ethics, but through subsequent discussions this evolved into a focus on teaching critical thinking. In early 2015 the new professor of higher education pedagogy became involved and suggested that the academic framework for the module be based on the concept of 'criticality' (Barnett 2012), which comprises both critical thinking and critical reflection in order to develop a more ethical and compassionate stance. This connection was developed from the Socratic idea of self-examination leading to a more ethical and compassionate engagement with the world and its dilemmas (Nussbaum 1997). It was thought that this would provide an academic framework to link the development of critical thinking abilities with the capacity to develop ethical perspectives. Although specific readings were sourced to provide more detail on the concepts of criticality, critical thinking and being ethical, it was actually quite difficult to pinpoint readings which connected the three in clear ways, suitable for an entry level 4 student audience. Accordingly, the introduction to the handbook was written to spell this out more clearly. The below quote from the module handbook describes how the connection was made:

> In its simplest form, the ability to be critical involves the ability to 'think beneath the surface' of something or to question what is apparently taken-for-granted. This often means being able to offer a different perspective than the mainstream view which is normally accepted or agreed upon.... You can then use this intellectual ability to analyse many things, such as documents, policies, or even other people's stories about a situation. Once you are able to question frameworks which are 'given', and come up with perspectives which might be outside the original frame of reference, or even just widely accepted views, you are applying a critical ability. This is the intellectual aspect of being critical, and normally we call this 'critical thinking'.
>
> However there is also an emotional aspect of being critical, which some people regard as being addressed through the ability to critically reflect. Critical reflection is sometimes referred to as the ability to learn from your own experience (Dewey). How does this compare with critical thinking? Critical reflection involves the ability to think critically about your own experience i.e. to think below the surface about what the experience means,

> and to question what you have taken for granted. When you do this of course, emotions also become important, as your own experience will be a combination of many aspects – ideas, feelings, memories, actions, perceptions, past experiences, meaning – not just ideas. Critical reflection therefore has the potential to unearth a whole range of ideas and their connection with a whole range of experiences, including emotions. When you critically reflect, you are, in a sense, thinking critically about your own story or experience (not other people's necessarily).
>
> Criticality is therefore made up of an intellectual (critical thinking) and an emotional (critical reflection) aspect. The advantage of being able to combine both is that there is greater potential for learning, since we ourselves as human beings function on intellectual and emotional levels. Combining the two maximizes the potential for learning, since sometimes (as we all know) it is one thing to be able to know about something, but quite something else to be motivated to do something about it.
>
> This brings us to two other important aspects about being critical. Of course there is an action element, but even more importantly, a social element. Taking action on the basis of our critical thinking and reflection always happens within a social context, and therefore is shaped by this context (e.g. where and when we are taking action, with who, etc) and also shapes this context (e.g. who is affected by what we think and do and how this changes a situation).
>
> It is this social or contextual level which is particularly important in learning and which is crucial to a good education. You will see from the readings that criticality is associated with things like being a good citizen and participating in one's community; being better able to make decisions; developing confidence, autonomy and responsibility; and appreciating different perspectives and developing an ethical stance in relation to these. Indeed, critical reflection also involves the ability to engage 'ethically and compassionately with the world and its dilemmas' (Socrates). Because these are all crucial objectives in education, we hope that providing you with a basic framework to do achieve them, in the form of helping you become critical, will not only help you benefit as much as possible from your university studies, but will act as a lifelong basis for your own learning and progression through life. This is central to the social justice mission of learning at [our university – name deleted] and we do hope that you find that becoming critical leads you to engage better with your own experience, your own studies, and the people you meet along the way.

A package of readings and notes was developed and provided to all staff who were interested in the module, particularly to those staff who might possibly act as seminar leaders. In conjunction with this, two training sessions were provided on the framework. These included discussion of how the framework might be implemented in specific programmes. Staff chosen to facilitate the seminars in each programme met together, and with the module leaders, as often as possible to plan the specific design of their seminars.

One of the logistical difficulties encountered initially was how to run the module when there was no space in the relevant programmes. This meant that each programme which agreed to pilot the module had to remove a module to be replaced by this new module. This created major problems for programmes that had honed their design and curricula over some years. Other programme leaders were somewhat resistant as they argued that critical thinking was already taught in their programmes. Others were hesitant as they felt that there were some very basic study skills which needed to be taught at this very early stage (such as awareness of plagiarism; how to write assignments) which they were reluctant to relinquish. While it is fair to say that there was a strong level of support for running the module in some quarters, there was also a strong degree of resistance, mostly because of these types of logistical difficulties, which proved very difficult to address, especially in a short time.

Description of module delivery

Module description

Students came from three different programme areas: sport/exercise, science journalism and education studies and totalled approximately 220.

The module was delivered with six two-hour lecture/panel sessions in which students came together as a whole group. A guest speaker presented on a contemporary topic (chosen by the planning group) for an hour, and then a panel asked questions, debated different viewpoints and engaged the student audience in discussion. Topics included: gender issues; the politics of university funding, fee-paying and learning ('who owns the university?'); business ethics for participation; issues surrounding contemporary 'toxic' childhood and the difficulties entailed in this; and the welfare state. Specific readings were supplied for each topic.

Additional weekly two-hour seminars were also organised for single groups of students in each academic pathway and facilitated by staff from the relevant programme area. These were flexibly organised and designed by each set of seminar facilitators so as to be more directly applied to the needs of students in each programme.

The stated module objectives were:

- Demonstrate an ability to learn from their own experience and others (critically reflect) (as a platform for later learning in the placement);
- Demonstrate an ability to begin to integrate critical thinking and critical reflection in relation to some major contemporary issues;
- Demonstrate an ability to identify theoretical approaches to debate and persuasion, including aspects of emotional intelligence and confidence practice;
- Show an ability to evaluate scholarly arguments for and against a given topic;

- Demonstrate a sustained ability to be aware of different perspectives on contemporary issues and engage with critical debate beyond subject-specific disciplines;
- Use primary and secondary texts to convey a particular argument.

Seminars for each programme

In seminar groups, students practised the skills of critical thinking and debate through a variety of approaches. The seminar leaders took responsibility for designing the content of the seminar sessions. This resulted in a variety of approaches between the groups.

In journalism, students were asked to identify pertinent issues. The students were divided into smaller groups and each group was asked to select a pertinent issue that they wanted to debate. Debates were not necessarily discipline-specific. They were asked to identify a specific question and between sessions the group researched into the issue they had identified. Upon arrival at the next session the seminar leader informed the group members which stance they had to take (i.e. for or against). This meant that all members of each group were required to research both sides of the debate because they did not know which side of the argument they would be adopting in the following session. Each group selected different topics for debate and therefore different topics were being discussed concurrently. The debates took place within small groups. After the small group debates had taken place, the group members were required to agree on an overall stance through a voting process. The debates that were selected did not always relate to the debates that they had observed in the presentations, although periodically the seminar leader asked the students to continue these debates in their smaller groups.

The sport and exercise science group was facilitated by two seminar leaders, who split the responsibility for the sessions. They did not team teach. Within the seminar sessions students were introduced to models of critical reflection. One seminar leader asked the students to debate subject-specific issues. Topics included: women's rugby; homophobia in sport; and drug testing in the Olympics. Students were also encouraged to debate topical issues including the refugee crisis and gun ownership in America. These 'general' topics were identified by the students as important and worthy of debate. The students were organised into small groups and each group was required to 'bid' for a topic. Topics include: ethics in sport; sport and politics; sporting identities; and gender issues in sport. Each group was then assigned a topic and asked to prepare a ten-minute presentation, which they delivered to the whole seminar group. The second seminar leader continued the debates they had observed in the larger group in the seminar.

The education studies students were taught by one seminar leader. Students were introduced to critical theory and critical frameworks and this was then applied to education. Students were asked to work in small groups. Each group selected a topic of interest and they researched into that. Topics related to education but students were expected to apply critical theory and critical frameworks to these. Each group then presented the issue to the rest of the seminar group. Issues included race, gender and sexuality in education.

Observations/reflections

Focus group discussions were held with staff involved in teaching of the module every month over the four months it was taught (September to December 2015). In addition, final focus groups were held with each group of students, and a final focus group was held with staff early in 2016. Students also completed module evaluation questionnaires. More generic focus groups were held with staff groups throughout the university, to try to gauge wider perceptions of the module and its implementation to date.

One of the early issues which arose was the low student attendance at lectures/panel sessions. These were held at 9:00 a.m. (mostly because of room availability, as a large venue was needed for the large number of students), which was regarded by students as too early. Students were sometimes almost outnumbered by staff in attendance, as there was often a small group of staff in attendance to conduct the filming of the events (in addition to staff on the discussion panel).

Students also raised the fact that the talks were not traditional 'debates', as they had been labelled, but were instead the presentation of one point of view (the speaker's) and then discussion of this by members of the panel (made up of a student from the group, two PhD students, and a number of staff from different programmes).

Most staff felt it was very difficult to stimulate student interaction, which negatively impacted upon the potential for interdisciplinary learning and subsequently the students' potential to differentiate between competing perspectives in this format. Although students were invited to ask questions and participate in discussion with the panel after the talks, this proved very difficult in a large lecture theatre. Not only was it difficult to hear but many students felt awkward about speaking up freely in a large inter-faculty group, which, as an inter-faculty cohort, was principally comprised of 'strangers'. In addition, it was difficult to facilitate many different views being aired and discussed fairly and openly in such a large group and venue.

In addition, many students expressed the view that they were not interested in all of the topics. It was indeed difficult to choose and provide topics which would stimulate equal interest across the three programme areas. For instance, education studies students found the topic on 'toxic childhood' more relevant, and these students could also more readily appreciate the need for reflection in general, given that this is a core skill that they are taught throughout the degree. Sports science students found that the whole idea of reflection sat outside what they thought they were at university to learn. As one student said, 'we are just here to learn the facts'. Paradoxically, however, the talk on 'who owns the university?', which was delivered by a senior member of the National Union of

Students, should have been of common interest, but seemed not to have been appreciated by many students because of its rather sophisticated critique of how a fee-paying culture and environment can be antithetical to learning; in effect, many present in the lecture completely disagreed. These observations led us to reflect upon whether students actually shared our expectations of what (and how) they were at university to learn. Were our expectations too high and/or were some of the students not prepared for the challenge of independent study at higher education level? For example, in one programme it was reported that students had a great deal of difficulty in negotiating their assessment, although many felt it was good that they were given some choice. These observations led us to question whether our learning outcomes were too ambitious. This query was also raised by some staff not directly involved in the teaching or design of the module.

A resounding theme from students was that they expected to learn material which was directly relevant to the programme of study they had chosen, and many could not see how the content of talks fitted this. Another issue was the naming of the module as 'critical thinking' when in fact the objectives covered a much wider range of skills (e.g. study skills).

This proved to be a complex issue because, as the module delivery continued, it became clear that, indeed, not all the teaching staff understood (in the same way) the connection of critical thinking to developing an ethical position, and indeed to critical reflection. This understandably is an issue when teaching staff come from a wide range of disciplinary backgrounds with differing perspectives on criticality.

Student module evaluation questionnaires also indicated a range of different responses from students, which was presumably the result of how material was specifically delivered in their separate seminar groups. It did appear that the programmes which made a very concerted effort to relate the material directly to the topic area of their programmes (as students perceived it) were rated more highly by students. However, this required a large amount of extra work from the seminar tutors in terms of convincing students of the rationale for the module, searching out other literature and devising exercises and seminar material which would translate the material for students' consumption. Discussion in all the staff focus groups indicated that there was a very large range of differing approaches taken to how the material was processed in seminars.

Overall, despite the high standard of the talks presented (as perceived by teaching staff involved), and the relevance of the topic to contemporary global issues, it was also felt that the core emphasis on ethics (including social justice issues and awareness of diversity) did not come through clearly enough. In this sense, there was seen to be a disparity between the intended objectives of the module and the perceptions of the staff and students involved in it.

Discussion

Our experience of the staff focus groups was that they were extremely helpful in gaining an understanding of not just different disciplinary approaches but also different pedagogical approaches. How critical perspectives are taught can be a major site for differences, ranging from the teaching of critical theory to more of a pragmatic focus on teaching/learning skills of argument. This point, in relation to both conceptualisations of critical thinking (Jones 2007) and conceptualisations of general attributes (Jones 2009) is of course borne out in other literature. In addition, there is research to indicate that students' own understandings of critical thinking may be limited, or, at the very least, be quite variable at this stage in their education (Phillips and Bond 2004).

A clear message from student feedback was that more direct links were needed between the material presented in the lecture/panel sessions, the objectives of the module, and the students' expectations of what they would be studying in their chosen programmes. Taking on board the idea that the lecture/panel sessions themselves were not perceived as relevant by students (on the whole), we needed to rethink the purpose of these, especially vis-à-vis the goals of the module. Again, this point is well made by McCowan, in summing up general points learned from attempts to introduce a citizenship curriculum in three English universities (McCowan 2012: 65). He notes:

> Possible resistance on the part of students must be taken into account, for instance if they see university as a place to learn a particular skill or profession, rather than develop broader qualities such as criticality and self-understanding.

In our further discussion of the feedback, we reaffirmed that the goals of the module were about teaching citizenship (including social justice, issues of diversity, ethics and the ability to be critical (thinking and reflection)). With this in mind, it seemed more appropriate to conceptualise the lecture/panel sessions as being a form of stimulus material, useful as providing content for debate and analysis. Rather than students believing that they needed to learn the content of these sessions, we reaffirmed that it was about using this material to learn about different perspectives, to be able to formulate opinions and argue for them, and to be able to develop ethical thinking in relation to them. They should also act as a stimulus for reflection on students' own experiences. With these principles in mind, it seemed important to conceptualise the lecture/panel sessions as only one form of possible stimulus material. Others might include examples of popular culture (e.g. TED talks, a piece of literature, TV programme, a blog, a news item or event, film etc). Conceptualising stimulus material in this broad way opens the potential for more student involvement in choosing what material to discuss.

We think maybe it is worth mentioning here the huge difference to the way that students are educated in school in a highly transmit and test way (this is in several other chapters), where the focus is on spoon-feeding content in order for children to perform on subsequent statutory assessments, and the fact that this module was therefore a bridge too far in the first year of university.

Given the difficulty in adapting a universal (on paper) module to specialist needs in specific programmes, we felt there was clearly a need to make the delivery more flexible. For instance, rather than requiring all students to meet together in one place to listen to one speaker on a regular basis (something that might become more difficult as programme numbers grow), it was decided that the number of common sessions could be reduced. Of the limited number that would be held, the speakers would be given more direct briefing on the focus of the talks, and a format would be devised which would allow for different viewpoints to be aired. Short podcasts on specific topics for discussion in seminar sessions would be a good idea.

Given the perceived possible discrepancy between teachers' and students' expectations about learning in higher education, we decided that it would be important to include some sessions on the transition into higher education, and more explicit preparation for the different learning and teaching approaches being used at university. We agreed that it would be important to model, and to introduce students to, some of the more prominent features of the university's Learning, Teaching and Assessment Strategy, such as small group learning, student responsibility for learning, and student-led inquiry.

Lastly, given the need to introduce students to the whole idea of citizenship, we felt it was important to reiterate the intellectual framework for this, and to retitle the module more appropriately. We decided to change the name of the module to 'Ethics and Society', and to make the framework for linking social justice, diversity, ethics and criticality with notions of citizenship more explicit.

Conclusion

What has our experience taught us about the process of developing such a module? Literature which relates to making changes in higher education does seem to indicate that quite long time frames are needed to bring about such an extensive change (Hall 2014). Even though we were only attempting to introduce one module, the knock-on changes which this involved were quite extensive. Even with much good will, it was sometimes difficult to make changes when other extensive changes were also occurring.

Clearly there is a need to allow enough time for consultation and development when instituting a new university-wide initiative. This includes the need to perhaps pre-empt logistical problems which might arise when introducing new compulsory and universal initiatives. Otherwise there is a risk that the pragmatic agenda will dominate, and that the new initiative may not be attempted if logistical difficulties prove insurmountable. This is an important consideration if there are other changes occurring at the same time and staff energies are stretched. It is also important for a more fundamental reason, which is that if pragmatic concerns rule then more substantial academic and value-based concerns may be forgotten. In this case the major motivating reasons for implementing changes, which should provide the impetus for changes, may be hijacked, and ironically be denatured.

The need for both teaching staff and student buy-in is also obvious, as noted elsewhere (McCowan 2012) but this can be more difficult to obtain when there are other pressures. It is also more difficult to obtain buy-in if pragmatic or logistical concerns cause staff to lose sight of the more important academic reasons for introducing such changes. It is also important to consider the wider policy and cultural context. In our case, we did not perhaps take into account students' own expectations of higher education, which might have been influenced by the current discourse about employability and perhaps a more outcome- or target-driven educational culture they had been exposed to in their school education to date.

Given that there were quite differing disciplinary approaches to notions of citizenship and criticality, it is important to recognise that there may need to be a degree of flexibility in how these concepts are interpreted and translated to differing groups of students. The university can clearly have an important role in educating different student groups to find a way of becoming good citizens, particularly in the case of a faith-sponsored institution, but what is needed is a much more complex understanding of different disciplinary approaches and needs in doing this. However, there is a need to understand not only disciplinary differences but also the more specific learning needs of both students and staff in relation to social justice and diversity. Does the use of critical theory and pedagogies help students (Manis 2012) and might staff also need training in issues such as diversity (Singleton and Fleming 2009)? In these senses, might both staff and students need to study citizenship and social justice in more depth before meeting the intricacy of ethical policy and practice within a complex, changeable world at the university level?

References

Ardovini, J. and Lopes, A. (2009). Teaching social justice: a proposal to innovate the liberal arts core. *Theory in Action*, *2*(2): 33–44.

Behar-Horenstein, L.S. and Nui, L. (2011). Teaching critical thinking skills in higher education: a review of the literature. *Journal of College Teaching & Learning*, *8*(2): 25–42.

Bourke, B., Bray, N.J. and Horton, C. (2009). Approaches to the core curriculum: an exploratory analysis of top liberal arts and doctoral-granting institutions. *JGE: The Journal of General Education*, *58*(4): 219–40.

Dearing, R. (1997). *The Dearing Report-National Committee of Inquiry into Higher Education. National Report–Future Demands for Higher Education.* London: Stationery Office.

Barnett, R. (ed.). (2012). *The Future University: Ideas and Possibilities*. New York, NY, and London: Routledge.

Dall'Alba, G. (2012). 'Re-imagining the university: developing the capacity to care', in R. Barnett (ed.) *Higher Education: A Critical Business*. Buckingham: Society for Research into Higher Education and Open University Press, pp. 102–22.

Gates, B.E. (2006). Religion as cuckoo or crucible: beliefs and believing as vital for citizenship and citizenship education. *Journal of Moral Education*, *35*(4): 571–94.

Hall, E.A. (2014). Co-Learners and Core: Education Reform at Saint Joseph's College. *International Social Science Review*, *88*(3), Article 4. Online. Available at http://digitalcommons.northgeorgia.edu/issr/vol. 88/iss3/4.

Jones, A. (2007). Multiplicities or manna from heaven? Critical thinking and the disciplinary context. *Australian Journal of Education, 51*(1): 84–103.
Jones, A. (2009). Redisciplining generic attributes: the disciplinary context in focus. *Studies in Higher Education, 34*(1): 85–100.
Lederhouse, J.N. (2014). Teaching and leading for human flourishing: creating a liberal arts framework for teacher preparation. *AILACTE* Z! (Fall 2014): 1–17.
McCowan, T. (2012). Opening spaces for citizenship in higher education: three initiatives in English universities. *Studies in Higher Education, 37*(1): 51–67.
Manis, A. (2012). A review of the literature on promoting cultural competence and social justice agency among students and counselor trainees: piecing the evidence together to advance pedagogy and research. *The Professional Counselor, 2*(1): 48–75.
Maskell, D. and Robinson, I. (2002). *The New Idea of a University*. Thorverton: Imprint Academic
Maxwell, N. (2012). 'Creating a better world: towards the University of Wisdom', in R. Barnett (ed.) *Higher Education: A Critical Business*. Buckingham: Society for Research into Higher Education and Open University Press, pp. 123–38.
Nelson, J., Smith, L.B. and Hunt, C.S. (2014). The migration toward ethical decision making as a core course into the B-school: instructional strategies and approaches for consideration. *Journal of Education for Business, 89*: 49–56.
Nussbaum, M. (1997). *Cultivating Humanity: A Classical Defense of Reform in Higher Education*. Cambridge, MA: Harvard University Press.
Phillips, V. and Bond, C. (2004). Undergraduates' experiences of critical thinking. *Higher Education Research & Development, 23*(3) (2004): 277–94.
Singleton, J.L. and Fleming, M.K.J. (2009). Transformation of learning and the learner: infusing cross-cultural content across the curriculum. *The International Journal of Learning, 15*(12): 131–39.

Conclusion

Where now for social justice?

Ann Marie Mealey and Pam Jarvis

As we reach the end of this book, we turn back to consider the varied chapters from the perspective of the overarching issues raised in the introduction. We do this from a position of troubled times for societal cohesion, in the wake of a heinous terrorist attack in northern England that specifically targeted young people: the Manchester Arena bombing in May 2017. This reminds us of the complexity of social justice, how those who have multiple experiences of disempowerment may in extreme circumstances seek empowerment through highly dysfunctional means, striking out at innocent targets who have, in the process of disempowerment, been mistakenly constructed as symbols of an oppressive 'other'. This reminds us of the high stakes that we negotiate when we engage in interactions at every level, from the political to the individual when we engage with interactions that impact upon everyday social justice

Empowerment and advocacy

Our initial constructions of social justice emerge from our earliest experiences of the world. Pam Jarvis, Jonathan Doherty and Helen Hanna consider issues arising in the home, the school and the wider society, where we all too often lose the opportunity to provide models of empowerment to children, with parents and teachers experiencing disempowerment through draconian 'accountability' experiences that focus intently upon human fallibility rather than human resilience, setting up a negative spiral in which human beings lose trust in one another and, through this process, develop low self-esteem. Graham Turner gives examples of how this can happen through sporting experience, which, in an attempt to encourage children to strive, may sometimes miss opportunities to celebrate smaller achievements, while Stefano Ba' describes the disempowering environment within which some families live: a world of zero-hours contracts and insecure employment while attempting to provide a secure base for their children.

Sue Elmer and John Battle explore contemporary ways in which vulnerable individuals may be empowered to challenge oppressive situations, while Patricia Kelly considers a historical example in which one inspirational man created a movement through which collective action was enabled through a faith perspective, assisting those whose vulnerability was being exploited to speak with one cohesive voice against the oppressor.

Ann Marie Mealey, Alana Vincent and Qari Asim explore the issue of social justice from the perspectives of three different faith bases, all picking up on the complex relationship between faith and social action; Vincent brings this debate into the sharpest relief, considering the relationships between 'justice' and 'advocacy' and how this has developed differently within the same religious tradition, in its realisation in different historical periods and cultural situations. Mealey stresses the need to take the practices of the local Churches into consideration as a means of enabling people to grow in virtue and to enter in the narrative story of their faith to extrapolate resources that can motivate and inspire change.

The faith sections of this volume show how different narratives help to motivate and to provide the framework for people to interpret what is going on in a situation and to decide 'why?' they should act. Reflections on social justice need narratives in order to ensure that the issues for which individuals are being encouraged to speak out about make sense to them in their community and in their interpretive frameworks. This is particularly brought into focus in Qari Asim's chapter.

However, it is also important that we remain critical and open-minded about such narratives. One of the risks of having such an interpretative framework is that it can become stagnant or that it can be misinterpreted somehow and used to justify immorality. In this sense, then, we need good leadership in our faith communities and expertise that can guide our interpretations of the Scriptures to avoid fundamentalism and such like. Listening to the voice of experience can be a useful tool in this regard. Listening to the Scriptures is important but we also need to listen to the 'signs of the times', as represented in *Gaudium et spes* in the Catholic tradition and the Talmud in the Jewish tradition for example, in order to ensure that our narratives continue to be relevant and inform us today.

Often, in both political and ethical discourse, however, we fail to listen. Indeed, we often fail to talk in detail about how we 'experience' policies, practices or issues on the ground out of a fear of being a 'lone voice', a 'radical' or a torment to those in authority. This book is an attempt to articulate the view that experience is a category of ethical discourse that informs judgements about whether policies and perspectives are genuinely supportive of and contribute to the flourishing of individuals in our communities. It is also an attempt to show that across the disciplines there is scope to discuss complex issues such as faith and morals; children and families; government policy and education. Each perspective may well view phenomena through a specific lens of interpretation but nevertheless there is common ground in the category of experience. How we experience policy, education, family and everyday life informs how we see 'being human' and living life to the full.

Dignity, redistribution and recognition

A further key factor to emerge from all the chapters in this book, whether they are constructed from a faith or secular perspective, is the human need for recognition as a human being who is respected as an equal among other human beings, regardless of ethnicity, 'race', faith, gender or socio-economic status. This maybe comes into the sharpest focus within Pam Jarvis's account of the twenty-first-century social media construction of 'yummy and slummy mummies', in which a demographic group which should be able to offer support and solidarity instead finds itself in a divisive situation, in which it begins to define itself in terms of internal differences rather than in terms of what is shared, and where mutual support could be secured. Within the dysfunctional relationships that arise within social media communication in which individuals are 'deindividuated', those who are most powerless are stripped of dignity and depicted as less deserving of respect. This creates the seeds of low self-esteem and resentment, a process which is also described in Helen Hanna's account of sectarianism and Stefano Ba's account of struggling families who feel that the socio-economic odds are stacked against them.

Social justice is a concept that has evolved over time. In England, the first document to be concerned with social justice, the Magna Carta of 1215, took a highly property- and liberty-based perspective; for example:

- No free man shall be seized or imprisoned, or stripped of his rights or possessions, or outlawed or exiled, or deprived of his standing in any other way, nor will we proceed with force against him, or send others to do so, except by the lawful judgement of his equals or by the law of the land.
- To no one will we sell, to no one deny or delay right or justice.

(The British Library 2014, online)

The text also refers to 'free men', which also excluded much of the male population and all of the female population; however, it was a start in the recognition that not all the people and land in England were the property of the king. As Pam Jarvis details in Chapter 7, Western recognition of individual rights developed over many centuries, for example through the 1628 English Petition of Right, the 1787 United States Constitution, the 1789 French Declaration of the Rights of Man and of the Citizen and the 1791 United States Bill of Rights (United for Human Rights 2016).

However, it was Karl Marx (1887) who suggested to a newly industrialised society that governance is based on oppression, in which workers are oppressed by employers who exploit their workers by paying them a wage that does not equal the full value of their labour, and that the only road to freedom is through a collective attempt to throw off the oppressor. Marxism in its purest form proposes that everyone in society should be responsible for everyone else, to avoid such oppression. In such a society, everyone would be responsible for financing the care and education of children, and industry would be managed by co-operatives where members shared profits equally. While pure communism – imposed by revolution – has been found to be unsustainable, modern Western states all make some attempt to redistribute wealth through their taxation systems, offering collectively funded services to their whole populations such as education and health care. In this sense, in the modern world there is general recognition that some amount of redistribution of wealth is necessary for social justice to be realised.

However, the level of redistribution differs between different societies; for example, taxation and provision of collective services are far more developed in the Scandinavian nations than it is in the United States of America, and the level of redistribution is a key difference between politicians on the right, who argue for low taxation and low public spending, and those on the left, who argue for higher levels of redistribution through higher taxation and more developed public services. While the redistribution argument is likely to continue for the foreseeable future, the issue that our chapters raise is that, while redistribution of wealth is certainly seen as a key issue within social justice, it is not the only issue that emerges in contemporary societies, with several authors articulating the deep need of individuals for recognition as a fellow human being with rights to his or her own self-determination, in an environment in which differences are not only permitted, but where they are also not viewed as deficits.

Helen Hanna proposes: '*A socially just citizenship education, in the view of this chapter, allows young people to define their own identities, recognising that young people are the adults and therefore decision makers of the future. It allows young people to move away from the 'copper-fastened' thinking of the past in order to create new, and sometimes even seemingly conflicting, identities rather than simply adhering to those categories that adults have defined*', which concurs with Graham Turner's point that '*Empowerment for young people is therefore reliant upon the establishment of democratic relations where interaction is built upon communication and collaboration*'.

Arguing for younger children to be accorded respect for their life stage, Pam Jarvis comments '*To effectively provide social justice for children, we need an overarching culture which authentically embraces childhood on its own terms as an integral life stage, rather than viewing it through a lens which constructs it as an inconvenient journey to a work-consumed adulthood within a wealth-obsessed society*'. In her subsequent chapter she also argues for empowerment for their mothers: '*we must now construct a new feminist approach which critically reviews the maternal situation for women within neo-liberal societies, with the intention of reviving the values of the social democratic tradition*'. This point is extended to the life of the family by Stefano Ba' in his comment that '*Social justice as dignity here is then linked to the fact that the call for dignity from families in precarious conditions refers to an existing class-divided society based on precarious employment which necessarily negates their dignity. In that sense, dignity is an everyday life concept*'. Finally, referring to the clients of social workers, Sue Elmer reflects '*The "delicate balance" to ensure social justice principles are adhered to involves a capacity to assess the service users' abilities to make informed decisions in a way which does not deny their dignity or autonomy*'.

In all these chapters, then, we hear authors redefining social justice in terms that go beyond Marx's call for redistribution and additionally make the point for recognition by our peers, to be defined by others as a fully human being with the right to an equal voice, regardless of life stage, ethnicity, religious belief, socio-economic status, gender or social vulnerability.

Listening at the 'grass roots'

In 2014, Michael Reisch wrote the following:

> [i]t has become increasingly clear … that the expansion of social provision alone cannot create a socially just society. The creation of socially just outcomes involves more than constructing policies which allocate societal 'goods' more equitably. It also requires the development of socially just means to formulate, implement, and evaluate those policies, coupled with a recognition that the translation of an idealized abstraction (social justice) into concrete terms may take different forms in different circumstances. The goal of social justice is, therefore, neither simple nor ever entirely realised. It is a goal which is constantly pursued rather than completely attained.
>
> (Reisch 2014)

This quote is important for understanding what we mean when we turn to the faith communities for answers. Since the goal of social justice is pursued constantly, it requires imaginative and ever-searching approaches to what is just, good and true in every age. Hard and fast principles are perhaps not the only answer here but, rather attunement to the 'See, Judge, Act' that is central to Catholic social teaching and to the Citizens UK project. Listening to the voice of experience is also key. Since our experiences are a source of wisdom and point to what might be going on in a situation, the voice of experience helps to inform people's attitudes and consciences regarding what ought to be done in a particular situation or with a particular set of issues. Listening to grass-roots organisations and individuals who have lived through particular experiences is therefore key to informing and understanding what principles should guide us and whether these need to be refined in the light of new experience. This is what the Citizens UK agenda is.

The listening that happens within this organisation is an example of how listening to the voice of experience can tell us about the root causes of a particular issue and inform us about what course of action to take. Of course, our narrative stories found in our faith communities, as pointed out by Vincent, Asim, Kelly, Battle and Mealey, also sustain the quest for moral goodness and the quest to find the best way to articulate 'what is going on?', 'what can be done?' and 'how should we act?' The various stories, parables and key texts can offer people a lens though which to consider what might be questionable about a particular situation and what virtues need to be enlisted in order to do something about it. Much like the moral search for truth, the search for social justice is constant. It requires constant reflection on what is means to be a moral human being in every age, in multiple and diverse settings and in the face of new moral issues that are the result of new phenomena that appear in our ever-changing world.

As Fook and Goodwin have pointed out at the beginning of this volume, the editors and authors 'deliberately introduce a reflexive approach, one which tries to understand how social justice actions and approaches develop from the experience of social justice exponents themselves. In this sense, this book makes a contribution to our appreciation of how social justice emerges from our own experiences and practices.'

This reflexive approach has highlighted the need to respect individual and collective dignity in relation to issues relating to work (Stefano Ba'), identity (Helen Hanna), parenting (Pam Jarvis) and social work practice (Sue Elmer). In addition, the faith sections highlight that being a person of faith is not simply about evangelisation (though it includes this) but that it also includes a social programme and a commitment to do what is good and just. While each chapter has taken a different perspective, the key threads that link them such as dignity, listening to the voice of experience, listening to our 'storied' communities make the search for social justice all the more complex. As Fook and Goodwin put it, 'the concept of social justice can be linked to a wide range of traditions, ideals and visions for society and has come to absorb all sorts of meanings, hopes and demands' (Fook and Goodwin, this volume).

Since the quest for social justice relates to how we might become more fully human both individually and collectively, it makes sense therefore that this will be a complicated business. We anticipate that what we have provided here will be of use to those who are interested in a clear, 'everyday' interpretation across multiple disciplines and 'everyday' examples of what living a fulfilled life might mean in today's ever-changing, diverse and multifaceted society.

In addition, we hope that this book will give a voice to some in the community who will relate the various chapters to their own perspective and that it will inform discussions and reflection in other communities who were perhaps 'not so sure' how their faith tradition or particular experience relates to the social justice perspectives presented by the various authors. We also hope that, in rather complex political times, people will feel empowered to speak out against injustices in our society in the realisation that they will find support in surprising quarters, in order to protect what is just and true.

References

British Library (2014). *Translation of the Magna Carta*. Available at www.bl.uk/magna-carta/articles/magna-carta-english-translation (accessed 25 May 2017).

Marx, K. (1887). *Capital: A Critique of Political Economy*. Available at www.marxists.org/archive/marx/works/1867-c1/index.htm (Marxists.org 1995, 1999) (accessed 25 May 2017).

Reisch, M. (2014). 'Introduction', in M. Reisch (ed.) *The Routledge International Handbook of Social Justice*. London: Routledge.

United for Human Rights (2016). *A Brief History of Human Rights*. Online. Available at www.humanrights.com/what-are-human-rights/brief-history/cyrus-cylinder.html.

Index

Page numbers in *italics* denote tables, those in **bold** denote figures.